Case Law
and
Common Sense

A Guide to
Pennsylvania School Law

Lawrence C. Korchnak, Ph.D.

Second Edition

2002

Printed in Korea

ISBN 0-9715747-0-7

Educational Services Publishers
P.O. Box 134
Allison Park, PA 15101-0134

To my wife, Karen,
and my son, Lawrence

TABLE OF CONTENTS

Page

Section II **Teacher Issues**

Section III Liability Issues

Section IV Equity Issues

LIST OF TABLES

Education is a **concern** of the Federal government,
a **function** of State government, and
the **responsibility** of local government

INTRODUCTION

In the real world, public school administrators routinely make decisions requiring knowledge of the law: student issues, teacher issues, questions of liability, issues of equity, and questions involving curriculum. Unfortunately, the solicitor for the Board of School Directors is rarely present for consultation. While it is true that not every administrative decision has grave consequences, knowing the limits of the school's authority in a given situation has the power to transform potential conflict and confrontation into cooperation and resolution.

Case Law and Common Sense is a handbook on school law. Its primary goal is to clarify the most important legal issues affecting educational decision making with an emphasis on the laws of the Commonwealth of Pennsylvania. Since litigation is an all-too-real fact of life in today's public school system, *Case Law and Common Sense* is designed to provide the professional educator with a knowledge base from which (s)he can make sound educational decisions and determine when to seek legal counsel. Information of this kind can reduce the number of lawsuits and spare school districts the financial burden and negative impact on a school's reputation that accompanies litigation. *Case Law and Common Sense* is also intended as a textbook and resource for teacher education programs as well as administrative preparation programs.

Case Law and Common Sense contains sections on Students, Teachers, Liability, Equity, and Curriculum. Each section includes alphabetically arranged chapters that address specific legal issues. Each chapter also contains a section with implications for parents and students as well as teachers and administrators.

Case Law and Common Sense was piloted in undergraduate and graduate classrooms. Students' comments and suggestions have been incorporated to create an overall design that is both manageable and challenging. The text is written in a direct, narrative style avoiding lengthy quotations. Practical examples are end-noted to the appropriate court cases along with comments and references to appropriate legislation. The reader will also find a select number of sample policies and procedures for easy reference.

It is important in law to use accurate language. Knowing the meanings of the Latin terms and Common Law phrases is essential to understanding and applying principles of law. Since legal terminology is largely unfamiliar to the layperson, a glossary of legal terms and a key to understanding standard citations and abbreviations are provided for easy reference.

Lawrence C. Korchnak, Ph.D.

LEGAL FRAMEWORK

Understanding the impact of the law on public education requires knowledge of the primary sources of law. The following framework is offered to help the reader understand the foundations and context of the law as it pertains to public education.

Common Law

Common law is the first source of law that affects public education. Under Common Law individuals possess certain rights and responsibilities that have become part of the American legal system by virtue of British common law. Such things as tort law, parental rights and responsibilities, property rights, and contracts are some of the common law principles that apply to the operation of public schools. These Common Law principles represent a host of legal issues that exist separately from constitutional and/or statutory provisions. Tort law, involving the commission or omission of an act by one person resulting in the injury to another, creates the basis for a large portion of liability litigation against school districts. Property rights and contract law are essential to any discussion of tenure, negotiations, or grievance arbitration. Likewise, parents or guardians assert their rights and responsibilities with respect to minor children resulting in challenges to schools' *in loco parentis* authority.

Common Law issues comprise at least as many incidences of litigation as constitutional and statutory challenges. Each issue carries with it the tradition that has been passed down for hundreds of years dating back to the Middle Ages.

Governmental Sources

Along with Common Law, knowledge of the legislative framework surrounding the governmental source of law is essential to understanding school law. This framework deals with constitutional issues and statutory provisions enacted by federal and state legislatures. The legislative framework can be summarized in a single statement:

Education is a concern of the Federal government,
a function of State government, and
the responsibility of local government.

Federal Law

There is no direct reference to education in the Constitution of the United States. The federal government's relationship to education can be traced to implied grants of powers that create a nexus for governmental involvement at the federal level. These implied powers come from a broad interpretation of the General Welfare Clause of the United States Constitution. This clause, Article 1, Section 8, gives Congress the power "...to provide for the...general welfare of the United States..." and to "...make all Laws which shall be necessary and proper for carrying into Execution the foregoing Powers..." Accordingly, Congress has passed legislation relevant to the operation of schools such as the Individuals with Disabilities Education Act (IDEA), the Equal Educational Opportunities and Transportation Act, and the Elementary and Secondary Education Act.

Another source of federal involvement comes from the Bill of Rights. These first ten amendments of the Constitution contain essential provisions protecting the rights of individuals. These rights have a direct bearing on public school policy and its routine administration:

The First Amendment ensures basic personal freedoms. It addresses the use of public funds for non-public schools, establishes a safeguard against violations of a person's religious beliefs such as school prayer, and establishes protections for an individual's freedom of symbolic, oral or written expression. How far may a school restrict the valid exercise of these enumerated freedoms?

The Fourth Amendment provides a safeguard against unreasonable search and seizure. It deals with questions that balance the individual's right to privacy with the school's responsibility to provide a safe and secure learning environment. What constitutes a legal search for weapons or drugs? Is random drug testing permissible?

The Fifth Amendment ensures that teachers and students have protected rights in criminal prosecutions: protections against self-incrimination and the taking of property without due process of law.

The Eighth Amendment assures that no person be subjected to cruel and unusual punishment. This has been interpreted by the United States Supreme Court to permit appropriately administered corporal punishment in public schools.

Although not a part of the Bill of Rights, the Fourteenth Amendment grants equal protection under the laws while guaranteeing substantive and procedural due process. The Fourteenth Amendment created dual citizenship with language stating that all United States citizens are citizens of the state within which they reside. Equal protection follows accordingly by applying the civil rights provisions of United States Constitution to the citizens of the individual states:

> No State shall make or enforce any law which shall abridge the privileges and immunities of citizens of the United States...nor...deny any person within its jurisdiction the equal protection of the laws.

Once applied, the Fourteenth Amendment guarantees that the personal liberties enumerated in the Bill of Rights are protected for all citizens. This guarantee is supported in case law.

In granting due process, the Fourteenth Amendment prohibits the states from depriving "...any person of life, liberty, or property, without due process of law." Due process is twofold: substantive and procedural. Substantive due process deals with legislation and its reasonable relationship to the purpose of its passage. Here the protection is against excessively unfair acts by the government or its political subdivisions. Procedural due process pertains to fairness in the decision-making process used to ascertain whether or not a law has been violated. Even though most school policy violations are not criminal, procedural due process applies just the same.

Equal protection and due process rights circumscribe issues of religion, equity, and discipline. Without the Fourteenth Amendment, states would not be held to the same restrictions as the federal government in matters of respecting personal liberties.

State Law

The questions of civil rights emanating from the Bill of Rights are high profile; yet, they are only a part of the complete legal picture. The second important component of the legislative framework is the State. Since the Constitution does not specifically delegate the responsibility of education to the federal government, education becomes a function of the state by means of the "reserve clause" of the Tenth Amendment that states, in part:

The powers not delegated to the United States by the Constitution…are reserved to the States respectively, or to the people.

Through these words, the power to maintain a system of public schools becomes an attribute of state government in the same sense as police power or the power to tax. The states have a responsibility similar to that of the federal government to promote the general welfare, but without the specific enumeration found in Article 8 of the United States Constitution. Hence, having retained a broad range of governmental powers, state government may promote the general welfare of its citizens by establishing a system of education for the purpose of producing "enlightened citizens." In Pennsylvania, this is accomplished by the legislature through Article 3, Section 14, of the State Constitution that states:

The General Assembly shall provide for the maintenance and support of a thorough and efficient system of public education to serve the needs of the commonwealth.

The legislature may, accordingly, organize the state for the purpose of education and distribute duties and responsibilities as it sees fit to the agencies that it creates. It can even choose not to establish a system of public education. However, if it chooses to set up a public school system, it must do so legitimately. That is to say, the legislature may only delegate its administrative powers, not its legislative powers. Here, the courts, by virtue of *Marbury v. Madison* (1803), have the right of judicial review acting as a check on the legislature's potential abuse of power. In this governmental process, the principle of separation of powers is periodically invoked to insure that the delegation of power is a proper one. A typical example is the state of Pennsylvania that delegates its administrative powers under the Public School Code of 1949, as amended, where the General Assembly has established the guidelines for operating its public school system.

State legislatures delegate power in many ways. One way is to delegate a portion of its administrative power to the Secretary of Education and the State Board of Education. They, in turn, issue directives and statements pertaining to the operation of the schools. In other words, they regulate. Their authority to regulate is grounded in Local Agency Law that creates governmental agencies and, accordingly, grants them the power to act and enforce their respective regulations.

Local Law

The last component of the legislative framework is the local government that has the responsibility to educate. The local government, in the form of the Board of School Directors, receives its power from the legislature to accomplish this end. The legislature delegates this power to local Boards because it is impossible for them to foresee the infinite possibilities and complex nuances involved in operating a school system. Even in the state of Hawaii, which operates a single school system, there is a separate administrative body that supervises the school system. A valid delegation of power, this frees the state legislature to legislate.

As a governing body, the local Board of Directors also possesses a wide range of operational freedom in the form of implied powers. The courts have broadly interpreted these implied powers, thereby granting local Boards the flexibility to meet the changing needs of society. A good example of this flexibility can be seen in *Stuart v. School District No.1 of the Village of Kalamazoo*, 30 Mich. 69 (1874), where the Supreme Court of Michigan upheld the extension of the existing common school system to create tax supported high schools in 1874.

Local boards may exercise powers necessarily implied to enable them to carry out the express powers granted. This exercise of power is known as the doctrine of necessity, and there may be no clearer recent example than that of Pennsylvania's Midland Borough School District. In 1986, Board of School Directors elected to tuition its secondary students to a neighboring Pennsylvania school district. When this agreement expired, the district entered into another tuition agreement with an out-of-state school district in nearby Ohio. Both actions received the approval of Pennsylvania's Secretary of Education and Department of Education, and, although there was considerable concern about using public funds from one state to fund the education of its children in another, no legislative or court action was taken.

Summary

The law of public education involves legal principles based on common law as well as specific laws emanating from governmental sources.

Common law relationships between individuals such as tort actions, contracts, and the establishment of property rights create the need for the court system to review individual rights and responsibilities. Parents also assert rights over minor children over the *in loco parentis* authority of the school.

Education is a concern of the federal government, a function of the state government and the responsibility of the local government.

The federal government's concern for education comes from the implied grant of power in Article I, Section 8, of the United States Constitution and the Bill of Rights as applied by the Fourteenth Amendment. Education is a function of the state because it possesses a wide range of powers reserved to it by virtue of the Tenth Amendment. The responsibility for education is expressly granted to the local government by the legislature with broadly interpreted powers of necessity that permit flexibility in addressing the changing needs of society.

School law, to a great extent, consists of balancing individual and collective rights. On the one hand there are laws defining the interests of the school district as a political subdivision and agent of state government. On the other hand, there are the individual rights and civil liberties of parents, students and teachers granted by the United States Constitution and applied to the states via the Fourteenth Amendment.

Various other laws exist on all three levels of government. These laws are also subject to the scrutiny of the courts as part of a rich dialogue that makes up the body of judicial renderings called school law.

Chapter 1 Activities

Sources:

> Title IX of the Educational Amendments of 1972, 20 U.S.C. Section 1681
> Pennsylvania Public School Code, 24 P.S. Code 5
> Political Subdivisions Tort Claims Act, 42 Pa. C.S.A. Section 854 *et seq.*

Schools do more than provide classroom instruction. In the classical sense, education addresses the developmental needs of the whole person. A significant part of any child's educational program includes the development of life skills involving physical and social elements as well as an opportunity to demonstrate achievement in any number of specialized areas. To these ends, schools provide activities outside the normal range of curricular offerings.

Activities have become a traditional part of public schooling. Athletics enjoy a great deal of support evidenced by the fact that sports programs often survive during times when other programs are eliminated. Co-curricular programs also abound in the form of clubs, organizations, and support groups. Some of these activities have curriculum-related purposes, such as language clubs, drama clubs, and journalism clubs. Many others activities or clubs are not related to the curriculum. Students learn social and leadership skills as members of Student Council, they enhance their personal development by joining religious clubs, and they explore their unique talents by participating in various specialized interest clubs.

It is well established in law that activities are considered an important, "integral and complementary part of the total school program."[1] Since education is the responsibility of state and local authorities, the United States Supreme Court is reluctant to intervene in matters concerning routine conflict resolution.[2] Federal courts have held similarly.[3]

The right to establish activities is granted to public schools by virtue of language contained in sections of the various states' school codes. Herein, school districts are able to establish reasonable rules and regulations as they may deem necessary and proper in the area of school athletics, publications, clubs and organizations.

Over the years, the courts have had to address numerous issues involving school activities. Major areas of litigation include:

1. Authority to regulate and control: Questions of control exist on two levels: the school district level and the level of the association to which it belongs.

2. Liability: Injury and the question of damages under the common law concept of torts, equity, and financial liability.

3. Assignment: Duties and responsibilities associated with coaching or sponsorship of an activity.

This chapter attempts to address these areas of athletics and co-curricular activities. Many issues involving religion, equity, discipline, liability, and expression are examined in greater detail in other chapters.

Regulation and Control

<u>Schools</u>

The courts generally regard local school officials as competent and better equipped than judges to make decisions where "legitimate educational concerns" exist.[4] For example, in Pennsylvania, schools have the absolute right to regulate participation in activities[5] (i.e., athletics) reserving judicial review to those cases beyond simple error in judgment to include such things as arbitrariness or abuse of discretion. This right includes:

1. The management, supervision, control, or prohibition of exercises, athletics, or games of any kind, school publications, debating, forensic, dramatic, musical, and other activities related to the school program, including raising and disbursing funds for any or all of such purposes and for scholarships, and

2. The organization, management, supervision, control, financing, or prohibition of organizations, clubs, societies and groups of the members of any class or school.

Students do not have a property right to participate in activities.[6] Activities are generally held to be privileges where education is considered a right. Reasonable rules may, therefore, include grade requirements. Regardless of a district's affiliation with local or national organizations, it may elect to set stricter standards for participation. This applies to athletics as well as co-curricular activities. If a student simply fails to meet the grade requirements, there is no deprivation of rights and, therefore, no cause of action.

Disciplinary actions for inappropriate behavior or violations of school policy have excluded many students from activities. For example, under Section 511a of the Pennsylvania Public School Code, the school district "may provide...for the suspension, dismissal, or other reasonable penalty in the case of any pupil... who violates any of such rules or regulations." The school code grants the board of directors the authority to set "reasonable rules and regulations" and the courts have upheld their authority to manage student conduct and discipline within the school district.[7]

Further disciplinary action may be taken by a coach, in conjunction with the principal, to discipline players for conduct unbecoming an athlete.[8] Similarly, students in co-curricular activities may be disciplined as a result of violating the activity's behavior code.

A frequent cause of action in recent years has grown from the use of alcohol and other controlled substances. A one-year suspension from extracurricular activities as a sanction for possession or use of alcohol was held not to be excessive.[9] Moreover, a school may even exclude a student from participating in all extracurricular activities as a result of underage drinking off school premises (where such an action is in violation of an existing policy on the use of controlled substances).[10]

Other rules may be enforced as well. Students may be denied the opportunity to participate in interscholastic competition for involvement in hazing, even if it occurs off school grounds at a summer camp.[11] A school may require immunization prior to participation in athletics,[12] the school board may limit the number of students that can participate,[13] and attendance requirements may be imposed.[14] Schools may also require attributes of character and leadership for participation in sports, clubs, and activities such as student council.[15] However, the regulation must be reasonable and related to the intended purpose of the activity. As long as no "partiality, prejudice, bias, or ill-will" has clouded the application of the regulation, it will more than likely be upheld, even if it results in the exclusion of a student from athletic participation as a result of an examination by a school physician.[16]

Associations

In the area of control, school districts have a right to affiliate with any local, district, regional, state or national organization whose purposes and activities are appropriate to and related to the school program. Schools elect to participate in state and national associations and, as such, are bound by their rules fairly and reasonably applied.

Courts have generally upheld association rules and regulations when the association has been within its legal authority to act, when the rule or regulation is deemed fair, and when the rule or regulation is applied in a consistent manner. Likewise, courts have long recognized an association's authority to manage its own affairs given the voluntary nature of participation.

Like school districts, associations may set grade requirements for eligibility to participate in an activity. Under certain athletic associations, a student must maintain a particular grade point average (i.e. a "C" average) to remain eligible for interscholastic competition. This standard is considered the minimum for eligibility. Schools may apply a stricter standard; however, they may not set a standard below that which has been set by the association if they wish to participate.

There is little room to question grade point averages set by academic affiliations such as the National Honor Society (NHS). The right of the NHS and other academic organizations to establish grade requirements have been traditionally accepted and are rarely challenged.

Discipline by an association for actions that violate association rules and regulations are seldom struck down by the courts. The usual practice is to submit to the association's procedure for resolving disciplinary issues prior to filing suit. Still, associations have had to face litigation. Statewide athletic associations have been held to act within the scope of their authority even when they declared the forfeiture of two complete seasons for the use of ineligible players.[17] Censure and probation for fighting after an athletic event have also been upheld.[18]

Other rules and regulations may be established by associations binding their membership in a number of areas. These areas cover, among others, periods of participation, attendance, transfers, age, and subjective evaluative criteria.

Most associations stipulate periods of participation in the activity that they represent. The Pennsylvania Interscholastic Athletic Association regulations state that a pupil cannot represent his/her school in interscholastic athletics for more than eight (8) semesters beyond grade eight. This is not uncommon. Statewide athletic associations often address questions of age, the complications involving students retained for academic reasons, and students who, by reason of some disability, may have progressed through the system at a different rate. Similar restrictions on participation are placed on local clubs and societies that are affiliated with larger associations such as the National Honor Society (NHS), Key Club (affiliated with Kiwanis), and Future Business Leaders of America (FBLA).

A key question is whether or not an association can regulate participation in outside activities during the regular season, i.e. tournament participation and games independent from the association's jurisdiction. As long as such rules are reasonably construed, fairly applied, and involve no substantive constitutional issue, the courts will uphold them.[19]

Regulation of activities beyond the regular season exceed the power of the association unless the participant receives compensation. Compensation of any kind will violate the student's amateur status, thereby rendering him/her ineligible.

An association may clearly regulate attendance just as a school district may establish attendance criteria for participation in activities. This becomes an issue in sports more so than extra-curricular activities. In Pennsylvania, a student who has missed a total of twenty (20) or more school days during a semester may not participate in any athletic contest until he/she has attended for a total of sixty (60) days following the twentieth (20) day of absence.[20] These types of regulation may create a waiver if the student misses five (5) or more consecutive days due to illness, injury, or quarantine. Most state interscholastic sports associations have adopted similar policies.

While transfer for the purpose of participating in an athletic program has been the issue in a number of court cases, non-athletic associations rarely view transfers in the same light. Controlled participation is considered necessary in athletics given the potential for abuse: pressures to win at any cost, over-zealous coaches and parents, de-emphasis of the value of education, exploitation of superior athletes, and recruitment schemes. As with most cases involving transfer, the courts are reluctant to hear cases unless all administrative remedies are exhausted prior to commencing litigation.[21] However, if the issue bears upon a constitutionally protected liberty right, the court will hear it. The association's regulation is usually attacked on the basis that it is arbitrary and capricious, thus denying the student due process and equal protection under the federal and state constitutions.

Courts have upheld transfers based on legitimate academic reasons, such as removing a student from an unhealthy home environment to live with another relative.[22] Other transfers involving a divorce and change in custody have been upheld. In one case, a student moved to another district after poor grades and disciplinary problems required him to move in with the other parent.[23] But, where a student voluntarily transferred from a private school to a public school after school district lines were redrawn, the court rejected the arbitrariness of the association's decision to permit eligibility because the public school students were required to change schools and private school students were not.[24] If an investigation reveals that a transfer was undertaken with the intent to circumvent policy, the association's policy will be upheld.[25] Thus, the courts will deny eligibility when it can be proven that a student relocated or transferred for athletic purposes.[26]

Age has been an issue in several cases that have reached the courts. Athletic associations have exhibited particular reluctance to relax regulations establishing an age limit on student participation. Again, non-athletic organizations do not hold so high a priority on age. Athletic associations may prohibit nineteen (19) year-olds from playing. In Pennsylvania athletes are limited to eight (8) semesters of continuous attendance beginning with the ninth grade. The reasons for establishing age requirements are sound: to prevent injury to younger or less mature athletes, to provide an arena of fair competition, and to avoid the manipulation of academics for the purpose of athletics.

When a challenge was brought against a state activity organization's rule that excluded nineteen (19) year-old students who have not made "normal educational progress," the court upheld the limit in face of the student's contention that he was retained in fifth grade at his mother's request.   The court upheld the rational basis for the rule; namely, preventing students from intentionally repeating a grade to participate in sports at an earlier age.[27]. The courts have supported age limits even when a.) earlier health problems affected the schooling timeline and excluded students from participating during their senior year,[28] b.) a student played in games while a restraining order was obtained against the association,[29] and c.) a student quit school for a period of time to support an ailing parent.[30]

Subjective evaluative criteria such as leadership, character, and service have been upheld on all levels of the court system. Since there is no constitutional right to be selected for membership in an organization, be it athletic, academic, or service, challenges are rarely made on this basis. When they are, the result has been consistent. In a challenge to the criteria employed by the National Honor Society (NHS), a school district's exclusion of a student who was otherwise academically qualified was upheld.   Here no detailed reason was required except that the faculty council decided it so.[31] In a widely publicized case involving the expulsion of an unmarried, pregnant high school student from the NHS, the court affirmed a school's regulation of conduct with emphasis on leadership and character. The issue of Title IX discrimination based on sex was dismissed since the decision to expel the student was based on character, not pregnancy.[32]

Liability

Liability for injuries sustained as a result of participating in school-related activities springs from several sources. One area of liability may grow from the <u>willful act</u> of a coach or sponsor causing an injury to a student under his/her supervision. In such a case, if intent can be proven, liability exists for the individual who harbored the intent. However, the district may not be held liable unless it knew, or had reason to know, that the offensive behavior was taking place, yet failed to act.

School districts are more commonly held to a degree of qualified immunity under common law by reason of the state's tort claims act. Here, liability exists for governmental entities such as school districts, but it does so in limited fashion. See Chapter 16, "Negligence and Tort Liability."

Further liability may be incurred by establishing policies that violate an activity's right to meet and express its views. Equal access to school facilities becomes an issue when no fair policy exists or there is no consistency in applying existing policy. See Chapter 18, "Equal Access."

Similar problems may arise if a school district, by reason of policy or tradition, promotes the recitation of a prayer before an activity. This applies to athletic events, club meetings, as well as graduation ceremonies. Refer to Chapter 8, "Religious Activity."

Schools must be careful not to establish rules and regulations for activities that create liability by reason of a misapplication of due process or a violation of some personal liberty as part of a discipline procedure. Refer to Chapter 4, "Due Process."

Title IX and related federal legislation support the premise that there is no rational basis for employing different standards for activities based on gender. This applies to academic standards[33] as well as physical standards. Although a Rhode Island court dissolved an injunction allowing a boy to participate on a girl's field hockey team,[34] Pennsylvania held to the contrary after a similar case was remanded to determine whether physical differences warranted different treatment.[35] Since contact was prohibited by anyone under the rules of field hockey, the male's physical characteristics did not dictate exclusion, as long as he complied with all other rules and regulations, including wearing the team uniform, a skirt! The sword clearly has two-edges.

The other edge of the sword is evident in another recent case. As long as equal treatment is required for both sexes, there is no duty to warn of obvious dangers when a female elects to participate in a contact sport with males. The courts have held that the female student assumes the risk of catastrophic injury by choosing to participate since the dangers of a sport, like football, are self-evident.[36]

The concept of "effective accommodation" should be considered when attempting to provide equal opportunities for both sexes. Essentially the courts will consider whether the selection of a sport or activity accommodates the interests (desire to participate) and abilities (talent, level of competition) of the members of both sexes.[37]

Students with disabilities have succeeded in obtaining court orders to participate in activities based upon the constitutional guarantees of the Fourteenth Amendment in the application of the Americans with Disabilities Act (ADA), 42 U.S.C. Section 1201 *et seq.*, Section 504 of the Rehabilitation Act (29 U.S.C. section 794), and the Individuals with Disabilities Education Act (IDEA). As mentioned earlier in this chapter, courts have upheld age requirements applied to students who have not progressed normally through the school system. This applies to regular, not special education students.

If a student's progress is slowed or interrupted (i.e. retention at a particular grade level) and there is no special education placement, age limitations for participation will be upheld. Exclusion has been sustained in one case where the parents recognized the child's disability but chose not to request special education services or an individualized educational program (IEP).[38] If the progress is slowed or interrupted as a result of a diagnosed disability and special education placement has been accomplished, the courts have permitted participation. A student diagnosed with attention deficit/hyperactivity disorder that failed to receive the number of semester credits required by the state athletic association was permitted to play a sport.[39] A Missouri court held similarly in the case of a student who was retained twice because of a disability, behavior disorder, and language impairment in auditory comprehension. Here the student was permitted to participate even though he entered his senior year beyond the required age limit.[40]

Financial liability exists for the person or persons who manage activity funds. As a rule of thumb, sound written policy indicating the nature and the use of such funds is essential. Management of activity funds should follow a set of general operating procedures that are in accordance with accepted accounting principles. When this is done within the framework of existing school laws and regulations set forth by local and state government, few problems will arise. School boards have clear authority to adopt reasonable regulations concerning raising, holding, use, and disposition of school-sponsored activity funds.[41]

Liability occurs in the intentional and unintentional handling of activities funds. Money can be raised for a particular activity and held by the activity under its own name and management.[42] The funds remain the property of that activity and cannot be used for any purpose other than the activity with one exception. It may be used by the board of education for purposes related to the educational program.[43] This usually occurs when funds are left unspent in an activities account.

Criminal charges can be filed against those who willfully mismanage funds for personal gain. Negligent behavior may be held liable because one knew or should have known the proper procedures. The consequences may be fines, incarceration, and/or loss of position. Great care should be exercised in developing policy, establishing procedures, and managing the system.

Teacher Assignment

School boards have discretion in assigning extra-curricular duties. However, the discretion is not unlimited[44] and an activity assignment must be reasonably related to the school program.[45] Furthermore, the assignment must be fairly and reasonably made.[46] In situations where contracts are offered requiring both instructional and extracurricular duties, courts have held school boards to be within their rights.[47]

Taking away an extracurricular assignment has met with mixed results in a number of jurisdictions, basing the decision on whether the activity was part of a collective bargaining agreement or not.[48] In Pennsylvania, case law supports activities contracts for specified periods of time;[49] however, supplemental activity contracts may be terminated without the same degree of notice and hearing that is applied to the termination of a teaching contract.[50]

Implications

<u>Teachers and Administrators</u>:

- Schools may control participation in activities in many ways, including setting achievement criteria (grades) and excluding students (disciplinary removal).

- School activities may affiliate with state and national associations. As such, they are subject to the association's criteria for membership or removal. Schools are minimally held to the association's standards; however, they may adopt stricter criteria as a matter of policy.

<u>Parents and Students</u>:

- Schools have the authority to make "reasonable rules and regulations" concerning student participation in activities.

- While education is a right, activities are considered a privilege. Grade requirements, personal character, attendance records, as well as other rules and regulations are held to be legitimate exercises of authority. Disciplinary removal for violating these rules will be upheld as long as they are reasonable.

Chapter 1 Endnotes

[1] Davis v. Meek, 344 F. Supp. 298 (N.D. Ohio 1972).

[2] Epperson v. Arkansas, 393 U.S. 97, 89 S. Ct. 266 (1968).

[3] Zeller v. Donegal School District, 517 F.2d 600 (3rd Cir. 1975).

[4] Bull v. Dardanelle Public School District No. 15, 745 F. Supp. 1455 (E.D. Ark. 1990).

[5] Crawshaw v. Meadville Area School District, 11 Crawford 39 (Pa. 1970).

[6] Adamek v. PIAA, 426 A.2d 1206, 57 Pa. Cmwlth. 261 (1981); Dallas v. Cumberland Valley School District, 391 F. Supp. 358 (M.D. Pa. 1975).

[7] Girard School District v. Pittenger, 392 A.2d 261, 481 Pa. Cmwlth. 91 (1978).

[8] Davis v. Central Dauphin School District School Board, 466 F. Supp. 1259 (D.C. Pa. 1979).

[9] Billman v. Big Spring School District, 27 D.& C.3d 488 (Pa. 1983).

[10] King v. Hempfield School District, 8 D.& C.4th 48 (Pa. 1990).

[11] Westhafer v. Cumberland Valley School District, SLIE, Vol. 38, No. 19 (2001).

[12] Calandra by Calandra v. State College Area School District, 512 A.2d 809 (Pa. Cmwlth. 1986).

[13] Mifflin County School District v. Monsell, 504 A.2d 1357 (Pa. Cmwlth. 1986).

[14] Woodring v. School Directors of Bald Eagle Area School District, 56 D.& C.2d 401 (Pa. 1972).

[15] Bull, *supra.*, Spitler v. Eastern Lebanon County School District, SLIE, Vol. 38, No. 18 (2001).

[16] Crawshaw, *supra.*

[17] Moreland v. W.P.I.A.L., 572 F.2d 121 (3rd Cir. 1978).

[18] School District of Harrisburg v. P.I.A.A., 309 A.2d 353 (Pa. 1973).

[19] Kite v. Marshall, 661 F.2d 1027 (1981), *certiorari* denied, 50 U.S.L.W. 3982 (1982).

[20] Moreland, *supra.*

[21] Sutterby v. Zimer, 594 N.Y.S.2d 607 (N.Y. 1993).

[22] Jordan by and through Jones v. I.H.S.A.A., 813 F. Supp. 1372 (N.D. Ind. 1993).

[23] Crane v. I.H.S.A.A., 975 F.2d 1315 (7th Cir. 1992).

[24] Alabama H.S.A.A. v. Scaffidi, 564 So.2d 910 (Ala. 1990).

[25] Kriss v. Brown, 390 N.E.2d 193 (Ind. App. 1979).

[26] Jobson v. P.I.A.A., 18 D. & C.3d 347 (Pa. 1981); P.I.A.A. v. Greater Johnstown School District, 463 A.2d 1198 (Pa. Cmwlth. 1983).

[27] Moody v. P.I.A.A., 11 Crawford 45 (Pa. 1970); Arkansas Activities Association v. Meyer, 805 S.W.2d 394 (Ark. 1991).

[28] Missouri State High School Activities Association v. Schoenlaub, 507 S.W.2d 394 (Mo. 1974).

[29] Cardinal Mooney High School v. Michigan H.S.A.A., 467 N.W.2d 21 (Mich. 1991).

[30] Smith v. Crim, 240 S.E.2d 884 (Ga. 1977).

[31] Dangler v. Yorktown Central Schools, 777 F. Supp. 1175 (S.D. N.Y. 1991).

[32] Pfeiffer v. Marion Center Area School District et. al., 917 F.2d 799 (3rd Cir. 1990).

[33] Fontes v. Irvine Unified School District, 30 Cal. Rptr. 521 (Cal. App. 4th Dist. 1994).

[34] Kleczek v. Rhode Island Interscholastic League, Inc., 612 A.2d 734 (D.R.I. 1992).

[35] Williams v. School District of Bethlehem, 998 F.2d 168 (3rd Cir. 1993).

[36] Hammond v. Board of Education of Carrol County, 639 A.2d 223, 100 Md. App. 60 (Md. 1994).

[37] Roberts v. Colorado State University, 814 F. Supp. 1507 (D. Colo. 1993).

[38] J.M., Jr. v. Montana H.S.A.A., 875 P.2d 1026 (Mont. 1994).

[39] Hoot by Hoot v. Milan Area Schools, 853 F. Supp. 243 (E.D. Mich. 1994).

[40] Pottgen v. Missouri State Activities Association, 857 F. Supp. 654 (E.D. Mo. 1994).

[41] Shade Central City School District v. Class of 1974, 1 D.& C.3d 376 (Pa. 1976).

14

[42] Twin Valley School District v. Student Activity Fund of the Twin Valley High School Class of 1981, et. al., (C.P. Pa. Berks Co. 1989); In re Indebtedness of Avoca Borough School District, 85 D.& C. 102 (Pa. 1953).

[43] Shade, *supra.*

[44] Lewis v. Board of Education, 537 N.E.2d 435 (Ill. App. 1989).

[45] Pease v. Millcreek Township School District, 195 A.2d 104, 412 Pa. 378 (1963); Monaca School District Appeal, 52 D.& C.2d 447 (Pa. 1971).

[46] Pease, *supra.*

[47] Lemmon Education Association v. Lemmon School District #52-2, 478 N.W.2d 821 (S.D. 1991).

[48] Sadler v. Board of Education of Cabool School District, 851 S.W.2d 707 (Mo. App. S.D. 1993); Board of Education v. Regala, 589 A.2d 993 (Md. App. 1991).

[49] Ringgold School District v. Abramski, 426 A.2d 707, 57 Pa. Cmwlth. 33 (1981).

[50] Moriarta v. State College Area School District, 601 A.2d 872 (Pa. Cmwlth. 1992).

Chapter 2   Attendance

Sources:

> Pennsylvania Public School Code, 24 Pa. Code 13
> State Board of Education Regulations, Pupil Attendance, 22 Pa. Code 11

Questions concerning school attendance have increased in recent years. Residence and entry requirements comprise one set of issues. School populations are more transient and students' rights in the form of special educational needs have become paramount. Therefore, questions of residence define not only the locus but also the limits of a school's responsibility to educate. Compulsory attendance, absence, and the penalties associated with compulsory attendance comprise another set of issues. While truant officers rarely scour the neighborhoods and drag youngsters into the classroom today, school attendance has felt the impact of the many diversions available to school-aged children: vacations, employment, shopping, and "mental health" days, to mention a few. Parents excuse absent students, district magistrates routinely turn their heads, and school districts are reluctant to prosecute in spite of clearly defined regulations in the School Code and State Board Regulations.

The attendance laws have seen few modifications over the years. Most of the changes exist in the form of revisions to the State Board of Education Regulations. Those attendance laws have been tested by the courts on a number of fronts.

Education is a statutory right subject to provisions set forth by the state legislature. School districts possess considerable discretion in setting criteria for admission as long as it is consistent with state law. For example, they may establish an age for admission to school as a beginner within the state guidelines provided that it is reasonably grounded, even though it may not be perfect or result in some "inequality of practice."[1] Pennsylvania guidelines will be used in this chapter to examine the various issues surrounding attendance.

Residence

The Pennsylvania Public School Code is clear on the issue of residence. Any resident child aged 6 to 21 may attend the public schools in the district of residence (24 P.S. Code 1301). The operative term is "may." Parents/guardians may elect to send a child but are not required to do so unless the child is of compulsory school age (8 years to 16 years). The term "resident" also includes foreign exchange students. Furthermore, the Code establishes provisions for a school district to assign its resident students to another school, under proper arrangement, even if such school is in another state (24 P.S. Code 1315).

The School Code states "a child shall be considered a resident of the school district in which his parents or the guardian of his parents reside." This applies to minors living with persons standing *in loco parentis*, such as an aunt.[2] A child may also reside with a parent or guardian who intends to keep and support the child "continuously and not merely through the school term" (24 P.S. Code 1302). A resident must file legal documentation demonstrating guardianship or dependency, or a sworn statement verifying residency to support the child *gratis* and assume the personal obligations of the child while intending to keep the child continuously.[3]

If a child's parents are separated and living in different school districts, the child does not have a choice to attend either school. Rather, the child's residence is that of the parent who has custody.[4] If residence is questionable, the burden of proof lies with the person claiming residence.[5] The minimum requirement to establish residency is the word of the resident guardian in the form of a signed affidavit.

When the issue of residency involves an immigrant student, a United States Supreme Court ruling declared that public schools may not deny admission based on their undocumented status. Furthermore, schools are prohibited from requiring students or parents to disclose or document immigrant status[6] as a safeguard to their privacy rights.

Emancipated students are also entitled to an education in the district of residence. Emancipated minors are children below the age of twenty-one (21) who have chosen to live apart from the control and support of parent(s) or guardian(s). For the purpose of attendance, "a minor living with a spouse is deemed emancipated" (Basic Education Circular (BEC) 55-13-87).

Resident students further include children attending non-public schools and those receiving home schooling. In both instances, these children are entitled to attend classes and programs on a part-time basis as long as they conform to the policies and practices of the full-time students.

In establishing a child's right to an education in a particular school district, the child's residence and domicile usually refer to the same physical location. But, this may not always be the case. A residence is defined as a physical presence with the intention to remain for a period of time. This includes homeless persons who have no legitimate address. A residence may also be different from a domicile. A domicile is defined in law as the true place of habitation. The distinction between residence and domicile is particularly important in the cases where non-resident children establish residency without changing domicile. The Pennsylvania School Code provides a free public education for three categories of non-residents:

1. Non-resident children living with a district resident without compensation or gain (24 P.S. Code 1302). The physical act of residence in the school district is the controlling factor and obtaining an affidavit of gratuitous keep should be required by the school district. Support such as Aid for Families with Dependent Children (AFDC) is not considered to be compensation under the School Code.

2. Non-resident children receiving full time, paid foster care[7] or custodial care in the home of a resident (24 P.S. Code 1305a). Once again, an affidavit of gratuitous keep should be on file with the school district.

3. Non-resident children living in facilities or institutions located within the school district (24 P.S. Code 1306) This provision addresses children in shelters as well as inpatient drug and alcohol or mental health facilities located within the school district. The school district may fulfill its obligation to these children in a number of ways apart from including the children in the regular school program. The district may offer its own program at the facility by hiring qualified teachers or even by assigning teachers in the district to provide limited tutoring. The district may enter into a contract with the facility authorizing them to provide an appropriate education. The district may also create an approved alternative education program.

Admission to School

Once residence is established and before a child is admitted to school, the child must have received the required immunizations and meet the age requirements set by statute and school board policy, especially in the case of beginners. Records of immunization are required for all students including beginners. (24 P.S. Code 1304) Those records should contain verification of the following immunizations:

- 3 doses of Dpt, Td or DT vaccine (for protection against tetanus and diphtheria). These are usually received in combined vaccines.
- 3 doses of Oral Polio vaccine or, if prescribed by a physician,
- 4 doses of Inactivated (Salk) Polio vaccine. Students 18 years of age or older are exempt.
- 1 dose of Measles vaccine or a blood test showing immunity.
- 1 dose of Rubella vaccine or a blood test showing immunity.
- 1 dose of Mumps vaccine or a signed statement from a physician stating that the child has had the disease.

By the 2002-03 school year, children entering school for the first time must have proof of varicella (chickenpox) immunity and students entering the seventh grade must have varicella immunity and 3 doses of hepatitis-B vaccine.

Four exemptions are worth noting. The first applies to a child who has partial immunization. This means that (s)he has at least one or more doses of all the required immunizations. In the event of partial immunization, parents should be informed of immunization requirements and be advised of any need to further comply with the law prior to or at registration. The student may then be provisionally enrolled for up to eight months, at which time (s)he may be excluded if not in compliance.

Secondly, a child may claim exemption based on religious grounds, whereby (s)he must provide a written statement to that effect. Third, a child may provide a statement by a physician verifying the medical need for an exemption. Fourth, homeless children may be admitted upon oral verification of immunization by the previous school (pending transfer of actual records).

A beginner is defined as "any child that should enter the lowest grade of the primary school or the lowest class above the kindergarten level" (24 P.S. Code 1304). Absent an early admission policy, the age required by the School Code is five years and seven months before the first day of September if the child is to begin in the fall. The age is five years and seven months before the first of February if the child is to begin at the start of the second semester. The district has the statutory right to refuse to accept beginners who have not reached the mental age of five. The courts have acknowledged that requiring a child to have attained the mental age of five years "establishes a colorable claim of unconstitutionality" by tending to stigmatize the child without a hearing.[8] Any child, however, whose admission has been so postponed is entitled to timely placement in an educational program consistent with Sections 1371-82 of the School Code dealing with exceptional children.

Admission to a new school also requires that there be a signed parental statement concerning any past or present expulsions/suspensions, particularly those involving controlled substances or weapons.

Compulsory Attendance

Although a resident child <u>may</u> attend the public schools in the district of residence, "compulsory school age" is defined in the Pennsylvania Public School Code as "eight (8) years, until the age of seventeen (17) years" (24 P.S. Code 1326). Since the Commonwealth of Pennsylvania does not statutorily mandate kindergarten, compulsory attendance does not apply to kindergarten programs. Age, not the existence of a school-sponsored program, is the controlling factor. Therefore, a parent cannot be held guilty of violating the compulsory attendance laws by refusing to send a child to kindergarten.[9]

For many years, the state's power to compel children to attend school has been interpreted to include the option of attending non-public schools. In *Pierce v. Society of Sisters*, the Supreme Court of the United States struck down an Oregon Statute requiring all students to attend public schools. In upholding the property right of two private schools, the Court affirmed a parent's right to "direct the education of children by selecting reputable teachers and places."[10] Non-public education has been a viable alternative to compulsory attendance laws for over seventy years.

The First Amendment has been the basis for litigation involving religious exceptions to compulsory attendance laws. In granting Amish parents the right not to send their children to school beyond eighth grade (or the age of fourteen), the Supreme Court rejected Wisconsin's contention that "its interest in its system of public education is so compelling" that it outweighs the parents' constitutional interests in the religious upbringing of their children.[11] In Pennsylvania, Amish children are compelled to fulfill attendance requirements because the Commonwealth has provided an alternative to formal public and private schools by granting the Amish the right to run their own schools.[12] In effect, the schooling of the Amish beyond the age of fourteen is comprised of performing farm and home chores while receiving a few hours of formal classwork per week under parental supervision.

Where the health and safety of a child is positively and immediately threatened, a parent or guardian may be justified in withdrawing a child from school.[13] The fact that minor altercations occur does not authorize withdrawal, even though a school district has a responsibility to provide a secure learning environment.[14]

Several other exceptions to compulsory public school attendance are listed in Section 1327 of the Pennsylvania Public School Code and Chapter 11 of the State Regulations:

1. Enrollment in a private trade or business school licensed by the Department of Education.
2. Enrollment in a licensed non-public school.
3. Home Education according to law.
4. Involvement in a tutoring program conducted by a qualified tutor with the approval of the superintendent (22 Pa. Code 11.31).

One other significant exception to compulsory attendance affects administration on the secondary level. According to the State Board of Education Regulations, students may be enrolled full-time in an approved post-secondary program (22 Pa. Code 11.4). Credit may be given for coursework completed at a college or university and/or be used to fulfill the requirements for high school graduation. Under this regulation, a diploma may be issued by a school district with the approval of the superintendent and the school board.

The School Code provides other exceptions to the compulsory attendance. A child may be excepted if (s)he:

1. Has attained the age of sixteen (16) years, is regularly engaged in useful and lawful employment, and holds an employment certificate issued according to law.

2. Has attained the age of fifteen (15) years, is engaged in farm work or domestic service, and has the recommendation of the superintendent.

3. Has attained the age of fourteen (14) years, is engaged in farm work or domestic service, has satisfactorily completed the equivalent of the highest grade in elementary school, has a demonstrated need,[15] has the recommendation of the superintendent, and as the approval of the Secretary of Education.

The issuance of a work permit need not be automatic. Nothing in the law prohibits discretion on the part of the school district in determining what is in the best interest of the student. There are two types of employment certificates. The first type is a regular certificate that entitles the minor (ages 16 to 18) to work the entire year. The second type is a vacation employment certificate. This entitles minors (ages 14 to 18) to work any day with the exception of those days when the student is required to be in school. When such certificates are issued, the following papers must be received, approved, and filed:

1. Proof of age
2. A certificate of physical fitness
3. A statement from the prospective employer indicating the type of work offered as well as the number of hours per day and per week

Absence

If a child is of compulsory attendance age, absence from the school setting may require action. Absence is non-attendance on those days (or half days) that school is in session. They may be excused, unexcused or unlawful.

Excused absences are absences that are deemed legal under the Pennsylvania Public School Code (24 P.S. Code 1329). These legal excuses include certification by a licensed practitioner of the healing arts showing that the student in question is prevented from attending school based on mental, physical, or other urgent reasons (keeping in mind a strict interpretation that does not permit irregular attendance): illness, health-related problems (24 P.S. Code 1417), quarantine, therapy (22 Pa. Code 11.23), impassable roads, death in the family, approved educational trips,[16] appearance in court, weather that might endanger the child's health, and religious instruction (up to 36 hours per school year) (24 P.S. Code 1546). Furthermore, a school district may excuse a pupil who engages in a non-school sponsored educational tour or trip if certain conditions are met.[17]

Generally speaking, excused absences are of short duration. The school district maintains considerable discretion in determining the nature and form of such excuses. The School Code says "...every principal or teacher...may...excuse any child for non-attendance during temporary periods" (24 P.S. Code 1329). This includes the power to formulate policies that describe the nature of legitimate excuses, require substantiation by the parent or guardian, and establish procedures. Sound judgment dictates that such school policies be communicated to parents and students on a regular basis. This communication can occur at the beginning of the school year, at open house, or in school district mailings.

Excuses from attendance for other than temporary reasons may be obtained "upon recommendation of the school physician and a psychiatrist or public school psychologist or both with the approval of the Secretary of Education" (22 Pa. Code 11.34). Long-term excusal is generally considered to be in excess of thirty days and must be reevaluated every three months.

If the absence does not fall in the excused category due to parent neglect, illegal employment or simple truancy, it is considered unexcused.

An unexcused absence is unlawful (illegal) for all students within the compulsory age requirement: ages eight (8) to sixteen (16). If a student is seventeen (17) years of age or older, an absence without legitimate cause is merely unexcused with no statutory sanctions or penalties. Sanctions may be applied by the school district; however, caution must be exercised to avoid arbitrary disciplinary action.

Penalties

When a violation of the compulsory attendance laws occurs, i.e. "absent three days or their equivalent, during the term of compulsory attendance, without lawful excuse" (24 P.S. Code 1332), the parent/guardian or offending child is subject to prosecution and fine by the District Justice (24 P.S. Code 1333). The three days may or may not be consecutive and adequate notice of such violation must be given by the school.

Adequate notice (24 P.S. Code 1354) was defined in *Comm. v. Grace.*[18] Two children, aged 15 and 13, were excused on three different occasions by their mother for "deer hunting," "a farm show," and "helping with work at home." Although the absences were adjudged to be unexcused and therefore unlawful, the school erred in not providing adequate notice.

The *Grace* court [19] asserts adequate notice for unlawful absence must state that:

1. The child was absent from school on a certain date or dates.

2. The absence was an unexcused absence.

3. The unexcused absence constitutes a violation of the compulsory education provision of the Public School Code.

4. The law requires that the parent, guardian, or person in legal custody of the student be notified of this fact.

5. An unexcused absence constitutes a summary offense under the Public School Code for which penalties may be imposed.

6. If the student is illegally absent again, charges will be brought before the District Justice without further notice from the school authorities.

The most recent amendment to Section 1333 of the Pennsylvania Public School Code declares that children thirteen years of age or older who fail to comply with compulsory attendance provisions commit a summary offense. Specifically, these students are considered "habitually truant" from school. Habitually truant is defined as absence from school for more than three (3) school days or their equivalent following the first notice of truancy.

Not long ago, only the parent or guardian incurred punishment for a child's unlawful absence assuming that, as adults in charge, they were totally responsible for the child's actions. Presently, the law holds the child responsible for being habitually truant where parents or guardians have taken every reasonable step to ensure attendance.

Parents or guardians who do not take every reasonable step to ensure the attendance of a child will be convicted of a summary offense. They will be ordered to pay a fine of up to $300 plus court costs, or be sentenced to complete a parenting education program.[20] In lieu of, or in addition to any other sentence, the parent or guardian may be ordered to perform community service in the school district in which the offending child resides, for a period of up to six (6) months. A parent or guardian who fails to pay the fine or costs, or complete the parenting education program may be sentenced to the county jail for up to five (5) days. Consequences such as these can be powerful incentives to promote school attendance if the law is dutifully pursued by the school district and applied by the District Justice.

The School Code requires parents to appear at the hearing before the District Justice. If the District Justice determines that a child is no longer habitually truant from school without justification, the sentence may be suspended in whole or part.

Parents or guardians who have taken every reasonable step to ensure the attendance of a child thirteen (13) years of age or older "shall not be convicted of a summary offense." Instead, the summary offense is charged to the offending child. The offending child is subject to "a fine not exceeding $300 or be assigned to an adjudication alternative program." Alternative programs include community service to the school district under the supervision of the administration.

In lieu of prosecution, the District Justice has the discretion to refer the child to the school district for services or possible disposition as a dependent child.[21] Similarly, if the child is no longer habitually truant from school, the District Justice may suspend the child's sentence or adjudication alternative in whole or part.

Conviction for habitual truancy is tied to the loss of operating privileges by the Pennsylvania Department of Transportation. A first conviction carries a ninety (90) day suspension and a second conviction requires a six (6) month suspension of driving privileges. Multiple suspensions are cumulative, not concurrent. If the child does not yet possess a valid operator's license, the issuance of the license shall be delayed for the appropriate time.

Children under thirteen (13) years of age who are habitually truant are not subject to a summary offense. They are to be referred by the school district for services or possible disposition as a dependent child.[22]

Implications

<u>Teachers and Administrators</u>:

- Establishing the residency of a student is important. It is a basis for establishing the level of subsidy that a school receives from the state. This not only refers to entering school at the elementary level (age 6), but also to secondary students who reach the age of 21 before graduation (24 P.S. Code 1301). Students reaching the age of 21 during a given school year may be counted for subsidy purposes if there has been a hearing, a court order, or prior approval by the state department of education to extend educational services beyond the statutory limit.[23]

- Residence establishes the district's legal standing to enter into an Individualized Educational Program (I.E.P.) for special education services.

- Residence (the locus of habitation) may be different from domicile (the place one calls "home").

- School district policy should reflect a procedure that insures that new students comply with all of the health requirements required by state law.

- The School Code establishes consequences for non-attendance and contains enforcement provisions if a parent/guardian or child thirteen (13) years of age or over fails to comply with the adjudication of the District Justice.

- School officials should be aware of the exceptions to compulsory school attendance.

Parents and Students:

- Residents of a school district have rights accompanied by responsibilities. Schools possess considerable latitude in determining what constitutes a legitimate excuse from school.

- The consequences for unlawful absence range from fines and alternative service for offending students to fines, parenting education programs, and imprisonment for parents or guardians who do not take every reasonable step to ensure the attendance of a child of compulsory school age.

- Families should maintain a file of student health records and immunizations. This becomes especially important when transferring from one school district to another.

- Upon enrolling their child in a new school, parents must sign a statement that informs the new district of any suspensions or expulsions from the previous school district, even pending actions. This applies particularly to exclusions from school for controlled substances and/or weapons.

PENALTIES FOR TRUANCY
UNDER PENNSYLVANIA LAW

NOTICE OF UNLAWFUL ABSENCE
(When a child of compulsory school age is habitually truant)

PARENT GUILTY

Fine   Parenting Course
and/or
Community Service

Non-Compliance

Jail

**PARENT NOT GUILTY
AND CHILD IS**

13 years or older   Less than
13 years old

Child Hearing   Refer to Children
& Youth Services
as a dependent child

Guilty

Fine   Suspension of driving
privileges

Adjudication Alternative
Program

If non-compliant, the child
is declared dependent and
referred to Family/Children
and Youth Services

1. Habitually truant: 3 days unexcused or the equivalent
2. The District Justice may suspend penalties if the child is no longer habitually truant
3. Fine: up to $300 plus court costs for each offense
4. Community Service: up to 6 months
5. Adjudication Alternative Program: i.e. community service
6. Suspension of driving privileges: first offense, 90 days; second offense, six months. If unlicensed, the student's driving privileges are deferred accordingly.

Chapter 2 Endnotes

[1] O'Leary v. Wisecup, 364 A.2d 770, 26 Pa. Cmwlth. 538 (1976).

[2] Confluence Borough School Dist. v. Ursina Borough School Dist., 88 Pa. Super. 299 (1926).

[3] In the Interest of Jessica Mae Curry, 79 Westmoreland 207 (1997).

[4] Mathias v. Richland School Dist., 592 A.2d 811 (1991), Lushen v. Peters Twp. School Dist., 65 D. & C.2d 712 (1974).

[5] Ferndale Area School Dist. v. Shawley, 313 A.2d 366, 11 Pa. Cmwlth. 185 (1973).

[6] Plyler v. Dow, 457 U.S. 202 (1982).

[7] Nancy M. v. Scanlon, 666 F. Supp. 723, (E.D. Pa. 1987).

[8] Association for Retarded Children v. Com, 343 F. Supp. 279 (Pa. 1972).

[9] Comm. v. Pasceri, 98 Montg. 276 (Pa. 1974).

[10] Pierce v. Society of Sisters, 268 U.S. 510, 45 S. Ct. 571 (1925).

[11] Wisconsin v. Yoder, 406 U.S. 205, 92 S. Ct. 1526 (1972).

[12] Comm. v. Smoker, 110 A.2d 740, 177 Pa. Super. 435 (1955).

[13] Zebra v. School District of the City of Pittsburgh, 296 A.2d 748, 449 Pa. 432 (1972), appeal after remand, 325 A.2d 330, 15 Pa. Cmwlth. 203.

[14] Comm. *ex rel.* School District of Pittsburgh v. Ross, 330 A.2d 290, 17 Pa. Cmwlth. 105 (1975).

[15] Smoker, *supra.*

[16] Comm. v. Hall, 45 A.2d 674 (Pa. Super. 1983).

[17] 22 Pa. Code 11.26.

[18] Comm. v. Grace, 48 D. & C.2d 331 (Pa. 1969).

[19] Id. at 366.

[20] 24 Pa. Code 13-1333(a)(1).

[21] As defined under 42 Pa.C.S. 6302.

[22] Ibid.

[23] Pennsylvania Department of Education Basic Education Circular, BEC 17-95.

Chapter 3 Discipline

Sources:

> First Amendment
> Fourteenth Amendment
> Common Law, *in loco parentis*
> Civil Rights Act of 1871, 42 U.S.C. 1983

Schools do not have unlimited control over student behavior. Discipline is limited to maintaining order and preserving the integrity of the educational environment. To fulfill its educational responsibility to students, schools may adopt such reasonable rules and regulations as are necessary for the management of school affairs. "In the absence of gross abuse...courts will not second guess policies of the...boards of school directors."[1] This authority is broad and firmly established in law.

Authority: Rules of Conduct

Right to Discipline

Discipline involves setting rules, enforcing them, and punishing offenders. The process is not always simple, but it is necessary. Discipline is essential to maintaining a safe, orderly environment. Clearly written and fairly administered rules and regulations help prevent confusion among students whose rights are already limited in the school setting.

Schools derive their right to discipline from the Common Law Principle of *in loco parentis* within Constitutional and statutory limitations. The context for defining a school's authority to discipline is described in case law as it applies to a.) the First and Fourteenth Amendments, and b.) where the undesirable behavior occurs.

School officials stand *in loco parentis* over students while they attend school.[2] If punishment is justified and administered appropriately, schools are within their authority to act.[3] However, action will be justified only when the control exercised is necessary to prevent incidents that interfere with the educational process.[4]

It bears repeating that the authority is substantial but not unlimited. For example, discipline is not justified if it can be established that the person administering the alleged discipline acted with malice.[5] Where malice is present, the issue is not constitutional; rather, it is a question of liability based on intent to harm.

Furthermore, discipline may not adversely affect academic achievement. This is generally interpreted as a caution against grade reductions or the use of academic sanctions for non-academic misconduct.[6]

School authority includes, but is not restricted to, establishing smoking policies. In one instance, known smokers were limited access to rest rooms except during specified five-minute intervals three times per day.[7] Likewise, regulations may prohibit driving to school and parking to ease congestion, prevent hot-rodding, deter smoking in the vehicles, and discourage leaving school grounds. A Pennsylvania court upheld such regulations even though pupils were required to walk in excess of one mile or have parents/guardians drive them.[8]

Schools may adopt and enforce reasonable rules and regulations regarding general conduct and deportment.[9] Students may even be transferred to another school within the same district because of disruptive activities, insubordination, defiance of authority, and insightful activities, as long as due process was followed.[10]

Legal Limits

There are statutory and constitutional limitations to a school's authority to discipline. The former establishes the right to discipline within the body of state and federal laws. The latter addresses due process considerations in terms of "vagueness" and freedom of expression in what the Supreme Court of the United States refers to as "overbreadth."

Legislation. A school district's authority over student conduct proceeds from the state's public school code. Here, the legislature grants local boards of education the authority to "adopt and enforce such reasonable rules and regulations as it may deem necessary and proper" with respect to managing school affairs. This includes the "conduct and deportment of all pupils attending the public schools in the district" while they are under the supervision of the school (board of directors) "including the time necessarily spent in coming to and returning from school."[11] An example is the Pennsylvania Public School Code that extends the school's authority to extra-curricular activities. A district may provide for "the suspension, dismissal, or other reasonable penalty in the case of any ... pupil who violates any of such rules or regulations."[12]

Like boards of directors who have broad powers under school laws, teachers and administrators have extensive authority over students. Teachers and administrators have the right to exercise nearly the same authority as the parents, guardians or persons in parental relationship to such pupils[13] (*in loco parentis*). This even includes prohibitions on the possession of telephone paging devices ("beepers") in school.[14] However, no action can be taken without due process since public school codes grant principals and teachers in charge of a public schools the power to suspend and expel pupils only after a proper hearing.[15]

A further look at state regulations yields a clearer definition of what constitutes proper conduct and deportment. The provision requires school districts to adopt conduct codes that include "a listing of student rights and responsibilities."[16] Most districts have adopted the state policy verbatim as board policy.

Federal legislation may also define a school's authority over student behavior. The Gun-Free Schools Act of 1994, part of the Improving America's Schools Act, clearly spells out the consequences for bringing instruments of violence into the school. Unlike earlier crime legislation that was ruled unconstitutional, this act required every state to pass a law requiring public schools to expel any student who brought a weapon to school for a minimum of one year. Under the law, a school may exclude violators who are identified with special needs. The exclusion would be considered a change in placement and it would be unilateral, that is, without the consent of the parent. For these special education students, such a change in placement may be up to forty-five (45) school days,[17] not a full year.

The Constitution. Though not all school rules are written, the constitutionality of disciplinary provisions hinge on some prior enactment (and subsequent notice) of the rules that spell out disciplinary responses to disruptive behavior.[18] The potential for litigation is significant when the rules are not sufficiently clear. If a person of "common intelligence" must guess at the meaning or application of a rule, it will not stand. The "vagueness" test has long standing in criminal prosecutions as a part of procedural due process (Fourteenth Amendment).[19] However, schools have been authorized to "impose disciplinary sanctions for a wide range of unanticipated conduct" that disrupts the educational process.[20] Therefore, school policies that address "vulgarity," "intentional disruption," and "willful disobedience" have been sustained by the courts in spite of vagueness challenges.[21]

In terms of protecting First Amendment free expression rights, court challenges are not limited to vagueness. The "overbreadth doctrine" is invoked to ascertain whether a rule, regardless of the nature of the conduct in question, applies to some constitutionally protected behavior. If that is the case, the school rule or regulation will be struck down as having a "chilling" effect on protected rights. Still it takes a great deal to strike down policy based on the overbreadth doctrine. Citing vagueness and overbreadth, a student challenged his three (3) day suspension under an anti-loitering rule. An Illinois court dismissed the case holding that the rule gave fair notice and had sufficiently clear meaning within the school context. Furthermore, a prohibition against loitering was within the discretion of the administration to control the coming and going of students. Here, after numerous complaints, the school declared an area adjacent to school property off-limits. The school notified students and parents that violators would receive a three (3) day suspension. As classes ended, a student left the building at the end of the day and met with friends on the property in question. A school security officer approached the students and wrote up a report, whereupon disciplinary action was taken.[22] In face of both constitutional challenges, latitude was granted by the court to restrict student gatherings extending the schools' authority to discipline off school grounds.

Even though school rules range from disciplinary suspension for academic dishonesty[23] to corporal punishment,[24] two areas create concern for both students and school officials. The first of these addresses in school -versus out-of-school conduct. The second deals with the extent to which a school may exercise control over participation in activities.

In-School v. Out-of-School

As a general rule, schools do not have the authority to discipline students for out-of-school behavior unless the behavior has a direct effect on school discipline or adversely impacts the "health, safety or welfare" of the student or others.[25] With this in mind, school authorities must draw a reasonable relationship to the disciplinary action and the school's educational purpose. If the relationship is not established, the school will exceed the limits of its authority.

The limits of authority begin with statutory grants of power that allow schools to regulate pupils "during such times as they are under the supervision of the board of school directors and teachers, including the time necessarily spent in coming to and returning from school."[26] For example, two students were expelled for smoking marijuana on a school bus while en-route from the school to their home.[27] Similarly, misconduct on school property but outside regular classroom hours is punishable. The suspension of a student attending a high school basketball game while under the influence of alcohol was sustained by the courts.[28] Relying on the reasoning in *Wood v. Strickland*,[29] the court had "no problem with the question of jurisdiction of the school authorities."

The school district's authority to regulate student behavior at "such times as they are under the supervision of the board," implies that there are times when students are not under the supervision of the board.

When, then, is a student properly considered under the supervision of the board of directors? From the above cases, it is clear that a student is "under the supervision of the board" when a student is on school grounds during or outside school hours,[30] while a student is off school grounds but going to and from school,[31] and while attending or participating in a school-sponsored or school-related activity off school property.[32]

Extra-curricular activities. In determining the limits of a school's authority over extra-curricular activities, one must consider reasonableness. Boards may prescribe, adopt, and enforce such reasonable rules and regulations as it may deem proper. It may be said that activities automatically fall under the jurisdiction of the board by virtue of the board action that created them.

In *King v. Hempfield*, *supra*, a school disciplined a student who was not attending or participating in a school activity. The misconduct did not take place in school or on school premises; yet, the student was barred from participating in an extra-curricular activity. This Pennsylvania court denied a preliminary injunction against the school's action. The student's suspension from the activity was upheld.

Participating in extra-curricular activities is viewed by the courts as a privilege rather than a right. It may, therefore, be restricted as a result of disciplinary code violations. Since extra-curricular involvement implies representing the school and depicting its character, eligibility is subject to greater authority by the school district.[33]

The issue of control in the area of extra-curricular activities is covered more completely in Chapter 1, "Activities."

Out-of-school conduct. The general rule concerning a school's authority to discipline for misconduct occurring out-of-school is that the conduct must have a direct, substantial, and adverse effect upon the school's educational program. In the classic 1859 case, *Lander v. Seaver*, a boy outside of school while in the presence of other pupils, used "contemptuous language, with design to insult" the school master. The Supreme Court of Vermont observed:

> ...Where the offense has a direct and immediate tendency to injure the school and bring the master's authority into contempt, as in this case when done in the presence of other scholars and of the master, and with a design to insult him, we think he has the right to punish the scholar for such acts if he comes again to school.[34]

In a more recent incident, the federal district court rejected a student's claim that discipline for out-of-school behavior was improper. A high school student, while off campus, called a teacher an obscene name. The teacher heard the comment and reported the student to the school administration. The student received a three-day in-school suspension. The court affirmed the school district's authority over out-of-school behavior as a means of maintaining order and discipline. "It may be deemed a matter for discipline in the discretion of the school authorities. To countenance such student conduct ...without imposing sanctions could lead to devastating effects.[35]

In another case, a brawl broke out after a sporting event when a student struck another student with a board off school grounds. The student was suspended and eventually expelled. The court reasoned that the participants were students and the behavior was precipitated by a school related incident; therefore, the administrative and board actions were justified.[36]

More recently, a Pennsylvania court upheld a school vandalism policy by acknowledging the school's authority to suspend a student who participated with others in throwing eggs at a teacher's house. The court declared that the misconduct clearly "intended to threaten and intimidate and requires a response from school authorities that makes it clear that such behavior will not be tolerated."[37]

Some jurisdictions concur;[38] some do not.[39]

It should be remembered that although the school has a right to maintain discipline, constitutional guarantees must be preserved,[40] and equity respected.[41] It is essential that notice of the prohibited conduct is given and adequate guidelines to prevent arbitrary enforcement are provided. The student must be afforded the full range of due process under the law. See Chapter 4, "Due Process."

Corporal Punishment

Teachers and principals are responsible for maintaining safety and order to preserve the educational environment. Because parents have placed their children under the charge of school officials, they have legally acquiesced their control of such children to educators who stand *in loco parentis* so that the educational program can function. Corporal punishment is one of the ways that control of the student is maintained.

The common law concept of *in loco parentis* has been upheld in most jurisdictions reserving the right to administer corporal punishment. A few states have banned corporal punishment and California requires written parental permission before administering it. However, the Commonwealth of Pennsylvania continues to adhere to the practice. The United States Supreme Court addressed the constitutionality of corporal punishment in *Ingraham v. Wright*. The Court declared that "The prevalent rule in this country today privileges such force as a teacher or administrator reasonably believes to be necessary for proper control, training and education."[42]

Ingraham held that the "liberty interest" of the child was adequately protected under traditional common law (*in loco parentis*). Furthermore, the Court adhered to the "long-standing limitation...that...the Eighth Amendment [cruel and unusual punishment] does not apply to the paddling of children as a means of maintaining discipline in public schools."

Glaser v. Marrietta[43] is an example of how the courts sustain a school's authority to discipline in Pennsylvania. After discovering that a certain 12-year-old was responsible for an altercation, an assistant principal administered three (3) paddling strokes. The court held that this administration of corporal punishment was in accord with school district regulations, without excessive force, and under a carefully controlled situation. Therefore, schools that enact corporal punishment policies and administer them under reasonable conditions do so within the scope of their authority.

The statutory right to discipline students comes from the school board's authority to adopt and enforce reasonable rules and regulations and the similar delegation of authority of teachers, vice-principals, and principals. Given reasonable rules, then, "teachers may impose reasonable but not excessive force to discipline a child . . ."[44] Even so, educators are not guaranteed the right to administer corporal punishment. Although permitted, corporal punishment is not mandated, and it is up to each district to determine how, if at all, it may be administered.[45]

Case law affirms that the use of any form or degree of corporal punishment where forbidden by a school board could result in a violation of the School Code.[46] Therefore, administering corporal punishment in opposition to policy might constitute grounds for dismissal.[47]

It is also clear that tort liability for negligence is a cause of action as a result of excessive punishment.[48] However, criminal action in assault and battery is rare due to the nature of proving malice on the part of the teacher. Slapping, particularly in the face will be construed as corporal punishment.[49] Likewise, punching,[50] pushing to the floor,[51] paddling,[52] throwing students about the room and against the walls[53] all constitute forms of corporal punishment. Mere touching without force does not.[54] However, the location of the touch may give rise to other causes of action such as sexual harassment. See Chapter 17, "Sexual Harassment." The rule of law in Pennsylvania is that school officials have the discretion to use corporal punishment; however, it must be reasonable, not malicious or excessive.[55]

Remedies have also been sought under Section 1983 of the Civil Rights Act of 1871 (42 U.S.C. 1983) prohibiting acts of discrimination by public officials. Under Section 1983, persons acting under state law who subject or cause any other citizen to be deprived of any "rights, privileges, or immunities...shall be liable to the party injured in an action at law." Although educators, as public officials, were granted "good faith" immunity from prosecution under Section 1983,[56] liability exists in the form of compensatory damages for proven actual injury[57] based on the test of reasonableness.[58] Most recently, the courts have given indication that Section 1983 may give rise to liability under the "state-created danger" theory. See Chapter 16, "Negligence and Tort Liability."

In one case, the court held that infliction of excessive corporal punishment violated substantive due process rights under Section 1983. The court was able to determine that the force in this case was "inspired by sadism rather than a merely careless or unwise excess of zeal."[59] A similar conclusion was reached by another court concerning a disciplinary action taken with a third grade child. On one occasion, the child was held upside down and struck on the thigh five times with a paddle. Later, the same child received two swats with a paddle before being made to "hunch over" a chair for three more. The court noted: "at some point excessive corporal punishment violates the student's substantive due process rights."[60]

In another instance, a second grade child was tied to a chair by a jump rope securing her waist and legs for an entire school day (with the exception of lunch time). This disciplinary procedure was repeated for the major part of the following day. Here, the court declared a violation of substantive due process as a result of the corporal punishment being "arbitrary, capricious" and "unrelated to maintaining an atmosphere conducive to learning."[61]

Given statutory language, it would seem that Section 1983 remedies apply only to public schools. However, at least one exception was made for a private school where numerous state-mandated placements occurred.[62] Contractual provisions between the state and the private school established significant financial involvement as well as regulatory compliance in a number of areas. The private school was held to be responsible in its actions related to controlling the learning environment.

Corporal punishment can be defined as physically punishing a student for an offense against a school discipline code. Teachers and school officials may administer corporal punishment when authorized by, and in accordance with policies and guidelines established by the board of school directors. If administered, such punishment must be reasonable and under no circumstances cause bodily injury.

Parents or guardians have a right to be notified of a corporal punishment policy. Once notified, they retain the right to prohibit its use on their child by notifying the school authorities (usually in writing).

Even where corporal punishment is prohibited by school policy, teachers and school authorities may employ reasonable force in certain situations. These situations generally include actions to quell a disturbance, to obtain possession of weapons or other dangerous objects, for the purpose of self-defense, and/or for the protection of persons.

Recognizing the danger of excessive corporal punishment, regulations caution against applying corporal punishment in the heat of anger. No disciplinary action should exceed in degree the seriousness of the offense and, while it might seem surprising, some regulations find it necessary to specify that under no circumstance should any student be required to remove clothing when being punished.[63]

Implications

Board of Education:

- While corporal punishment may be legal, policy considerations dictate caution in specifying why and how it should be administered. Litigation is expensive, even where the challenge is unsuccessful.

Teachers and Administrators:

- Schools have the legal authority to discipline their students for misconduct in school or while engaged in a school-related activity.

- School discipline may also extend to out-of-school behavior. The authority beyond school grounds; however, is limited to such acts that have a direct, substantial, and adverse effect upon the school's educational program.

- Codes of conduct should be written in a clear and understandable fashion to avoid confusion and discourage litigation.

- Even though not all school rules and regulations have to be in writing, it is advisable to codify them. They should be written in such a way as to provide the flexibility to cover unanticipated circumstances and incidents.

- Parents and students should always be given notice of the rules and regulations contained in the code of conduct. They should also receive prompt notice of any changes

- Direct reference to the actual document (policy) adopted by the Board of Directors is advisable.

- Corporal punishment is legal but not mandated. If your school district prohibits its use, do not attempt to circumvent the policy.

- Liability may be incurred if corporal punishment is not administered with reasonable force.

- Never administer corporal punishment in anger or with malice.

- It would make good sense to have another responsible adult present to witness the administration of any form of corporal punishment.

Parents and Students:

- Schools not only have the power to discipline students for in-school behavior; they may, within limits, control out-of-school behavior as well.

- Education is a right; extra-curricular activities are a privilege. School policies that address misconduct resulting in removal from extra-curricular activities have been upheld by the courts.

- Corporal punishment is legal and school officials may employ reasonable force in administering it. Such force may also be employed in certain situations that are not of a disciplinary nature. Even in the absence of a corporal punishment policy, the use of such force will be upheld in a court of law.

- Parents or guardians may request (in writing) that corporal punishment not be used on a child in a school where a corporal punishment policy exists.

- Corporal punishment is generally associated with touch; however, not all touching is considered corporal punishment.

- It should be noted that even if the legislature has chosen to permit teachers to use reasonable physical force, no legislature has sanctioned the use of physical force by a student.[64]

Chapter 3 Endnotes

[1] Comm. v. Hall, 455 A.2d 674 (Pa. Super. 1983).

[2] Axtell v. LaPenna, 323 F. Supp. 1077, (D.C. Pa. 1971).

[3] Comm. v. Allen, 1 D.& C.3d 742, (Pa. 1976).

[4] Axtell, *supra*.

[5] Thrasher v. General Casualty Co. of Wisconsin, 732 F. Supp. 966 (W.D. Wis. 1990).

[6] Smith v. School District of the City of Hobart, 811 F. Supp. 391 (N.D. Ind. 1993); Katzman v. Cumberland Valley School District, 479 A.2d 671, 84 Pa. Cmwlth. 474 (1984).

[7] Figuero v. Thompson, 1 D.& C.3d 266 (Pa. 1975).

[8] Alman v. Fox Chapel Area School District, 4 D.& C.3d 288 (Pa. 1977).

[9] Woodring v. School Directors of Bald Eagle Area School District, 56 D.& C.2d 401 (Pa. 1971).

[10] Lee v. School District of Philadelphia, 51 D.& C.2d 504 (Pa. 1971).

[11] 24 P.S. Code 5-510.

[12] 24 P.S. Code 5-511(a).

[13] 24 P.S. Code 13-1317.

[14] 24 P.S. Code 13-1317.1 with noted exceptions:

1. Members of a volunteer fire company, ambulance or rescue squad.
2. Students who may require the device as a result of a medical condition of an immediate family member.

[15] 24 P.S. Code 13-1318.

[16] 22 Pa. Code 12.3(c).

[17] Public Law 103-783, Section 615(e)(3) of the Individuals with Disabilities Education Act, 20 U.S.C., Section 1415(e)(3).

[18] Bethel v. Fraser, 478 U.S. 675, 686 (1986).

[19] Connally v. General Casualty Co., 269 U.S. 385 (1926).

44

[20] Bethel, *supra*.

[21] Williams v. Board of Education, 626 S.W.2d 361 (Ark. 1982); Murray v. West Baton Rouge Parish School Board, 472 F.2d 438 (5th Cir. 1973). See also Bethel, supra.

[22] Weimerslage v. Maine Township High School District 207, 824 F. Supp. 136 (N.D. Ill. 1993).

[23] Rauer v. State University of New York, 552 N.Y.2d 983 (A.D. 3d Dept. 1990).

[24] Ingraham v. Wright, 430 U.S. 651, 97 S. Ct. 1401 (1977).

[25] 22 Pa. Code 12.6.

[26] 22 Pa. Code 12.3, 24 P.S. Code 5.

[27] Abremski v. Southeastern School District, 421 A.2d 485 (Pa. 1980).

[28] Quier v. Quakertown Community School District, 27 Bucks Co. L. Rep. 199 (Pa. 1975).

[29] Wood v. Strickland, 420 U.S. 308, 95 S. Ct. 1042 (1978).

[30] Quier, *supra*.

[31] Abremski, *supra*.

[32] King v. Hempfield School District, 8 D.& C.4th 48 (1983).

[33] Bunger v. Iowa High School Athletic Association, 197 N.W.2d 535 (Iowa 1972).

[34] Lander v. Seaver, 32 Vt. 114 (Vt. 1859).

[35] Fenton v. Stear, 423 F. Supp. 767 (W.D. Pa. 1976).

[36] Porter v. Board of School Directors, 445 A.2d 1386 (Pa. 1982).

[37] Patrick Shaw v. John McCracken, Superintendent, and the Corry Area School District, (W.D. Pa. 1995).

[38] R.R. v. Shore Regional High School District, 263 A.2d 184 (N.J. Super. 1970); State *ex rel.* Dresser v. Board of School District No. 1, 116 N.W. 232 (Wisc. 1908); O'Rourke v. Walker, 120 Conn. 130 (Conn. 1925).

[39] Klein v. Smith, 635 F. Supp. 1440 (D. Me. 1986); Board of Education v. Ambach 45 N.Y.S. 2d 77 (1983); Stanley v. Northeast Independent School District, 462 F.2d. 960 (5th Cir. 1972); Weeds v. Wright 334 F.2d 369 (5th Cir. 1964).

[40] 22 Pa. Code 12.3.

[41] 22 Pa. Code 12.4.

[42] Ingraham v. Wright, 430 U.S. 651, 97 S. Ct. 1401 (1977).

[43] Glaser v. Marietta, 351 F. Supp. 555 (D.C. Pa. 1972).

[44] Ingraham, *supra*.

[45] Harris v. Comm., Secretary of Ed., 372 A.2d 953, 29 Pa. Cmwlth. 625 (1977).

[46] Belasco v. Board of Public Education of School District of Pittsburgh, 486 A.2d 538, 87 Pa. Cmwlth. 5 (1985); Van Hooser v. Warren County Board of Education, 807 S.W.2d 230 (1991).

[47] Blascovich v. Board of School Directors of Shamokin Area School District, 410 A.2d 407, 49 Pa. Cmwlth. 131 (1980).

[48] Thrasher v. General Casualty Co. of Wisconsin, 732 F. Supp. 966 (1990).

[49] Harris, *supra*.

[50] Blascovich, *supra*.

[51] Caffas v. Board of School Directors of Upper Dauphin Area, 353 A.2d 898, 23 Pa. Cmwlth. 578 (1976).

[52] Belasco, *supra*.

[53] Caffas, *supra*.

[54] Harris, *supra*.

[55] Chodkowski v. Beck, 106 P.L.J. 115 (Pa. 1958).

[56] Wood v. Strickland, 420 U.S. 308, 95 S. Ct. 992 (1975).

[57] Carey v. Piphus, 435 U.S. 247, 98 S. Ct. 1042 (1978).

[58] Harlow v. Fitzgerald, 457 U.S. 800, 102 S. Ct. 272 (1982).

[59] Hall v. Tawney, 621 F.2d 607 (1980).

[60] Garcia v. Miera, 817 F.2d 650 (1987).

[61] Jefferson v. Ysleta Independent S.D., 817 F.2d 303 (1987).

[62] Milonas v. Williams, 691 F.2d 931 (1982), *certiorari* denied, 460 U.S. 1069 (1983).

---

[63] 22 Pa. Code 12.5e.

[64] Edwards v. Jersey Shore Area School District, 301 A.2d 116 (Pa. Cmwlth. 1973).

Chapter 4   Due Process

Sources:

> Improving America's Schools Act, 20 U.S.C. 6301 *et seq.*
> Individuals with Disabilities Education Act, 20 U.S.C. Sections 1400-1485
> Rehabilitation Act of 1973, 29 U.S.C. 794
> Fourteenth Amendment
> Common Law, *in loco parentis*

For regular education and special needs students, a suspension may be an exclusion from classes for varying lengths of time or an exclusion from school for a period of one to ten days. For regular education students, an expulsion is an exclusion from school by the board of education for a period exceeding ten consecutive days. For special needs students, an expulsion is an exclusion from school beyond ten consecutive days *or* fifteen cumulative days. Even with *in loco parentis,* schools do not have a blanket authorization to suspend or expel students.

School has been held to be an entitlement,[1] and, as such, only certain types of behavior are serious enough to warrant a removal from school. Specific behavior must be spelled out in a student discipline code or at least be made clearly known to students.[2]

The determination to suspend or expel must consider balancing the student's right to remain in school, the student's right to reasonably know that the misconduct is a basis for suspension or expulsion, and the student's right to due process. This should be balanced with the school's right to maintain order and safety in order to preserve the educational environment. If a student's rights are violated, the act of suspension or expulsion will be nullified; if the individual's rights are preserved, the act of suspension or expulsion will be sustained.

Suspension and Expulsion of Regular Students

<u>In General</u>

Case law supports the school board's authority to make and enforce reasonable rules as it deems necessary and proper.[3] See Chapter 3, "Discipline, Authority: Rules of Conduct."

Exclusion from school may involve graduation. In one case a high school senior's suspension carried through graduation ceremonies. Such a suspension was held not be the equivalent of expulsion even though the student never returned to school. The student had, in fact, graduated and a person may not be considered expelled when becoming an alumnus.[4] In another case, requirements for graduation were not considered beyond the State Board of Education's scope of authority. Graduation requirements are not simply separation requirements, they are a part of educational process. Hence, suspensions and expulsions apply to them. They are considered to be a part of the school system and its functions.[5]

With the passage of the Improving America's Schools Act, board actions to expel students who bring weapons to school have been upheld consistently.

Drug-related incidents have justified grounds for suspension and expulsion.[6] Local school boards have the power to suspend students for smoking marijuana on a school bus and expel a student for such behavior.[7] Students smoking marijuana on school grounds have also been permanently expelled, giving evidence of the broad discretionary power of the board where they believed that the student in question might be a hazard to other students by providing the substance to others.[8] Alcohol consumption might result in a suspension or expulsion even if it occurs on a school-sponsored trip.[9] Board action is not limited to the academic program; it may extend to exclusion from extracurricular activities.[10]

It is clear that acts of vandalism perpetrated against the student's school might result in suspension or expulsion. However, if the vandalism is to another school district, it may not be sufficient to disrupt the educational process in the student's own school and, thereby, warrant expulsion. The same reasoning applies to vandalism to the student's own school over a vacation period.[11]

Suspension for disrespect to a teacher is a reasonable exercise of school board authority.[12] Likewise, the courts have upheld the expulsion of a student who assaulted other students off school grounds after illegally consuming alcohol.[13]

Disciplinary transfers are held to be within a school board's power when not technically interrupting a student's educational program. It may be viewed as an internal matter.[14] As long as due process rights are preserved in all other respects, immediate suspension may be utilized in an emergency situation where there is a potential for physical harm.[15]

In any case, suspension or expulsion may require a school district to establish provisions for make-up work.[16] In the event of a long-term exclusion from school, the courts usually impose a continuing duty of care to educate compulsory school-age children. Long-term suspensions or expulsions may require tutoring. Parents generally have the authority to secure what they consider an appropriate education for an expelled child. However, if they are unable to bear the burden, the school district will assume both the responsibility for educating the child and the ensuing costs for a student of compulsory education age.

Procedural Requirements

A school district's responsibility to preserve individual rights begins at the inception of the disciplinary process. School officials are required to obtain information and gather evidence in order to sustain a disciplinary action. The context of a school district's action to suspend or expel a student is clearly civil, not criminal. As such, *Miranda*[17] warnings are not required to be given to the accused in school disciplinary actions.

A Michigan court addressed the civil/criminal context by noting that the "*Miranda* rule is not a constitutional right but, rather, a procedural safeguard" to protect an individual "against self-incrimination."[18]

Miranda warnings contain the following:

1. The right to remain silent
2. The caution that anything said can be used against the accused in a court of law
3. The right to have an attorney present
4. The right to court appointed counsel

Questioning students without giving *Miranda* warnings has been challenged as a "custodial interrogation," namely, one where there is reason to believe that the accused is being significantly deprived of freedom to act. Courts have held to the contrary. Since the context of a school investigation is not restrictive by nature, questioning by school personnel does not fall within the definition of a "custodial interrogation."[19] The courts have even upheld student interrogations by security personnel hired by the school district because the school's primary mission is education, not law enforcement.[20] Numerous jurisdictions concur. *Miranda* warnings are required in a criminal context, in a "custodial interrogation," or when the interrogation is initiated or conducted by law enforcement officials.[21] They do not apply to school officials or school personnel.

Another procedural issue arising from the need to obtain evidence at the inception of a school-based disciplinary action is search. The school is not held to the same strict standard in conducting a search as police officers. Schools need only have "reasonable suspicion" as opposed to "probable cause." See Chapter 9, "Student Searches."

Once the disciplinary action goes beyond the initial stages, students are accorded procedural rights through the application of the Fourteenth Amendment.[22] The landmark decision, *Goss v Lopez*,[23] deals specifically with the matter of exclusion from school. *Goss* held that all the procedural safeguards required in a criminal proceeding are not extended to public school hearings. However, the Court established that, since education was an entitlement, it is a property right protected by the Fourteenth Amendment.[24] *Goss* established minimum standards that apply to suspensions of ten days or less. The Court reasoned that due process for in-school suspensions (i.e. exclusion from classes) should be flexible based upon the seriousness of the misbehavior and the severity of the penalty. As the misconduct becomes more serious and the penalty becomes more severe (i.e. exclusion from school), the procedural due process requirements become correspondingly stricter.

Since most disciplinary action resulting in suspension or expulsion is based on a violation of school regulations, the language of the regulation must be specific and reasonably understood by the student. Merely restating the language of a judicial opinion does not guarantee specificity,[25] especially when applied to constitutionally guaranteed rights such as free speech. But, in Pennsylvania when a student's behavior includes "flagrant disregard of teachers," "loitering in areas of heavy traffic," and "rowdy behavior in the area of heavy traffic" the court rejected the student's claims of vagueness.[26] It appears that regulations should be written in such a fashion as to be clearly understood by parent and student. Furthermore, such rules should be publicized and made known to all. This is an advisable practice in any jurisdiction.

The Pennsylvania Public School Code contains typical language describing due process requirements in suspension and expulsion cases:

Every principal or teacher in charge of a public school may temporarily suspend any pupil on account of disobedience or misconduct, and any principal or teacher suspending any pupil shall promptly notify the district superintendent or secretary of the board of school directors. The board may, after a proper hearing, suspend such child for such time as it may determine, or may permanently expel him.

This forms the basis of due process actions in the public schools.

In-School Suspension. In-school suspension requires oral notice of suspension to the student with an opportunity to respond to the charges.[27] This usually occurs in the office of the administrator. Parents/guardians must be notified within a reasonable amount of time. Educational opportunity must be available to the student while serving the suspension.

Out-of-School Suspension. *Goss v. Lopez* has essentially defined the terms of due process for short-term suspensions, exclusions from school for a period not exceeding 10 days. In *Goss*, nine junior high school students were suspended for 10 days following a lunchroom disturbance involving some damage to school property. One of the suspended students, Dwight Lopez, testified that he was not a party to the destructive conduct. He further claimed that no one from the school testified to the contrary. Therefore, there was no evidence "in the record indicating the official basis for concluding otherwise." Simply stated, he never had a hearing.

In another aspect of the case, a female student was arrested with other students and taken to the police station, whereupon, she was released without being formally charged. Before school the next day, the student was notified of her 10-day suspension. It was clear from the record that she, too, had no hearing.

A third student suspended in the incident had no record of the suspension in his files, even though the files of six others "contained either direct references to the suspensions or copies of letters sent to their parents advising them of the suspension."

On the basis of the evidence, the Supreme Court affirmed the lower court decision that the students "were denied due process of law because they were 'suspended without hearing prior to suspension or within a reasonable time thereafter'. . ."[28]

The Court essentially held that certain minimal procedures are required before a student can be removed from school. Some kind of notice and hearing must be given when a student is suspended for ten days or less. The notice may be oral or written, and the student must have an opportunity to present the other side of the story after being given an explanation of the evidence. Since the Court did not specify that a delay should occur between the notice and hearing, it held that basic due process requirements would be satisfied by an informal discussion immediately following the alleged misconduct. The student should be told what the infraction was, why the accusation was made, and be given the opportunity to tell his/her side of the story.

Suspensions of three (3) days or less can be given by the principal or any other person in charge of the public school. Oral notice is sufficient[29] and the student need only be informed of the reasons for such suspension and given an opportunity to respond. If a danger to the school community exists, the student may be immediately excluded from school pending a hearing.[30]

It is further required that parents be notified in writing when the suspension is between three (3) and ten (10) days. Notice must be given within a reasonable time in advance of an informal hearing. Where parents had received oral but not written notification prior to the hearing in a four-day suspension, the court held that due process was violated.[31]

If it is clear that the health, safety or welfare of the school is threatened, prior notice is not necessary and a student may be suspended immediately. This also holds for violations of school weapons policies based on state law.[32]

A hearing enables the student to meet with the appropriate official and explain why he/she should not be suspended. Normally, the hearing should occur before the suspension. Retroactive suspensions have been held a violation of due process on appeal. For example, when students were directed not to attend classes on a Tuesday morning when, in fact, suspensions were imposed on Wednesday, this constituted evidence that suspension took place prior to the hearing.[33] Hearings held one day after suspensions for drug activity met due process guidelines especially since students requested an adversarial hearing with attorneys present.[34]

Suspensions are not permitted to run consecutively beyond ten (10) school days and students have the responsibility to make up work missed while on suspension. In the words of the *Goss* court:

> If school administrators follow procedures which result in a fair factual determination made after notice and an opportunity to defend against the charges of misconduct, then no matter how informal the procedure, the student has been accorded the minimum requirements of the due process clause of the Fourteenth Amendment.[35]

As mentioned earlier, the student must be afforded the opportunity to make up schoolwork or exams missed while excluded from school.

Expulsion. Since, by definition, any exclusion from school for a period of more than ten days is considered an expulsion the procedural requirements are necessarily stricter.

Written notice describing the misconduct, containing specific reference to the rules violation, and setting the time and place of the hearing must be sent certified mail to the student's parents or guardian.

A formal hearing must be held "with all reasonable speed" and shall be held in private unless the student or parent requests a public hearing. The hearing must be impartial, separating judicial and prosecutorial functions. As such, the school board solicitor shall not act as the presiding judge. Yet, in at least the expulsion hearing, it was not violative of due process to have the solicitor prosecute the case against a student, rule on evidentiary questions, and advise the school board as long as the student was represented by counsel and given the opportunity to provide his side of the story.[36]

A student may not only have the right to be represented by counsel in a formal hearing, but the student may also request the names of the prosecution's witnesses and copies of statements/affidavits of those witnesses. Furthermore, those witnesses against the student may be required to appear at the hearing to answer questions and be cross-examined. The accused student may testify or present witnesses on his/her own behalf.

Since a school exclusionary hearing is a civil rather than a criminal proceeding, the Fifth Amendment right against self-incrimination does not apply. The student is required to testify against him/herself, and while such testimony may eventually be used in criminal proceedings, such use of information and testimony does not constitute double jeopardy. Even information used in a prior suspension is not improper when applied to a subsequent expulsion for the same offense.[37]

The courts have reasoned that it is not necessary for the guilt of the student to be proven "beyond a reasonable doubt." Rather, it is only necessary to establish guilt based on "substantial evidence." The standard consists of evidence that a reasonable person would accept as adequate to determine guilt as opposed to preponderance of the evidence in criminal cases. Furthermore, evidence that is technically "hearsay" or circumstantial may be properly heard and considered. Local agencies are not bound by technical rules of evidence at agency hearings, and all relevant evidence of reasonably probative value may be received.

Conversely, evidence substantiable in a criminal case would be acceptable in a hearing to determine whether or not to expel a student. Where a board accepted in evidence a criminal citation for underage drinking and payment of a fine, the court upheld the violation of the school alcohol policy and the student stood expelled for 20 days.[38]

The hearing shall be made before the board, a duly authorized committee of the board, or a qualified hearing examiner appointed by the board. A record of the hearing must be kept and a copy may be provided at the student's expense.

Local Agency Law requires a written decision based on a majority vote of the full board (a total of five votes) containing findings of fact and conclusions. Where findings of fact and conclusions of law were not set forth, the decision will be rendered invalid[39] and either a new hearing or adjudication must take place[40] or the appeal court may modify the decision on a hearing *de novo*.[41] In one instance, a court modified a school board's decision by eliminating an expulsion where students took a second sip from a soft drink mixed with whiskey and realized that the drink contained alcohol. The court's discretion was considered proper when it based its findings on the facts that the students were good students with no prior discipline problems.[42]

School boards and officials have comprehensive authority within constitutional bounds to maintain order and discipline including permanent expulsion where necessary.[43] When this occurs, the continuing duty of care for the education of the student lies with the school district if parents are unable to bear the cost.

School districts are permitted by law to continue an expulsion from another school district without a hearing in the new district. Furthermore, records may follow from one district to another in cases where a student has been adjudicated in the juvenile court system.

Appeals to the decisions by the board of school directors may be made to the state courts at the appropriate level if the student disagrees with the results of the hearing. If a constitutional question is involved, the appropriate court of appeals is the Federal District Court.

Suspension and Expulsion of Students with Disabilities

In General

Under the Individuals with Disabilities Education Act (IDEA), handicapped students cannot be deprived of a free and appropriate public education. Where schools have attempted to discipline exceptional students by suspension, expulsion or transfer, case law has developed guidelines for disciplining exceptional students in conformity to the Individuals with Disabilities Education Act (IDEA) and the State Board Regulations for Special Education.

Mentally Handicapped Students

In-school suspensions of less than 10 days for mentally retarded students are treated the same as for regular education or gifted students as long as adequate instruction is provided to the student while suspended. Here, suspension is not considered a change in placement. However, in-school suspensions for more than ten (10) days would constitute a change in placement and, as such, requires the procedural due process. This requires an evaluation involving a multidisciplinary team (MDT) meeting, evaluation report (ER), a review of the individualized educational program (IEP), notice of recommended educational placement (NOREP), right to a hearing, and other special education due process considerations.[44]

Short-term out-of-school suspensions, or exclusion from school for one (1) to 10 days, constitutes a change in placement. Any exclusion from school for mentally retarded students invokes the full range of special education procedures: MDT, ER, IEP, NOREP, etc.

Long-term out-of-school suspension, exclusion for more than 10 days, requires the special education team to conduct a functional behavioral assessment and a manifestation determination to ascertain if the behavior in question is related to the handicap. Parents/guardians must then approve action to provide appropriate educational services or change the placement for the suspended student.

Bus suspensions, or the revocation of transportation privileges, for mentally retarded students may also require procedural due process. Short-term bus suspensions (10 days or less) are not considered changes in placement unless such a change substantially affects the student's educational experience.[45] An exclusion of more than 10 days from the bus constitutes a change in educational placement.

Keep in mind that a suspension or expulsion of a special needs student other than mentally handicapped for conduct unrelated to his/her disability is constitutional and not a violation of the IDEA. In a recent case in the Seventh Circuit, the court reasoned that if the misbehavior does not stem from the disability "there is simply no justification for exempting [the student] from the rules applicable to other students."[46]

There are four exceptions to the due process requirements outlined in the IDEA. First, the office of the Secretary of Education may approve an interim change in placement for students with mental retardation for periods not exceeding 10 consecutive or cumulative days. Second, if a student brings a weapon to school or has "knowing possession" of illegal drugs, change in placement is immediate and permitted for up to 45 days.[47] Third, school districts may obtain a court order to override the right of a parent/guardian to have the student remain in the original placement pending due process. Fourth, when a student poses a threat to him/herself or to other students "beyond a preponderance of the evidence" the student may be removed for up to 45 days.[48]

Other Eligible or Thought-to-be Eligible Students

Students who are not mentally retarded yet possess some other disability may also be identified as exceptional. These students and those whose status is pending placement or in question of placement also have rights under the IDEA.

In-school suspensions of other exceptional or thought-to-be exceptional students are handled in the same manner as that of regular students. In-school suspension is not considered a change in placement for them.

The procedures for short-term out-of-school suspensions, or exclusions from school for less than 10 consecutive days, for exceptional or thought-to-be exceptional students are the same as for regular students. Short-term exclusions, therefore, do not call for special education procedural requirements. Even so, the new IDEA cautions against a *cumulative* total of more than 10 days exclusion from school for such students.

The long-term out-of-school suspension of these students is considered a change in placement. Long-term suspensions are defined as exclusions from school for a period of more than 10 consecutive or cumulative days. The change in placement invokes the full range of procedural requirements. Specifically they are:

1. Evaluation (ER)
2. IEP meeting
3. Procedural safeguards for parents/guardians
    a. notice of recommended educational placement (NOREP) for a change in placement
    b. the right to challenge the result
    c. "stay put" provision for the student.

The "stay put" provision of the IDEA is a safeguard against inappropriate placement. It requires the school district to maintain the student's current placement until due process is completed or the parents/guardians and the school district agree otherwise. This holds true even if the student, who was not identified as needing special education prior to the rules infraction, is in the process of a special needs assessment. Schools are, thus, prevented from circumventing due process by denying an appropriate special education placement to disruptive students.[49]

With the exceptional or thought-to-be exceptional student frozen in his/her placement, due process should commence with a determination as to the relationship of the misconduct to the disability.[50] In the past schools have skirted the link between the behavior and the handicap by "creative" means. Deviating from normal school policy is one way of dealing with the issue. Without a consistent, systematic application of board policy, even providing home instruction for exceptional students will not stand court scrutiny if home instruction is not normal policy for similar actions involving all students.[51]

Serial suspensions are yet another way that schools have dealt with misconduct by exceptional or thought-to-be exceptional students. The mere fact that a behavior or a set of behaviors reoccur raises the question of behavior related to the disability as well as possible re-evaluation and revised placement.[52]

Likewise, indefinite suspensions may not be used to mask expulsion and thereby circumvent special education due process requirements.[53]

If a student's misconduct is not related to the disability, disciplinary action may be taken with the parent/guardian's approval for the exclusion from school. Any expulsion (long-term exclusion from school in excess of 10 consecutive or cumulative days) must follow from the determination that the student's behavior is not related to the handicap. If it is, special education due process requirements consistent with a change in placement must be followed.[54]

Seriously Emotionally Disturbed and Socially Maladjusted

Considerable confusion exists when school officials deal with students who are socially maladjusted or seriously emotionally disturbed (SED). Schools should be careful to understand the distinction. Disciplinary consequences depend on it. As a matter of definition, a student is SED if he or she meets specific psychological criteria, exhibits behaviors to a marked degree over a long period of time, and such behavior adversely affects the student's educational performance. Evidence of SED is when a student is *unable to control* inappropriate behavior or sustain appropriate peer and teacher relationships.[55]

Social maladjustment is different. Unlike SED where an inability to control one's behavior is paramount, social maladjustment is demonstrated through continued behavior outside acceptable norms, behavior from one who understands society's expectations but chooses not to follow them. Like a conduct disorder where a student would engage in drinking, use of controlled substances, and risk-taking, bad conduct alone does not warrant an SED designation.[56]

Gifted Students

Gifted students may be disciplined in the same manner as non-handicapped students.

Disciplinary Transfer

Transfers to approved schools are considered changes in placement requiring special education due process. Parents may reject the transfer; but, if the school can establish 1.) that it cannot meet the student's needs, 2.) that normal procedures were followed, and 3.) that the change is to ensure a safe school environment, the transfer will be upheld.[57] This includes emergency placement pending completion of due process.[58]

Implications

<u>Teachers and Administrators:</u>

- Student discipline requires a comprehensive understanding of due process. Actions involving separation from the regular school program (in-school suspension), short-term exclusion from school (out-of-school suspension for up to 10 days), or long-term exclusion (out-of-school suspension for more than 10 days) dictates a different set of procedural requirements.

- Due process for short-term in-school suspension is easily satisfied. If the suspension results in exclusion from school, the due process requirements become stricter for both regular and special education students.

- The educational placement status makes a difference for students who are involved in disciplinary exclusions.

- Exceptional students may not be excluded from school on a long-term basis for behavior that is related to their disability. Suspension or expulsion for conduct unrelated to the disability, however, is permitted. Mentally handicapped students may not be excluded for any period of time without the full range of due process.

- Exclusion from school for any period of time is considered a change in placement for students who are mentally retarded. Other exceptional, or thought-to-be exceptional, students require special education due process when excluded for more than 10 days or a cumulative total of more than 15 days.

- If it is clear that the health, safety, and welfare of the student or other students is threatened, prior notice to parents/guardians is not necessary and the student may be excluded from school immediately.

<u>Parents and Students:</u>

- To a degree, schools have the right to impose discipline on exceptional students.

- While the school possesses limited unilateral authority to exclude exceptional students, the law requires a certain set of procedures to ensure that the rights of the student and parent/guardian are not violated.

- There are exceptions to the due process requirements for excluding regular and exceptional students.

DUE PROCESS SUMMARY for STUDENT DISCIPLINE

EXCLUSION FROM CLASSES: In-School Suspension

I. <u>Regular and Gifted Students</u>

1 to 10 Days

A. Notice: 1. Oral notice to student prior to suspension
(in administrator's office).
2. Notify parent/guardian within a reasonable time.

B. Hearing: Student given the opportunity to respond prior to the suspension.

C. Responsibility: Provide educational opportunity for the suspended student.

Beyond 10 Days

A. Notice: 1. Oral notice to student prior to suspension
(in administrator's office).
2. Immediate notification to parent/guardian and
superintendent in writing.
    a. State reason(s) for the suspension
    b. Indicate time and place for informal hearing

B. Hearing: 1. Student given the opportunity to respond prior
to the suspension.
2. Informal hearing scheduled by the 10th day.
    a. Student has the right to speak
    b. Student may question witnesses
    c. Student may produce own witnesses

C. Responsibility: Provide educational opportunity for the suspended student.

II. <u>Mentally Handicapped Students</u>

Follow the same procedures that apply to regular and gifted students insuring educational opportunity for the suspended student.

III. <u>Other Eligible or Thought-to-be Eligible Students</u>

Follow the same procedures that apply to regular and gifted students insuring educational opportunity for the suspended student.

EXCLUSION FROM SCHOOL: Out-of-School Suspension

SHORT-TERM Exclusion from School

I. <u>Regular and Gifted Students</u>

1 to 3 Days Exclusion

A. Notice: 1. Oral notice to student prior to suspension
                (in administrator's office).
          2. Immediate notification to parent/guardian and superintendent in
             writing.

B. Hearing: Student is given the opportunity to respond prior to the suspension.

C. Responsibility: Student may make up all schoolwork including examinations.

4 to 10 Days Exclusion

A. Notice: 1. Oral notice to student prior to suspension (in administrator's
           office).
          2. Immediate notification to parent/guardian and superintendent in
           writing.
               a. State reason(s) for the suspension
               b. Indicate time and place for informal hearing

B. Hearing: 1. Student is given the opportunity to respond prior to the
           suspension.
          2. Informal hearing is scheduled by the 5th day.
               a. Student has the right to speak
               b. Student may question witnesses
               c. Student may produce own witnesses

C. Responsibility: Student may make up all schoolwork including examinations.

II. <u>Mentally Handicapped Students</u>

A. Maintain current placement: "stay put."
B. Initiate the full range of special education due process.

III. <u>Other Eligible or Thought-to-be Eligible Students</u>

Follow the same procedures that apply to regular and gifted students insuring
educational opportunity for the student.

LONG-TERM Exclusion from School (Expulsion)

Regular Education

Beyond 10 Consecutive Days

I. <u>Regular and Gifted Students</u>

   A. Notice: 1. Oral notice to student prior to suspension (in administrator's office).
              2. Immediate notification to parent/guardian and superintendent in writing.
                  a. State reason(s) for the suspension
                  b. Indicate time and place for informal hearing

   B. Hearing: 1. Student is given the opportunity to respond prior to the suspension.
              2. Informal hearing is scheduled by the 5th day.
                  a. Student has the right to speak
                  b. Student may question witnesses
                  c. Student may produce own witnesses

   C. Responsibility: Education must be provided pending formal board hearing.

ADDITIONALLY:

   A. Notice: Notify parent/guardian by certified mail of the time and place of the formal board hearing.

   B. Hearing: Provide a formal hearing with the board of school directors, its committee, or designees.

        1. The student is granted the full range of procedural rights under law
        2. Alternative educational assurances must be given for students of compulsory education age if parents are unable to provide for it within 30 days

   C. Exceptions: If the student is a threat to him/herself or other students, the student may be excluded from school immediately. If there is a weapons policy violation, exclusion will be immediate and at least for the remainder of the school term.

   D. Timeliness: If the formal board hearing is not unreasonably delayed, the exclusion may be extended beyond the 10 days. If not, the student should be returned to his/her original placement pending the formal board hearing.

LONG-TERM Exclusion from School (Expulsion)

Special Education

Beyond 10 Consecutive or Cumulative Days

II. Mentally Handicapped Students

    A. Maintain current placement: "stay put."

    B. This action constitutes a change in placement necessitating the full range of special education due process. The multidisciplinary team must conduct a functional behavioral assessment and manifestation determination prior to a change in placement.

    C. If the student is a threat to him/herself or other students, interim placement can be obtained through the Office of the Secretary of Education or by court order.

    D. If the student is involved in a drug or weapons policy violation, exclusion and alternate placement will be immediate for up to 45 days.

III. Other Exceptional or Thought-to-be Exceptional Students

    A. Maintain current placement: "stay put."

    B. The multidisciplinary team must conduct a functional behavioral assessment and manifestation determination prior to a change in placement. If the behavior is related to the student's suspected disability, special education due process must be implemented before changing placement.

    C. If the misconduct is not related to the disability, the student receives the same procedural consideration as regular and gifted students. However, the school district is responsible for providing appropriate educational services immediately.

    D. If the student is a threat to him/herself or other students, interim placement can be obtained through the office of the Secretary of Education, hearing officer, or by court order.

    E. If the student is involved in a drug or weapons policy violation, exclusion and alternate placement will be immediate for up to 45 days.

Chapter 4 Endnotes

[1] Goss v. Lopez, 419 U.S. 565, 95 S. Ct. 729, 42 L.Ed.2d 725 (1975).

[2] Alex v. Allen, 409 F. Supp. 379 (W.D. Pa. 1976).

[3] Harris v. Commonwealth, Secretary of Education, 372 A.2d 953, 29 Pa. Cmwlth. 625 (1977).

[4] Mifflin County School District v. Stewart by Stewart, 503 A.2d 1012 (Pa. Cmwlth. 1986).

[5] Girard v. Pittenger, 392 A.2d 261, 481 Pa. 91 (1977).

[6] Morgan v. Board of Education of Girard City School District, 630 N.E.2d 71 (Ohio App. 11th Dist. 1993).

[7] Abremski v. Southeastern School Board of Directors, 421 A.2d 485, 54 Pa. Cmwlth. 292 (1980).

[8] In re Giles, 367 A.2d 399, 27 Pa. Cmwlth. 588 (1976).

[9] Tomlinson v. Pleasant Valley School District, 479 A.2d 1169, 84 Pa. Cmwlth. 518 (1984); Appeal of McClellan, 475 A.2d 867, 82 Pa. Cmwlth. 75 (1984); Burns by and Through Burns v. Hitchcock, 683 A.2d 1322 (Pa. 1996).

[10] Billman v. Big Spring School District (C.P. Cumberland County 1983); Davis v. Central Dauphin School District School Board, 466 F. Supp. 1259 (D.C. Pa. 1979).

[11] Rudi v. Big Beaver Falls Area School District, 74 Pa. D. & C.2d 790 (C.P. Beaver County 1976).

[12] Fenton v. Stear, 423 F. Supp. 767 (W.D. Pa. 1976).

[13] Porter v. Board of School Directors of Clairton School District, 445 A.2d 1386, 67 Pa. Cmwlth. 147 (1982).

[14] Jordan v. School District of City of Erie, Pa., 583 F.2d 91 (D.C. Pa. 1978).

[15] Everett v. Marcase, 426 F. Supp. 397 (D.C. Pa. 1977).

[16] Katzman by Katzman v. Cumberland Valley School District, 479 A.2d 671, 84 Pa. Cmwlth. 474 (1984).

[17] Miranda v. Arizona, 383 U.S. 436 (1966).

[18] Birdseye v. Grand Blanc Community School, 344 N.W.2d 342 (Mich. App. 1983).

[19] State v. Wolfer, 693 P.2d 154 (Wash. App. 1984).

[20] Id.

[21] In re Carey L., 250 Cal.Rptr. 359 (Cal. App. 1st Dist. 1988).

[22] In re Gault, 387 U.S. 1, 87 S..Ct. 1428, 18 L.Ed.2d 527 (1967); Tinker v. Des Moines Ind. School District, 393 U.S. 503, 89 S. Ct. 733, 21 L.Ed.2d 731 (1969).

[23] Goss, *supra*.

[24] Mifflin, *supra*.

[25] Jacobs v. Board of School Commissioners, 490 F.2d 601 (7th Cir. 1973).

[26] Alex, *supra*.

[27] Fenton, *supra*.

[28] Goss, *supra*.

[29] White by White v. Salisbury Township School District, 588 F. Supp. 608 (D.C. Pa. 1984).

[30] Popp v. Western Beaver County School District, 9 D. & C.3d 514 (1979).

[31] Mifflin, *supra*.

[32] Draper v. Columbus Public Schools, 760 F. Supp.131 (S.D. Ohio 1991); Armstead v. Lima City Board of Education, 600 N.E.2d 1985 (Ohio App. 3d Dist. 1991).

[33] Id.

[34] White, *supra*.

[35] Goss, *supra*., at 1302.

[36] Alex, *supra*., Fenton, supra.

[37] Porter, *supra*.

[38] Appeal of McClellan, *supra*.

[39] Big Spring School District Board of Directors v. Hoffman by Hershey, 489 A.2d 998, 88 Pa. Cmwlth. 462 (1985).

68

[40] Norristown Area School District v. A.V. By and Through V.V., 495 A.2d 990 (Pa. Cmwlth. 1985).

[41] McKeesport Area School District Board of Directors v. Collins 423 A.2d lll2, 55 Pa. Cmwlth. 548 (1980).

[42] Tomlinson, *supra*.

[43] Scoggin v. Henry County Board of Education, 549 So.2d 99 (Ala. Cir. App. 1989).

[44] Stuart v. Nappi, 443 F. Supp. 1235 (D. Conn. 1978).

[45] DeLeon v. Susquehanna Community School District, 474 A.2d 149 (3rd Cir. 1984).

[46] John Doe v. Board of Education of Oak Park and River Forest High School District, No. 96-3014 (No. 663014 7th Cir. 1997).

[47] Improving America's Schools Act, 20 U.S.C. 8001.

[48] Honig v. Doe, 108 S. Ct. 592 (1988).

[49] M.P. by D.P. v. Governing Board of Grossmont Union High School District, 858 F. Supp. 1044 (S.D. Cal. 1994).

[50] Doe v. Maher, 793 F.2d 1470 (9th Cir. 1986); School Board of the County of Prince William v. Malone, 762 F.2d 1210 (4th Cir. 1985).

[51] Lamont X. v. Quisenberry, 606 F. Supp. 809 (1984).

[52] Doe v. Koger, 480 F. Supp. 225 (N.D. Ind. 1979).

[53] Sherry v. New York State Education Department, 479 F. Supp. 1328 (W.D. N.Y. 1979).

[54] Id.; Stuart, *supra*.; Blue v. New Haven, 552 EHLR 401 (1981); Kaelin v. Grubbs, 682 F.2d 595 (6th Cir. 1982); S-1 v. Turlington, 635 F.2d 342 (5th Cir. 1981).

[55] Dallas School District v. Richard C. , 24 IDELR 241 ((Pa.) May 23, 1996).

[56] Springer v. Fairfax County School Board, 27 IDELR 367 ((4th Cir.) January 23, 1998).

[57] Everett, *supra*.; Jackson v. Franklin County School Board, 606 F. Supp. 152 (1985).

[58] Victoria L. v. District School Board, 552 EHLR 265 (11th Cir. 1980)

Chapter 5   Free Expression

Source:

> First Amendment
> Fourteenth Amendment

Many actions can be considered forms of expression. Accordingly, it is necessary to distinguish what forms of expression are considered constitutionally protected "speech."   The Supreme Court has held that certain conduct becomes a First Amendment issue when "intent to carry a particular message" is present and there is likelihood that those who receive the message would understand it.[1] This speech, or free expression, may be symbolic, oral, or written and restrictions on it may be challenged in a number of ways.

Court Challenges

"Vagueness" is one basis for challenging restrictions on free expression. The vagueness test has been applied to criminal proceedings where laws have been held to be unclear because a person of common intelligence must guess at the meaning or application of a rule. However, in a school setting, school officials have the authority to impose sanctions on anticipated or unanticipated conduct that disrupts the educational process. Here, vagueness has been narrowly applied. The courts have permitted rules that prohibit expressive behavior using general terms such as "vulgarity," "willful disobedience," and "intentional disruption."   A vagueness challenge is directed at the rule as it applies to the nature of the conduct. As long as a rule is clear in how it describes the limit of acceptable behavior, it will be sustained.

A second basis for challenging restrictions of free expression is "overbreadth."   The overbreadth doctrine focuses on whether a rule or regulation, regardless of the nature of the conduct, applies to a constitutionally protected behavior. This means that any rule or regulation that attempts to control a constitutionally protected behavior will be struck down as having a "chilling effect" on a person's right to free expression. Such was the case where a school's anti-harassment policy was struck down because not all obnoxious speech poses a "realistic threat of substantial disruption,"[2] even if it is directed towards a teacher.[3]

A third basis for challenging restrictions on free expression bears a relationship to the nature of the "forum." A forum may be defined as the context used by individuals to express themselves. There are three types of forums and each, respectively, carries its own restrictive standards.

The first type of forum deals with government property such as parks, street corners and the like. Here, individuals may mount a "soapbox" and express their personal views. This is called a "traditional public forum" and it requires a compelling state interest to restrict free expression.

The second type of forum is a "designated open public forum" where the context for expression is specified toward a particular use. Since the general public may have certain rights to expressive conduct in such a forum, a compelling state interest is necessary to restrict free expression. However, attempts to restrict expression must be narrowly construed and must address a particular need or interest. The right to restrict is limited to the time, place, and manner of the expression. Schools are considered designated open public forums.

The third type of forum is a "non-public forum." Here, indiscriminate expressive conduct has not been granted to the general public. Furthermore, the general public has no reason to believe that such expression is justified. Access may be controlled in a non-public forum by specifying who may engage in expression and what may be expressed. These may be reasonably regulated so long as the rule is neutral and appropriate to the purpose of the forum.

Forum analysis has particular significance in establishing the boundaries of control in cases dealing with non school-sponsored free expression in the form of publications and the distribution of printed materials.

What is clear from the record is that students do not lose their rights to free expression when they enter school. Schools are a microcosm of the society at large and, as such, students are permitted to express personal views within limits. Those limits were outlined in *Tinker v. Des Moines Independent School District* when the Supreme Court confirmed the right of students to express themselves "in absence of constitutionally valid reasons to regulate their speech."[4]

Curiously, in at least one jurisdiction, elementary students have no clearly established free speech rights. An Indiana elementary student was prohibited from wearing a T-shirt that protested that racism was the basis for her poor grades. Disciplinary action was taken and the appeals court affirmed the lower court's dismissal of the student's lawsuit. The appeals court held that while Tinker established certain speech rights for senior high school students, no case recognized such a right for elementary students![5]

Symbolic Expression

Tinker v. Des Moines established its standard for free expression by citing two earlier cases out of the Fifth Circuit that involved wearing political buttons. In the first case, student suspensions were overturned because there was no disruption to the educational process.[6] In the second case, the school district's disciplinary suspensions were sustained because hostile behavior, confusion, and disruption resulted from wearing the buttons.[7]

The facts in *Tinker* revolve around wearing an armband as a protest to the Vietnam War. In December, 1965, a group of adults and students met and agreed to publicize their objection to hostilities by fasting and wearing armbands on December 16 and New Year's Eve. The school administrators discovered the group's intentions and, two days prior to the event, adopted a policy requiring students to remove armbands or face suspension.

Thirteen year-old, Mary Beth Tinker, and sixteen year-old, Christopher Eckhardt, wore black armbands on December 16. Fifteen year-old, John Tinker, wore his the next day. They were all sent home and suspended. A complaint was filed by the parents in the U.S. District Court and dismissed after an evidentiary hearing supporting the school's action.

Tinker reversed the District Court citing that there was "no indication that the work of the school or any class was disrupted." *Tinker* described protected speech in three ways. First, protected speech does not create disturbances or disorders on the school premises. Second, protected speech should not give reason to forecast substantial disruptions or material interference with school activities. Third, protected speech should not invade the rights of others. This means that mere "disagreement with the thoughts expressed or a generalized fear of disruption" is not sufficient to warrant regulation. "There must be substantial facts which reasonably support a forecast of likely disruption."[8]

The Supreme Court opined that "undifferentiated fear or apprehension is not enough to overcome the right to freedom of expression." Students are "persons" under the law and, therefore, possess fundamental rights that the state must respect. The students "neither interrupted school activities or sought to intrude in the school affairs or the lives of others."

Four years later, the *Tinker* standard was employed by the Sixth Circuit. The Sixth Circuit held that disruption could be foreseen in wearing anti-war buttons in a school where the climate was racially tense and the students were urged not to create situations that polarized opinions.[9]

Wearing armbands and buttons are not the only forms of symbolic free expression. Demonstrations are viewed as free speech subject to the *Tinker* standard. As such, flag burning enjoys First Amendment protection.[10] Individuals are also permitted to express political dissatisfaction with the government or withhold political allegiance due to religious beliefs. Accordingly, students are not obligated to salute the flag in the traditional Pledge of Allegiance based on personal and/or religious grounds.[11]

If a demonstration causes disruption, it will not be protected. Such was the case with picketing,[12] wearing berets to symbolize "Chicano Power,"[13] and protestations against school policy.[14] Even where racial opposition to playing the school song, "Dixie," created disruption, a five-day suspension was upheld by the court.[15]

T-shirts bearing messages and displaying gang colors are subject to regulation using the Tinker standard. Gang identification is subject to even stricter scrutiny. However, clothing bearing certain types of messages enjoys some jurisdictional protection. See Chapter 6, "Grooming and Dress Codes."

Demonstrating sexual preference became a recent issue when two gay students petitioned for the right to attend the school prom together. The court viewed its role as "not mandating social norms or imposing its own view of acceptable behavior." In this instance, the undifferentiated fear or apprehension of disturbance that was claimed was not enough to outweigh the individual student's right of free expression. There was no material or substantial interference with the operation of the school. Hence, the student's First Amendment right to free expression and association was upheld.[16]

Seven years later two students, a brother and his sister, brought a civil rights action against an Ohio board of education for being denied the opportunity to attend the prom cross-dressed as a couple. Their claim was dismissed in a summary judgment. The Sixth Circuit found no infringement of the students' constitutional rights since the school board's dress regulations were reasonably related to the valid educational purposes of teaching community values and maintaining school discipline.[17]

Oral Expression

It is well established in law that certain kinds of oral expression can be controlled. The test employed by the courts is the substantial disruption standard set in Tinker. In balancing the individual's rights with the government's interest in providing an appropriate public education, the "special characteristics of the school environment" grant school officials the right to prohibit speech that materially and substantially disrupts the school. School officials may also control speech that can reasonably be foreseen to materially and substantially disrupt the school or invade the rights of other students.

Obscenity, vulgarity, and lewdness fall into the category of unprotected speech. The Supreme Court in *Bethel v. Fraser* has held that such expression is subject to control and discipline by school authorities.[18] Using an "elaborate, graphic, and explicit sexual metaphor," a student delivered the following speech at a high school assembly supporting a candidate for student government:

> I know a man who is firm - he's firm in his pants, he's firm in his shirt, his character is firm - but most ...of all, his belief in you, the students of Bethel, is firm.

> [N] is a man who takes his point and pounds it in. If necessary, he'll take an issue and nail it to the wall. He doesn't attack things in spurts - he drives hard, pushing and pushing until finally - he succeeds.

[N] is a man who will go to the very end - even to the climax, for each and every one of you.

So vote for [N] for A.S.B. vice-president - he'll never come between you and the best our high school can be …

The Supreme Court labeled the speech as "offensively lewd" and "indecent" in the context of public education. Its "sexual innuendo" was held to be "offensive to both teachers and students" and clearly within the authority of the school to regulate. In a concurring opinion, Justice Brennan said "in light of the discretion school officials have to teach high school students how to conduct civil and effective public discourse, and to prevent disruption of school educational activities, it was not unconstitutional for school officials to conclude … that the respondent's remarks exceeded permissible limits …"

In cases involving lewd expression, at least one of the following criteria[19] must be present for the speech to be considered obscene:

1. Does the expression appeal to prurient interest?
2. Is it patently offensive?
3. Taken as a whole, does the expression lack substantive value?

School plays containing sexual themes or vulgarity may be restricted or canceled using the above criteria.[20]

"Fighting words" fall into the category of controlled speech in public schools. School officials have the authority to prohibit "fighting words" as long as there is a basis for doing so as part of the school's "legitimate pedagogical concern."[21] While limitation on expressions characterized as "fighting words" is considered unconstitutional outside school, it is not the case in the school context. Such language may be limited when it violates the *Tinker* standard by causing interference or material disruption to the educational process or being reasonably perceived as causing disruption.

The school's authority to control obscenity and "fighting words" is established in case law: language that disrupts is essentially unprotected by the First Amendment. Fighting words are defined as "personally abusive epithets which, when addressed to the ordinary citizen, are, as a matter of common knowledge, inherently likely to provoke violent reaction."[22] Hate speech and sexually harassing expression falls into the same category using *Tinker*'s disruption standards.[23]

Guest lecturers/speakers are subject to restrictions as well. In a lecture showing the link between mathematics and film making, a sitting member of the board of education who was a former filmmaker, showed a film clip depicting two women and a man naked from the waist up to tenth-grade students. When the principal directed him to refrain from showing the questionable scene, he did so. Later, he objected to the principal's action on constitutional grounds. The Second Circuit dismissed the lecturer's constitutional challenges stating that "a guest in the classroom, was entitled to no more deference than a trained educational professional."[24]

Schools may exercise a great deal of authority over criticism of school officials if the criticism is expressed during a school-sponsored activity. Discourteous and rude remarks about an administrator during an assembly have been held to fall within the school's authority to regulate. A student made such remarks as a candidate for student government and added that "the administration plays tricks with your mind," causing school officials to suspend him. Citing *Hazelwood v. Kuhlmeier*, the Sixth Circuit said that civility is a legitimate pedagogical concern. Therefore, schools do not offend the First Amendment by exercising control over school-sponsored activities.[25]

In an earlier decision by an Idaho court, students were denied a preliminary injunction against a suspension for wearing a T-shirt characterizing three school administrators as drunks.[26] The court relied on *Tinker* and *Bethel* in concluding that students were not entitled to First Amendment protection for their satirical depiction of the administration. The court further reasoned that the school is "statutorily charged with teaching about the effects of alcohol." As role models, such a characterization would compromise the administration's position as authority figures in charge of maintaining an orderly educational environment.

Clearly, criticism in the school context invites a greater likelihood of control. What about expression off school grounds? It appears that the courts adhere to the view that criticism of school officials off school grounds must have some impact on the educational process for it to be unprotected by the First Amendment. Refer to the web site discussion on page 82.

On the one hand, disciplinary action was upheld when a student made disrespectful remarks to a teacher in the presence of other students.[27] And, a recent Maine court held that a vulgar gesture made one-on-one to a teacher off school grounds and after school hours was an exercise of free speech.[28] Here, the court did not view the gesture as "fighting words" in the context of the operation of the school. The gesture was seen, rather, as an expression of personal opinion outside school. Therefore, the action by the student was too attenuated to support discipline by the school having caused no disruption to the educational process.

A Pennsylvania student was not so lucky. His loud comments at a local restaurant was met with a three-day suspension that was affirmed by the court which said, "To countenance such student conduct ...without imposing sanctions could lead to devastating effects."[29]

Written Expression

Students using the printed word to criticize the school are subject to standards similar to oral expression. Publications that are a part of the school curriculum are subject to greater control than those printed off school premises. Generally, the expression must reasonably forecast disruption of or materially interfere with school activities.[30] This section addresses written expression in greater detail.

The forum analysis made earlier in this chapter indicated that the context used by individuals to express themselves defines the limits of a school's authority to control free expression. The government's authority to control free expression depends on the nature of the forum[31] and it has been established that schools are "designated public forums" during the day.[32] Accordingly, schools have the right to set reasonable rules and regulations governing the time, place, and manner of the expression.

The limits of a school's authority to control written expression depends upon whether the expression is a school-sponsored publication, originating within the school, or whether it is non school-sponsored, originating off school premises. The former gives greater authority and control to the school. The latter limits the school's authority and control to Tinker's disruption standard and regulating the time, place and manner of the expression.

School-Sponsored Publications

School-sponsored publications were at issue in *Hazelwood v. Kuhlmeier* where an administrator exercised "editorial control over the contents of a high school newspaper as part of the school's journalism curriculum."[33] The principal objected to two articles scheduled to appear in the school newspaper (The Spectrum) exercising "prior restraint" or censorship.

The principal's action was grounded in his concern that the articles were written in such a way that students who read them would be able to identify the "anonymous" persons in the articles. One article addressed students' experiences with pregnancy while the other focused on the impact of divorce on students in the school. In the article on pregnancy, the principal felt that certain references to "sexual activity and birth control were inappropriate for some of the younger students at the school." The article on divorce contained the name of a particular student. The principal felt that it denied the student's parents an opportunity to respond or consent.

The Spectrum was written by the Journalism II class and published every three weeks or so. This May 13 issue would have been the last one before the end of the school term. The board of education allocated funds for the newspaper and the principal's normal practice was to review the articles prior to publication. The facts of the case reveal that the principal directed the journalism teacher to publish the issue without the articles in question. He based his decision on concerns about the two articles and the unlikelihood that revised versions would be ready before summer vacation. When the principal informed his superiors, they concurred. Action was brought by three former students from the newspaper staff contending that "school officials violated their First Amendment rights by deleting two pages of articles" from The Spectrum.

The *Hazelwood* decision defined the context for the students' claims. It reaffirmed their rights under *Tinker* to express themselves short of substantial disruption of the school or infringing on the rights of others. Citing Bethel, it recognized that students' rights are "not automatically coextensive with the rights of adults in other settings." The court reasoned that schools need not tolerate student expression inconsistent with its educational mission even though the government would not censor similar expression outside school.

Relying on the "forum analysis," the Supreme Court declared that it was not the intent of the school to open the facilities "for indiscriminate use by the general public...or by some segment of the public, such as student organizations."[34] The school was, therefore, not a traditional public forum. The Court stated that school facilities are "reserved for other intended purposes," making it a designated open public forum where limited discourse is permitted. The school, thus, reserves the right to make reasonable restrictions on the free expression of students, teachers, and other members of the school community.[35]

The Court distinguished between tolerating speech (*Tinker*) and affirmatively promoting particular speech (*Hazelwood*). The former addressed "educators' ability to silence a student's personal expression that happens to occur on school premises." The latter addressed "educators' authority over school-sponsored publications, theatrical productions, and other expressive activities that students, parents, and members of the public might reasonably perceive to bear the imprimatur of the school."[36] The Court concluded that school officials are entitled to regulate the contents of school-sponsored publications "in any reasonable manner" consistent with legitimate pedagogical concerns. The courts may interfere only when the decision to censor school-sponsored vehicles of student expression "has no valid educational purpose."

In a footnote, the *Hazelwood* majority made clear its intent to apply the ruling to school-sponsored publications only.

A Ninth Circuit decision extended the definition of school-sponsored publications to include yearbooks and athletic programs when it upheld a school's authority to prohibit advertisements from a family planning organization.[37]

In another case involving written expression, school officials were sustained in their refusal to permit a survey of sexual attitudes to be distributed to eleventh and twelfth grade students for publication in the school newspaper. The survey required "rather personal and frank information about the students' sexual attitudes, preferences, knowledge and experience" covering a range of specific topics such as pre-marital sex, contraception, homosexuality, and masturbation. The court believed "that the school authorities did not act unreasonably in deciding that the proposed questionnaire should not be distributed because of the probability that it would result in psychological harm to some students."[38]

Two decisions suggest that *Hazelwood* does not apply to publications produced outside the classroom.   While recognizing the school's authority over school-sponsored publications, one federal district court held that a school newspaper funded by the board of education but produced outside of the classroom is a co-curricular activity. Accordingly, it is not subject to the strictures imposed in *Hazelwood*.[39] In another case, a student, not a teacher, was in sole "control" of a school-affiliated literary magazine as editor-in-chief. Attempts at prior restraint were held to be unconstitutional.[40] It appears that prior restraint over the educational curriculum requires control by the school officials over the content of what is taught.

Non School-Sponsored Publications

Having established that school officials may exercise prior restraint to the content of school-sponsored publications and distributions, the question remains: To what extent may a school district censor independent publications originating off school premises?

Independent Student-Initiated Expression.   Certainly, the *Tinker* standard of material and substantial disruption may be invoked. Students were suspended from school for using vulgarity and profanity in an independent student publication that disrupted the school based on *Tinker*.[41] When the independent student publication was designed as a specific act of defiance against a school policy aimed at underground newspapers, the result was the same.[42] The Seventh Circuit recently confirmed the school's right to take disciplinary action where a student wrote an article in an underground newspaper detailing how to gain access to the school's computer files citing reasonable expectation of disruption.[43]

However, not all courts agree. The Second Circuit approved broad review and censorship of non school-sponsored student publications,[44] while the Seventh Circuit held that any prior restraint of independent student-initiated publications is unconstitutional.[45]

What guidelines, then, can schools follow to ensure that students' rights have not been violated since the presumption against prior restraint has existed for many years?[46] Prior restraint of independent student-initiated publications requires "precise criteria sufficiently spelling out what is forbidden so that a reasonably intelligent student will know what he may write about and what he may not write."[47]

A number of courts view prior restraint of independent student-initiated publications as suppression of speech different from discipline of individual students after the expression has occurred.[48] Even when the language was "potentially disruptive," censorship by school officials was not upheld in the Fourth Circuit.[49] In one recent case, students who produced a satirical publication printed outside of school and sold exclusively off school premises were suspended as a result of community pressure. The newspaper contained questionable topics yet the school's disciplinary action was overturned because "the risk is simply too great that school officials will punish protected speech and thereby inhibit future expression."[50]

In most jurisdictions, independent student-initiated publications are "in no sense 'school sponsored.' They are, therefore, not within the purview of the school's exercise of reasonable editorial control."[51] They may, however, be regulated as to the time, place, and manner of distribution.[52]

Courts scrutinize such attempts to censor independent student-initiated expression. In jurisdictions that permit prior restraint, a prior restraint policy must be in place. It should define "distribution" and its application to different types of printed material; it must provide for prompt approval of disapproval specifying the effect of failure to act promptly, and it should contain an adequate and prompt appeals procedure.[53]

Independent Expression of a Non-School Nature. When a student brings material into school for distribution, school officials may act within certain bounds to protect the interests of other students. Distributing leaflets that solicit funds was held to be impermissible on the grounds that schools may protect students from the annoyances and pressures that usually accompany requests to donate.[54] But, if there is no perceived intrusion, as was the case when students themselves attempted to raise funds for an underground newspaper, the school's prohibition was held to be unconstitutional.[55]

School officials still maintain the right to prohibit distribution of material that advertise products or services not permitted by law to minors.[56] And, in Pennsylvania, a policy was upheld by the court that prohibited the distribution of hate literature attacking ethnic, religious, or racial groups, material promoting disorder or violence, and material that is libelous.[57]

Distribution of religious material has created a large body of law striking down school policies on claims of vagueness and overbreadth. First, the courts have addressed the issue in light of the Equal Access Act (20 U.S.C. Section 4071). See Chapter 18, "Equal Access." Second, they have applied the *Lemon* test to determine that the rule or regulation does not have a secular purpose, neither advances nor inhibits the exercise of religion or avoids excessive government entanglement.[58] See Chapter 8, "Religious Activity." Third, the courts have focused on the school context as a designated open public forum.

Using the forum analysis, student distribution of religious material in a Pennsylvania school district was held to be permissible where school officials thought otherwise. The school policy in question required prior approval, specifically addressing religious material. The policy also "set forth the time and place of distribution so that distribution does not materially or substantially interfere with the educational process, threatened immediate harm to the welfare of the school or community, encourage unlawful activity, or interfere with another individual's rights." However, since the policy singled out material of a religious nature, it was not content neutral with respect to time, place, and manner restrictions.[59] Other courts have reached he same conclusion.[60]

Students have no right to distribute materials during a class.[61] Furthermore, students may be prohibited from distributing religious literature and otherwise proselytizing in the hallways.[62] A Colorado court reasoned that such a restriction on time, place, and manner was not a serious infringement on free expression since students could always express themselves off school premises. Since the hallways were not public forums, regulating the time, place, and manner was not intended to curtail free expression. Rather, it is designed to preserve the orderly use of space in an otherwise crowded environment. This applies to changing classes, while students are coming into the building in the morning, and while students are leaving school at the end of the day.

Given the nature of the forum, the issue of students distributing material of a non-school nature in the public schools can be complicated. Nonetheless, it is manageable under content neutral restrictions as to time, place, manner of distribution, and reasonable relationship to legitimate pedagogical concerns.[63]

Given the nature of the forum, the issue of students distributing material of a non-school nature in public schools can be complicated.

Nonetheless, it is manageable under content neutral restrictions as to time, place, and manner of distribution.

Web Sites

With the increasing development of technology, schools are faced with addressing questionable expression generated by students who create web sites at home. While acknowledging the distinction between constitutionally protected and unprotected speech, the courts are faced with defining what constitutes sufficient grounds for disciplinary action against students whose home-based web sites criticize, disrupt, mock, embarrass or threaten school employees.

Constitutionally protected speech precludes disciplinary action by school districts. A Washington state court granted a temporary restraining order against the five-day suspension of a student who's web page criticized the school administration and faculty.[64] The web site included disclaimers alerting visitors that the content of the web site was not school sponsored and existed solely for entertainment purposes. The web site also featured mock obituaries of two students (inspired by a creative writing class project) and the invitation to vote who to select would "die" next, i.e., be the subject of the next obituary. Even though the a local TV news broadcast characterized the obituaries as a "hit list," the court found no disruption of the educational process and insufficient evidence of intimidation or harassment to warrant disciplinary suspension in excess of one day. The court reasoned that the student's expression must go beyond criticism and embarrassment; it must create a material and substantial disruption of the educational process.

A similar conclusion was reached in Missouri[65] where a student was wrongfully suspended for a home-created web page that used vulgar language to criticize and convey his opinion about the principal and teachers. The seldom-visited web site was revealed when another student, angry with Beussink, told the principal about its existence. The principal ordered Beussink to "clean up his homepage" or "clear it out." The student wasted no time and removed the web page. The student's suspension was overruled by the court because the school disciplined Beussink simply because the principal objected to the content, not because it was disruptive or substantially interfered with the school's order or discipline.

In *J. S. v. Bethlehem Area School District*, a student's web site entitled "Teachers Sux" was viewed in a different light. His discipline was upheld on two grounds, disruptive expression and advocating violence. The court opined that disruptive expression was inferred from 136 repetitions of phrases condemning a teacher. Furthermore, a list of why the teacher "should die" and the plea to collect "$20 to help pay for the hit man" was viewed as a serious threat of bodily harm. The site even depicted the teacher being shot in the head. Students repeatedly accessed the web site causing the staff to be genuinely fearful. The teacher was forced to take a medical leave for the remainder of the year as well as the following year. In short, J. S.' web site resulted in material and substantial disruption of the educational process.[66]

Implications

Teachers and Administrators:

- Students have rights to free expression although their rights are not coextensive with those of adults.

- Case law demonstrates that intent to convey a specific message understood by others that does not materially disrupt the school is protected expression.

- Expression that disrupts school, can be reasonably foreseen to disrupt school, or invades the rights of others may be regulated.

- If a school wishes to prohibit verbal harassment of students by students, it should do so based on the concept of "fighting words" or foreseeable disruption.

- Guest lecturers are not entitled to any more free speech protection than professional employees. Schools are urged to establish rules for guest lecturers addressing what is permitted to be covered, assuring that it is related to the curriculum, and provides a mechanism for review.

- School-sponsored publications imply control over the curriculum with control over what is taught. Therefore, publications produced outside the classroom are not considered school-sponsored.

- School authorities may exercise control over student expression in school-sponsored activities as long as the restrictions are related to legitimate pedagogical concerns.

- Using the forum analysis, schools may regulate the time, place, and manner of expression for non school-sponsored expression whether originating from within the school or off school premises.

- Policies that include prior approval before allowing the distribution of non school-sponsored material should have clear criteria describing acceptable and unacceptable literature. They should also provide for prompt determination by administration and have a mechanism for appeal.

- Freedom to express one's views does not include the right to trouble others. This applies to questionnaires where a response to questions might result in harmful consequences. Likewise, students should be kept free from the distractions and impositions created by soliciting funds.

Parents and Students:

- Although students have legitimate rights to free expression in the school context, limitations on speech that would be unconstitutional outside the school are not necessarily unconstitutional within it.

- The decision as to what type of speech is appropriate to the school setting essentially rests with the school board, not with the individual who wishes to express an idea.

- A student's rights in a school-sponsored activity are more restricted than in a non school-sponsored activity.

- A student may be subject to restrictions on the time, place, and manner of distribution of literature on school premises. However, such restrictions must be reasonable and content neutral.

Chapter 5 Endnotes

[1] Texas v. Johnson, 491 S. Ct. 397 (1989); Spence v. Washington, 418 U.S. 406 (1974).

[2] Saxe v. State College Area School District, No. 99-4081 (3rd Cir. 2001).

[3] Killian v. Franklin Regional School District, 136 F. Supp. 2d 446 (WD Pa. 2001).

[4] Tinker v. Des Moines Independent School District, 393 U.S. 503 (1969) at 511.

[5] Baxter v. Vigo County School Corporation, 26 F.3d 728 (7th Cir. 1994).

[6] Burnside v. Byers, 363 F.2d 744 (5th Cir. 1966).

[7] Blackwell v. Issaquena County Board of Education, 363 F.2d 749 (5th Cir. 1966).

[8] Vail v. Portsmouth School District, 354 F. Supp. 592 (D.N.H. 1973).

[9] Guzik v. Drebus, 431 F.2d 594 (6th Cir. 1971).

[10] Texas, *supra*.

[11] West Virginia v. Barnette, 319 U.S. 624 (1943).

[12] Pickens v. Oklahoma Municipal Separate School District, 594 F.2d 433 (5th Cir. 1979); Karp v. Becker, 477 F.2d 171 (9th Cir. 1973).

[13] Hernandez v. School District #1, 315 F. Supp. 289 (D. Colo. 1970).

[14] Barker v. Hardaway, 394 U.S. 905 (1969).

[15] Tate v. Board of Education of Jonesboro, Arkansas, 453 F.2d 975 (8th Cir. 1972).

[16] Fricke v. Lynch, 491 F. Supp. 381 (D.R.I. 1980).

[17] Harper v. Edgewood Board of Education, 655 F. Supp. 1353 (S.D. Ohio 1987).

[18] Bethel School District No. 403 v. Fraser, 478 U.S. 675 (1986).

[19] Miller v. California, 413 U.S. 15 (1973).

[20] Seyfried v. Walton, 668 F.2d 214 (3rd Cir. 1981).

[21] Chandler v. McMinnville School District, 978 F.2d 529 (9th Cir. 1992).

[22] Cohen v. California, 403 U.S. 15 (1971).

[23] R.A.V. v. City of St. Paul, 505 U.S. 377 (1992).

[24] Silano v. Sag Harbor Unified School District, 42 F.3d 719 (2nd Cir. 1994), *certiorari* denied, 115 S. Ct. 2612.

[25] Poling v. Murphy, 872 F.2d 757 (6th Cir. 1989).

[26] Gano v. School District No. 411, 674 F. Supp. 796 (D. Idaho 1987).

[27] Lander v. Seaver, 32 Vt. 114 (Vt. 1859).

[28] Klein v. Smith, 635 F. Supp. 1440 (D. Me. 1986).

[29] Fenton v. Stear, 423 F. Supp. 767 (W.D. Pa. 1976).

[30] Scoville v. Board of Education of Joliet Township, 425 F.2d 10 (7th Cir. 1970).

[31] Gregoire v. Centennial School District, 907 F.2d 1366 (3rd Cir. 1990).

[32] Slotterback by Slotterback v. Interboro School Dist., 766 F. Supp. 280 (E.D. Pa. 1991).

[33] Hazelwood v. Kuhlmeier, 484 U.S. 260 (1988).

[34] Perry Education Association v. Perry Local Educator's Ass'n, 460 U.S. 37 (1983).

[35] Cornelius v. NAACP Legal Defense and Education Fund, 473 U.S. 788 (1985).

[36] Hazelwood, *supra*.

[37] Planned Parenthood v. Clark County School District, 941 F.2d 817 (9th Cir. 1991).

[38] Trachtman v. Anker, 563 F.2d 512 (2nd Cir. 1977) cert. denied, 435 U.S. 925 (1978).

[39] Romano v. Harrington, 725 F. Supp. 687 (E.D. N.Y. 1989).

[40] Koppel v. Levine, 347 F. Supp. 456 (E.D. N.Y. 1972).

[41] Baker v. Downey City Board of Education, 307 F. Supp. 517 (C.D. Cal. 1969); Sullivan v. Houston Independent School District, 438 F.2d 1058 (2nd Cir. 1971).

[42] Graham v. Houston Independent School District, 335 F. Supp. 1162 (S.D. Tex. 1970).

[43] Boucher v. School Board of the School District of Greenfield, 7th Circuit Court of Appeals No. 97-3433 (1998).

[44] Eisner v. Stamford Board of Education, 440 F.2d 803 (2nd Cir. 1971).

[45] Fujishima v. Board of Education, 460 F.2d 1355 (7th Cir. 1972).

[46] Near v. Minnesota, 283 U.S. 697 (1931).

[47] Baughman v. Frienmuth, 478 F.2d 1345 (4th Cir. 1973).

[48] Eisner, *supra*; Fujishima, *supra*; Baughman, *supra*; Nitzberg v. Parks, 525 F.2d 378 (4th Cir. 1975).

[49] Quarterman v. Byrd, 453 F.2d 54 (4th Cir. 1971).

[50] Thomas v. Board of Education, 607 F.2d 1043 (2nd Cir. 1979) *certiorari* denied, 444 U.S. 1081 (1980).

[51] Burch v. Barker, 861 F.2d 1149 (9th Cir. 1988).

[52] Slotterback, *supra*; Shanley v. Northeast Ind. School Dist., 462 F.2d 960 (5th Cir. 1972).

[53] Baughman, *supra*.

[54] Katz v. McAulay, 438 F.2d 1058 (2nd Cir. 1971).

[55] Pliscou v. Holtville Unified School District, 411 F. Supp. 842 (J.D. Cal. 1976).

[56] Bystrom v. Fudley High School, 822 F.2d 747 (8th Cir. 1987).

[57] Slotterback, *supra*.

[58] Lemon v. Kurtzman, 403 U.S. 602 (1971).

[59] Thompson v. Waynesboro Area School District, 673 F. Supp. 1379 (M.D. Pa. 1987).

[60] Johnson-Loehner v. O'Brien, 859 F. Supp. 575 (M.D. Fla. 1994); Rivera v. East Otero School District, R-1, 721 F.Supp 1189 (D. Colo. 1989); Nelson v. Moline School District No. 40, 725 F. Supp. 965 (C.D. Ill. 1989).

[61] Shanley, *supra*.

[62] Hemry by Hemry v. School Board of Colorado School Dist. No. 11, 760 F. Supp. 856 (D. Colo. 1991).

[63] Denno v. School Board of Volusia County, 218 F3d 1267 (11th Cir. 2000).

[64] Emmett v. Kent School District No. 415, 92 F. Supp.2d 1088.

[65] Beussink v. Woodland R-IV School District, 30 F.Supp 2d 1175 (E.D. MO 1998).

[66] J.S. v. Bethlehem Area School District, 757 A.2d 412 (Pa. Cmwlth. 2000).

Chapter 6 Grooming and Dress Codes

Sources:

> First Amendment
> Fourteenth Amendment

Even though schools may enact necessary rules that are reasonably connected to furthering the educational process, grooming and dress codes have been litigated on a number of legal fronts: 1.) governance of in-school as opposed to out-of-school behavior, 2.) freedom of expression, 3.) free exercise of religion, and 4.) due process and equal protection.   The litigation typically involves the balance of the school's authority over a person's autonomy to act within the school context.   This was described in *Tinker* v. *Des Moines*[1] as the point at which a student's right to freedom of expression materially and substantially interferes with the school's discipline requirements or the rights of others.[2] The tendency of the Court has been to grant school districts authority to establish and enforce rules designed to accomplish the school's educational purpose. Accordingly, the Supreme Court has declined to review the decisions of lower courts that denied students protection from school regulations involving grooming and dress codes.

Grooming

The court's position is aptly stated in *Kelley v. Johnson*, a non-school case involving grooming regulations for police officers in Suffolk County, New York. A lower court dismissed the police union's challenge to the grooming regulations; however, the Second Circuit Court of Appeals reversed. The United States Supreme Court reversed the Appeals Court decision placing the burden on the plaintiff to demonstrate that the regulation in question was so irrational that it was arbitrary. In its decision, the Supreme Court recognized that a liberty interest in a person's appearance may not be infringed upon without showing the rational basis for its relationship to a legitimate government interest.   The Court considered the context of the regulations and held that appearance was not on the same plane as marriage, procreation, or rights associated with family life.   Therefore, the government had "wide latitude" to regulate such behavior.[3] While police officers are different from students, students like police officers, function in a restricted context. That is to say, they have certain personal limitations imposed upon them as a result of who they are and what they do.

Kelley may or may not hold the key to interpreting all school grooming and dress scenarios. A few courts contend that hair length regulations are beyond the authority of the school to regulate.[4] In at least one jurisdiction, the issue "comes down to the question of whether or not there is any reasonable connection between long hair and education in a public school." Furthermore, "the impact of a hair length rule is to regulate out-of school conduct more than in-school conduct."[5] Schools must be careful to recognize the differences between what is reasonable in the classroom as opposed to what is reasonable on the street corner.[6]

In ruling on hair length, most free speech challenges have been unsuccessful because hair length is generally not considered a form of expression.[7] Other claims made on the basis of the free exercise of religion have failed as well. The courts insist that for a First Amendment religious challenge to succeed, the rule or regulation must violate a significant, established religious tenet, not merely a custom or preference.[8] Recently, however, a Texas court granted a preliminary injunction against the enforcement of dress code provisions prohibiting long hair on male students based on First Amendment grounds. The long hair was worn by Native Americans who were the only students disciplined under the dress code. The long hair in this case was held to be a protected activity that did not disrupt the educational process or interfere with the rights of other students. In balancing individual versus collective rights, the court noted that the potential injury to the students would be greater than the potential injury to the school.[9]

When challenged on Fourteenth Amendment grounds, circuit courts are split on the grooming issue. The Third, Fifth, Sixth, Ninth, Tenth, and Eleventh Circuits acknowledge the school's authority to regulate students' hair length. A typical example of the court's reasoning was made by the Fifth Circuit in reversing a trial court decision striking a dress code provision prohibiting the wearing of long hair and earrings by male students. This Texas tribunal ruled that it was inappropriate for the courts to intervene in matters where the state constitution vests power to the local district to manage the schools. Although the plaintiff argued that such a policy created sex discrimination, the court found it insufficient to warrant an injunction against the enforcement of the dress code.[10]

In the Third Circuit, Pennsylvania courts have held similarly. Regulations drawn by students and faculty that limit the length of students' hair have been determined to have a rational basis and, therefore, were held to be a reasonable exercise of a school's authority.[11]

The First, Second, Fourth, Seventh, and Eighth Circuits have upheld students' challenges to school district efforts to regulate grooming.[12] Early on, *Breen v. Kahl* held that there is a fundamental right to wear one's hair at any length.[13] Later decisions reflect the same right to govern one's personal appearance. Arguments have been made that hair length compromises the school's safety and hygiene while causing a distraction and creating disruption. One court dismissed these arguments as a pretext for imposing a style preference.[14]

Dress Codes

The courts have upheld a school's statutory authority to make and enforce reasonable rules and regulations with respect to student dress. Challenges to school dress codes have generally followed two lines of reasoning. The first addresses freedom of expression, a First Amendment interest guaranteed under the Bill of Rights. The second deals with the school's right to pursue its educational mission free from distractions, without harming instructional effectiveness, without endangering the safety of students, and without injuring student morals.[15]

Tinker confirmed the former by establishing the right of students to express themselves "in absence of constitutionally valid reasons to regulate their speech."[16] In this instance, the speech was an armband worn by students to protest the Vietnam War. The issue was one of communication by type or style of dress and, as such, was a free speech issue. Chapter 5, "Free Expression," explains this in more detail.

The second line of reasoning establishes the school's right to enforce reasonable clothing regulations so long as the rules are designed to accomplish the school's educational purpose.

Generally, schools may enforce dress codes that are deemed necessary to maintain the integrity of the educational process without undue disruption or distraction. This authority exists in face of the constitutional right of students to control their own appearance. It is easier to justify clothing regulations than hair or grooming regulations.[17]

At times, balancing these interests can be tricky. The courts have upheld prohibitions where excessively tight pants or skirts are the issue.[18] This applies to skirts more than six inches above the knee as well. However, longer skirts, frayed trousers, and tie-dyed clothing cannot be controlled without showing cause for disrupting the educational process.[19] One curious line of reasoning was offered by an Idaho court prohibiting wearing T-shirts depicting school administrators with alcoholic beverages. The court opined that school officials "would be seriously compromised" by such attire, and it is within the statutory obligation to teach students about the deleterious effects of alcohol.[20]

As long as the regulations are clearly related to maintaining discipline, even the teaching of community values might sustain the authority of the school district over student dress. In requiring attire that conformed to the community standards, a brother and sister were barred from an Ohio prom because they were cross-dressed.[21]

Most recently, gang attire has become a serious concern due to the potential for disruption as a concern of students, parents, and the school. Courts have acknowledged a rational basis for establishing rules and regulations designed to curb gang activity. Rules that prohibit wearing T-shirts with gang logos, symbols or drawings have been upheld. Even wearing earrings that demonstrate gang affiliation have met with judicial approval.[22]

It is not necessary to prove with certainty that disruption will occur when applying dress code regulations designed to curtail gang activity. However, the courts still demand that the facts must "reasonably lead school officials to forecast substantial disruption." This was the essence of a recent decision where a California school district's dress code was held to apply only to the high school since there was no proof that gangs existed in the elementary or middle school level.[23] With no evidence of gang activity at the elementary and middle school levels, substantial disruption could not be reasonably expected. Therefore, attempts to govern student dress could not pass the constitutional muster.

Implications

Teachers and Administrators:

- Grooming and dress codes have the courts' selected support. Know your jurisdiction and its position.

- It is more difficult to regulate hair length than clothing. Policies that attempt to do so must address the potential for disruption to the educational environment in the absence of such regulations.

- The recent Texas case defending the right of Native Americans to wear long hair may indicate a growing sensitivity to cultural diversity.

- A school should establish a clear purpose for any grooming or dress code before implementing policy. There is no need to invite litigation.

Parents and Students:

- Students have recognized liberty rights that cannot be infringed upon in an arbitrary or capricious manner in controlling their appearance. However, it is difficult to sustain arguments against a school's contention that dress codes bear a reasonable relationship to the school's educational purpose.

- One may expect greater personal freedom in grooming than in dress.

- Schools may exercise authority to regulate grooming and dress. Students' rights are limited in the restricted context of the school setting.

Chapter 6 Endnotes

[1] Tinker v. Des Moines Independent Community School District, 393 U.S. 543 (1969).

[2] Id. at 513.

[3] Kelley v. Johnson, 425 U.S. 238 (1976).

[4] Independent School District No. 8 v. Swanson, 553 P.2d 496 (Okla. 1976).

[5] Neuhaus v. Federico, 505 P.2d 939 (Ore. 1973).

[6] Ferrel v. Dallas Independent School District, 392 F.2d 697 (5th Cir. 1968).

[7] Jackson v. Dorrier, 424 F.2d 213 (6th Cir.), *certiorari* denied, 400 U.S. 850 (1970).

[8] Moody v. Cronin, 484 F. Supp. 270 (C.D. Ill. 1979); Hatch v. Goerke, 502 F.2d 1189 (10th Cir.).

[9] Alabama and Coushatta Tribes of Texas v. Trustees of Big Sandy Independent School District, 817 F. Supp. 1319 (E.D. Tex. 1993).

[10] Colorado Independent School District v. Barber, 846 S.W.2d 806 (Tex. App.- Eastland 1993).

[11] Casper v. Micken, 54 D.& C.2d 218 (Pa. 1971); Seville v. West Shore School District, 12 Adams L.J. 3 (Pa. 1970); Thomas v. Carbondale Area School District, 71 Lack. Jur. 67 (Pa. 1970).

[12] Davenport by Davenport v. Randolph County Board of Education, 730 F.2d 1395 (11th Cir. 1984); Zeller v. Donegal School District, 517 F.2d 600 (3rd Cir. 1975).

[13] Breen v. Kahl, 419 F.2d 1034 (7th Cir. 1969).

[14] Bishop v. Colaw, 450 F.2d 1069 (8th Cir. 1971).

[15] Fowler v. Williamson, 251 S.E.2d 889 (N.C. Ct. App. 1979).

[16] Tinker, *supra*, at 511.

[17] Wallace v. Ford, 346 F. Supp. 156 (E.D.Ark. 1972).

[18] Bannister v. Paradis, 306 F. Supp. 189 (D.N.H. 1970).

[19] Ibid.

[20] Gano v. School District No. 411, 674 F. Supp. 796 (D. Idaho 1987).

[21] Harper v. Edgewood Board of Education of School District No. 228, 655 F. Supp. 1353 (S.D. Ohio 1987).

[22] Oleson v. Board of Education of School District No. 228, 676 F. Supp. 820 (N.D. Ill. 1987).

[23] Jeglin v. San Jacinto Unified School District, 827 F. Supp. 1459 (C.D. Cal. 1993).

NOTES

Chapter 7   Home Instruction

Sources:

Pennsylvania Public School Code, 24 P.S. 1-111, 13-1327, 13-1327.1
Pennsylvania State Board of Education Regulations, 22 Pa. Code 11.25
Criminal History Record, 18 Pa. C.S. 9121

States have provisions in public school codes permitting certain forms of home instruction for students of compulsory school age. Home education, defined herein, refers to an educational program conducted at home as an alternative to regular education at a "day school" site. It provides an option to attending a public school or approved private school such as bona fide church or religious schools, trade schools, or business schools. Although terminology differs among the states, there are three basic types of home instruction: private tutoring, home schooling, and homebound instruction. Pennsylvania guidelines will be used as a basis for discussion in this chapter.

Private Tutoring

The first type of home instruction is private tutoring. Private tutoring is included as a form of home instruction because it normally occurs in the home even though it may take place at an alternate site. The Public School Code, Section 13-1327, describes it as a legal alternative to public education under a properly qualified private tutor. A "properly qualified private tutor" is defined as a person who has teaching certification recognized by the Commonwealth of Pennsylvania. The designated tutor must provide the majority of instruction to one or more children of a single family. The tutor must also receive a fee or other consideration for the instructional services rendered. Tutors may not have any felony convictions within five years of initiating services to pupils. Criminal violations that would disqualify a prospective tutor range from homicide to involvement in obscene and other sexual materials.[1]

Before private tutoring is initiated, the tutor must file a copy of his/her state certification and criminal history record information (pursuant to 18 Pa. C.S. 9121) with the superintendent of the school district of the children's residency. Students who receive private tutoring are neither counted in attendance for the purpose of reimbursement as part of the state education subsidy nor do they receive a high school diploma from the district of residency.

Private tutoring must consist of "regular daily instruction in the English language" in "subjects and activities prescribed by the standards of the State Board of Education." Compliance with these statutory provisions satisfies the conditions for a child's exclusion from attending school.

Home Schooling

A second type of home instruction is home schooling. Home schooling is described in the Pennsylvania Public School Code as "home education." "Home schooling" (common usage) is substituted here for Pennsylvania's statutory terminology (home education) since most educators prefer the common usage.

Home schooling, therefore, describes "a program conducted . . . by the parent or guardian or such person having legal custody of the child or children" (24 P.S. Code 1327). The provisions set forth in the School Code are designed to allow parents/guardians to conduct their children's education as a "supervisor," responsible for providing instruction. The supervisor, who must hold a valid high school diploma or its equivalent, is given a great deal of responsibility in educating the child.[2]

Students engaged in home schooling are not counted in attendance for the purpose of reimbursement as part of the state subsidy.

Once established, home-schooling sites may relocate to other school districts. The law provides that a letter of intent be sent to the new district of residence 30 days prior to the proposed relocation. If the program in question is involved in a hearing process to determine if it is in compliance with state law, the new district must continue the home schooling "until the appeals process is finalized." This balances the parents/guardians' right to home school with the school district's authority to hold the program accountable.

Applying for Home Schooling

Prior to initiating a home schooling program, supervisors of home-schooled children must file an affidavit with the superintendent of the district of residency. The affidavit is required to contain the following:

- The name of the supervisor and the name and age of each child in the home schooling program.

- The address and phone number of the program site.

- An outline of "proposed educational objectives by subject area."

- Evidence of proper immunization and appropriate health services.

- Assurance that the home schooling is in compliance with the law.

- A criminal background check of the supervisor.

If a child has special needs, the educational objectives must address "the specific needs of the exceptional student and [be] approved by a teacher with a valid certificate... to teach special education or a licensed clinical or certified school psychologist" (24 P.S. Code 1327(d)). These objectives must be submitted with the home schooling affidavit.

Home schooling supervisors of exceptional students may request the school district or Intermediate Unit to provide services consistent with the exceptional student's needs. Upon mutual agreement between the supervisor and school district/Intermediate Unit, specific services must be provided in the public school or a private school licensed to provide such programs and services.

Home schooling supervisors are entitled to educational support materials including copies of the district's planned courses, texts, and any curriculum materials appropriate to the student's age and developmental level. However, the district retains discretion over a number of services provided to home school students. The district may or may not permit a home-schooled student to participate in certain classes, field trips, special events, or extra-curricular activities. Special services, such as counseling and career planning, may be withheld as well as a high school diploma.

A sample affidavit is provided for reference at the end of the chapter.[3]

Demonstrating Educational Progress

The supervisor must maintain a detailed portfolio containing records and materials that demonstrate that an appropriate education is taking place. "The portfolio shall consist of a log, made contemporaneously with the instruction, which designates by title the reading materials used." The record must contain samples of writings, worksheets, workbooks, and creative materials used by or developed by the students.

Standardized test results must also be included. These results may come from the statewide testing program or from one or more of the Department of Education's list of "nationally normed standardized achievement tests."[4] The standardized test requirement may be satisfied by including the home-school student in the regular standardized testing program of the school district. If the supervisor elects not to have the home schooled student included in the school's testing program, the supervisor must ensure that the "nationally normed standardized tests … shall not be administered by the child's parent or guardian."

Evaluating the Home Schooling Program

The portfolio must be evaluated on an annual basis by either an appropriately certified public school teacher, a non-public teacher with at least two years of applicable teaching experience within the past ten years, or a licensed clinical or school psychologist. "At the request of the supervisor, persons with other qualifications may conduct the evaluation with the prior consent of the district of residence superintendent. In no event shall the evaluator be the supervisor or their spouse."

The evaluation must be written and it should consider "class work, homework, quizzes, class-work based tests and prepared tests related to class work subject matter."

The portfolio and annual written evaluation must be submitted to the school superintendent who is responsible for determining if the child is receiving an "appropriate education" as demonstrated by "sustained progress in the overall program." Any determination by the superintendent must be based on substantive fact and affirmative knowledge, not presumption.[5]

The superintendent may exercise his/her authority to monitor the home schooling program at any time during the school term if there is reason to believe that appropriate education is not taking place. The superintendent may require submission of the portfolio. Notice for such action must be made by certified mail, return receipt requested. The home schooling supervisor must submit the portfolio within 15 days and the written evaluation within 30 days.

If the superintendent finds that the program is not in order, the home schooling supervisor must be notified of the inadequacies in a certified letter, return receipt requested. The portfolio and written evaluation will then be returned to the supervisor who has 20 days to demonstrate that an appropriate education is taking place.

If the supervisor does not resubmit the documents within the 20 days, the home schooling will be considered out of compliance and the child must be enrolled in school.[6] If the documentation is resubmitted and found to be adequate, the home schooling program shall stand. If the documentation is found to be inadequate, the superintendent shall notify the home schooling supervisor of a school board hearing on the matter. Once again, notification for the board hearing must be sent by certified mail, return receipt requested.

The board hearing shall be conducted by an impartial hearing examiner[7] within 30 days and a decision must be rendered within 15 days. The hearing examiner's decision may be appealed to the Secretary of Education or to the Commonwealth Court by either the supervisor or the superintendent.

If there is no appeal after the hearing examiner determines that an appropriate education is not taking place, the home schooling program will be considered out of compliance and the child must be enrolled in school.[8] The supervisor of such a program is rendered ineligible "to supervise a [home schooling] program for that child . . . for a period of twelve (12) months from the date of such determination."

Homebound Instruction

Unlike private tutoring and home schooling, students on homebound instruction are counted in attendance for the purpose of reimbursement as part of the state educational subsidy. Homebound instruction is provided to students attending the public schools who require temporary excusal for "mental, physical, or other urgent reasons."[9] The term "urgent reasons" must be strictly construed so as not to permit irregular attendance. Temporary excusal is based upon a diagnosis made by a physician, psychiatrist, or licensed psychologist. The school district is ultimately entrusted with the responsibility to enact policies that "define the responsibilities of both the district and the pupil with regard to these instructional services." The discretion is broad, and the school's authority is considerable.

Once temporary excusal is verified, the student is entitled to instructional services from a teacher at the home site. The school district pays the cost of the teacher and receives partial reimbursement from the state according to the mandated minimum hourly rate times the school district's aid ratio.[10]

Homebound instruction applies to public school students only. If a non-public or private school student desires homebound instruction from the public school, the student must enroll in the public school for the period of time that homebound instruction is sought.

Homebound instructors may be a public, non-public, or private school teachers provided that they have the required criminal background clearance. Tutoring services may also be called upon to provide homebound instruction as long as the instructor possesses state certification. Employing a tutoring service may have financial advantages to a school district; however, districts should exercise caution in light of the collective bargaining agreement between the board of education and the professional employees.

Implications

Teachers and Administrators:

- Private tutoring, home schooling, and homebound instruction have substantive and procedural differences.

- Of the home education options, only homebound instruction counts students in attendance for the purpose of reimbursement as part of the state educational subsidy. It also receives partial reimbursement for instructional costs.

- Before a school district resorts to using an outside tutoring service for homebound instruction, it should consider the nature of the relationship between the professional employees and board of education.

- Cooperation with parents/guardians in matters of home education is preferable to confrontation.

Parents and Students:

- When home education is an option for compulsory school-aged children, make certain that procedures are followed to ensure compliance with state laws.

- Although it is up to the school district to decide if it will award a high school diploma to resident students who have been home-schooled, it is rarely done.

AFFIDAVIT OF THE SUPERVISOR OF
A HOME EDUCATION PROGRAM

To the superintendent of the (name of the school district) **School District:**

    1. I attest that I _(name of the supervisor)_ am the parent, guardian or legal custodian of _(name of the student(s))_, that I am the supervisor of the home education program and that I have earned a high school diploma or its equivalent, evidence of which is attached. The program will be conducted at _(address)_. The phone number at this site is _(phone number)_.

    2. I attest that the home education program will be in compliance with Section 13-1327.1 of the Pennsylvania Statutes Annotated.

FOR ELEMENTARY STUDENTS

    3. I attest that the subjects listed in paragraph four (4) below will be offered in the English language for a minimum of 180 days of instruction or a minimum of 900 hours.

    4. I attest that the following courses shall be taught: English (to include spelling, reading, and writing), arithmetic, science, geography, history of the United States and Pennsylvania, civics, safety education (including regular and continuous instruction in the dangers and prevention of fires), health and physiology, physical education, music, and art.

FOR SECONDARY STUDENTS

    5. I attest that the subjects listed in paragraph four (4) below will be offered in the English language for a minimum of 180 days of instruction or a minimum of 990 hours.

    6. I attest that the following courses shall be taught: English (to include language, literature, speech, and composition), science, geography, social studies (to include civics, world history, history of the United States and Pennsylvania), mathematics (to include general mathematics, algebra, and geometry), art, music, physical education, health and safety education, including regular and continuous instruction in the dangers and prevention of fires. Other courses may be included at the discretion of the supervisor.

    7. I attest that the educational objectives in the home education program are by subject area as attached to this affidavit. (attach objectives)

    8. I attest that the _(student name(s))_ has been immunized against the following diseases and I have attached evidence thereof that said student has a medical or religious exemption pursuant to Section 1303a(c) and (d) of Pennsylvania Statutes Annotated:

a. Diphtheria	d. Measles (Rubeola)	g. Hepatitis B
b. Tetanus	e. Rubella	h. Varicella
c. Poliomyelitis	f. Mumps	

9. I attest that __(student names(s))__ has/have received the health and medical services required by Article XIV of the Public School Code, and I have attached evidence thereof or a religious exemption under Section 14-1419 of the Pennsylvania Statutes Annotated.

Article XIV requires that every child of school age be given through methods established by the state's Advisory Health Board, an annual vision test, a hearing test, a measurement of height an weight, tests for tuberculosis under medical supervision and other tests required by the Advisory Health Board. Children upon entry into school and in the 6th and 11th grades must have a medical examination and comprehensive health appraisal by a physician. Children upon entry into school and in the 3rd and 7th grades must have a dental examination by a dentist. A comprehensive health record shall be maintained for each child.

10. I attest that no adult living in the home, including the undersigned supervisor and no person having legal custody of __(student names(s))__ has/have been convicted of any of the following offenses under Title 18 of the Pennsylvania Consolidated Statutes:

     Chapter 25, relating to criminal homicide
     Section 2702, relating to aggravated assault
     Section 2901, relating to kidnapping
     Section 2902, relating to unlawful restraint
     Section 3121, relating to rape
     Section 3122, relating to statutory rape
     Section 3123, relating to involuntary deviate sexual intercourse
     Section 3126, relating to indecent assault
     Section 3127, relating to indecent exposure
     Section 4303, relating to concealing the death of a child born out of wedlock
     Section 4304, relating to endangering the welfare of children
     Section 4305, relating to dealing in infant children
     Section 5902(b) felonies relating to prostitution and related offenses
     Section 5903(c) or (d), relating to obscene and other sexual materials
     Section 6301, relating to corruption of minors
     Section 6312, relating to sexual abuse of children

     Signed and Notarized:

                                 _____
                                   Supervisor's Signature

ATTACHMENTS:

     Evidence of a high school diploma or equivalent
     Educational objectives by subject matter
     Evidence of immunization
     Evidence of health and medical services

Chapter 7 Endnotes

[1] The complete list is found in 24 P.S. 111(e): criminal homicide, aggravated assault, kidnapping, unlawful restraint, rape, statutory rape, involuntary deviate sexual intercourse, indecent assault, indecent exposure, concealing the death of a child born out of wedlock, endangering the welfare of children, prostitution or other related offenses, obscenity, corruption of minors, sexual abuse of children, and felonies under the "Controlled Substance, Drug, Device, and Cosmetic Act" (P.L. 233, No.64 of 1972). Recently added to these are stalking, sexual assault, incest, indecent assault, and indecent performances.

[2] Jeffrey v. O'Donnell, 702 F. Supp. 513 (M.D. Pa. 1987).

[3] Pennsylvania Department of Education, Basic Education Circular (BEC) 15-94.

[4] They are:
   Iowa Test of Basic Skills
   California Achievement Test
   Stanford Achievement Test
   Metropolitan Achievement Test
   Science Research Associates
   Comprehensive Test of Basic Skills
   Comprehensive Testing Program (CTPIII)
   Wide Range Achievement Test
   Peabody Individual Test

[5] Stobaugh v. Wallace, 757 F. Supp. 653 (W.D. Pa. 1990).

[6] That is, the public school district of residence, a non-public school, or a licensed academic school.

[7] "Impartial hearing examiner" is defined as someone who is not an officer, employee, or agent of the school district of residence or the Department of Education.

[8] The public school district of residence, a non-public school, or a licensed academic school.

[9] 22 Pa. Code 11.25

[10] 24 P.S. 2510.1

Chapter 8   Religious Activity

Sources:

> First Amendment
> State Constitutional Provisions

The limit of government's authority over the free exercise of religion has been defined by the Supreme Court in a long history of cases based on the Establishment Clause of the First Amendment. The founding fathers' notion that "Congress shall make no law respecting an establishment of religion, or prohibiting the free exercise thereof" stems from the recognition that each citizen has a right to freely choose a spiritual course without governmental interference. Even though free public education was virtually non-existent in the late 18th century, the lessons of history warned against the fusion of government and religion by groups that would compel individuals to their form of worship. Therefore, the architects of our government inserted the Establishment Clause of the First Amendment to ensure "wholesome neutrality" in matters of religion.

Constitutional Limits

What is the nature of government's neutrality and society's perception of its role in providing for the health, education, and welfare of its citizens? As far back as 1879, the Supreme Court used the words of Thomas Jefferson to interpret the Establishment Clause to mean creating "a wall of separation between church and State."[1] Fifty years later, the "wall of separation" was tested by a Louisiana statute providing free textbooks for all public and private school children. The challenge to the statute was based on the use of public funds for nonpublic purposes. The Supreme Court upheld the statute on the grounds that the beneficiaries of the state's action were the children and not the schools.[2] This "Child Benefit Theory" has endured over the years. As recent as 1968, the Court affirmed the authority of the state of New York to require local school boards to loan books to nonpublic school children in grades seven to twelve.[3]

In one way or another, the concept of benefiting individuals, regardless of their religious affiliation, has been applied by the Court to justify government's role in providing services to its citizens. Such was the case in *Everson v. Board of Education* when transportation for nonpublic school children was upheld as a public service akin to police, fire, and health protection.[4] These and other cases addressing aid to nonpublic or parochial schools form an area of law commonly referred to as "parochaid."

Parochaid covers a number of issues. While transportation to and from school has been held to be constitutionally valid, public monies for transporting nonpublic school children on field trips was declared unconstitutional. Field trips for nonpublic school children were prohibited because they were curricular in nature making them a part of the instructional function of the nonpublic school.[5] Likewise, a tuition reimbursement plan was invalidated because it provided special economic benefit to a particular class of citizen.[6] The Supreme Court also barred the loans of instructional materials and equipment to nonpublic schools holding that there was a predominantly religious character to the schools benefiting from the loan.[7]

The most notable parochaid decision was handed down in *Lemon v. Kurtzman*.[8] In *Lemon*, the Court refused to permit "secular services" from public schools based on "excessive entanglement" between government and religion. *Lemon* is significant in that it "considered the cumulative criteria developed by the Court over many years." Three tests were "gleaned" from case law:

1. The statute must have a secular legislative purpose;
2. Its principal or primary effect must be one that neither advances nor inhibits religion...
3. The statute must not foster an excessive government entanglement with religion...[9]

The *Lemon* test is now used by the courts to analyze Church and State issues. For example, a portrait of Jesus Christ that hung for 30 years in a public school was found to "advance religion" and be without "secular purpose." It, therefore, had to be removed.[10] In another case, Halloween observances were permitted where students and teachers dressed as witches. The court felt that the secular purpose of the celebration was in accordance with contemporary tradition without religious emphasis. It did not advance religion despite the contention that it bore similarity to Wicca, a witches' religion.[11]

Recently, a complex Louisiana statute authorized, among other things, contractual arrangements between public school employees and sectarian schools for special education services. This portion of the law was struck down as creating excessive entanglement in *Helms v. Cody*.[12] Consistent with *Everson*, the free transportation provision of the statute was upheld because students were the prime beneficiaries of the aid. However, direct payments for the cost of transporting students were a different story. Direct payments to two private academies were classified as unconstitutional direct subsidies. However, payments to parents were permissible because the parents (children) were direct beneficiaries and not the parochial schools.

The child benefit theory was also used to uphold a request for the services of an interpreter for a deaf student at a parochial school.[13] Objecting to the school district's reasoning that the interpreter could be used to communicate non-secular (religious) ideas, the court viewed the service as providing direct benefit to the student.

Finally, in a narrow 5-4 opinion, the Supreme Court lifted barriers to remedial instruction to eligible students in religious schools. *Agostini v. Felton* rejected earlier rationale that prohibited the presence of public school teachers on parochial school premises. Mere presence no longer creates a "symbolic union" as long as money is allocated based on neutral criteria.[14] It is important to note that *Agostini* addressed New York City's Title I program which contained a number of conditions that the Supreme Court felt preserved the Constitutional integrity of sending instructors on to parochial school grounds. Rules were in place that stressed the secular purpose of their work. They were accountable only to their secular supervisors who alone were able to determine which students were eligible for the service. No intermingling of teaching duties (i.e. team teaching, cooperative instructional activities) and the use of materials and equipment was permitted. Title I instructors were also not permitted to be involved in any religious activities. Other safeguards included the provisions that only secular employees could be assigned without regard to religious affiliation as Title I personnel, religious symbols had to be removed from the classrooms, and a secular field advisor had to make one unannounced visit to the instructor's classroom per month.

In *Mitchell v. Helms*, the United States Supreme Court held that private religious schools that receive educational materials and equipment under Chapter II of the Educational Consolidation and Improvement Act of 1981 did not violate the Establishment Clause of the First Amendment.[15] The Court neither challenged the secular purpose of Chapter II nor questioned the matter of excessive entanglement (re: *Agostini*). It did, however, consider Chapter II's effect, namely, that it "neither results in religious indoctrination by the government not defines the recipients by reference to religion." The Court held that Chapter II did not advance religion because 1.) the aid did not contain impermissible content relying on the private choices of parents and students, and 2.) it allocated and used neutral, secular criteria that applied to both secular and non-secular schools on an equal basis.

Religious activity may occur before, during, and after school. It may involve prayer, released time for religious instruction, or even the Pledge of Allegiance. An analysis of each of these areas reflects the controversial nature of church and state issues as the courts attempt to balance the government's authority with the individual's right to practice religion.

Religious Activity During School

Religious Activity During School

School Sponsored (Organized)

Recitation/Readings.   State-sponsored prayer was declared unconstitutional in 1962 when a 22-word invocation used at the beginning of each day was prohibited by the Supreme Court.[16] A year later, the prohibition was extended to Bible reading when Unitarian and atheist parents raised objections. [17]   The Court cautioned that, while the Establishment Clause clearly prohibits the state from denying the free exercise of religion to anyone, it has never meant that the majority could use that machinery of the state to foster the practice of any particular belief. This includes the efforts by state legislatures to remove official sponsorship of prayer in its schools under the mask of free expression.

Moment of Silence.   Subsequent Supreme Court challenges were based on state laws requiring a "moment of silence." In *Wallace* v. *Jaffree*, an Alabama statute authorizing a one-minute period of silence in all public schools "for meditation" was declared unconstitutional in 1985 using the *Lemon* test. Affirming a Federal District Court ruling, the Supreme Court invalidated the statute based upon facts that revealed no clear secular purpose. On the contrary, records of the legislative discussion supporting the law's passage reflect just the opposite.[18] Similar conclusions were reached in the 3rd and 4th Circuits.[19]

Some concern has surfaced over the Court's strict interpretation of "secular legislative purpose." Justice Sandra Day O'Connor suggested an "endorsement test" in her concurring opinion in *Wallace*. Justice O'Connor proposes that the *Lemon* test should be modified "as to the purpose and effect of a statute. . . to examine whether government's purpose is to endorse religion and whether the statute actually conveys a message of endorsement." She argues that this would give the Court analytic jurisprudence as opposed to rigid adherence to the *Lemon* test's "constitutional signpost, to be followed or ignored in [each] particular case." Justice O'Connor believes that an endorsement test "would not preclude government from acknowledging religion or taking religion into account on making law and policy." It would, nevertheless, still preclude government from "conveying or attempting to convey a message that religion or a particular religious belief is favored or preferred."

Justice O'Connor's reasoning may indicate a new direction for the Court. If the Court adopts the endorsement test, silent meditation statutes may pass the Court's scrutiny and be declared constitutional. As such, silent meditation would be viewed as constitutionally protected private speech, not as government sponsored prayer.

Graduation Ceremonies. The issue of prayer at graduation ceremonies applies to baccalaureate exercises as well as commencement exercises.

Baccalaureate exercises may not be organized or sponsored by the school. The nature of the ceremony is ostensibly religious and the constitutional prohibition is clearly established in law. However, a private group such as a multi-denominational ministerium, may organize traditional religious baccalaureate exercises using school facilities on the same terms as any other outside group. The school district must be careful not to extend special benefits to the group organizing the baccalaureate exercises that are not enjoyed by any other group using school facilities. For example, the district may not waive the building use fee if school policy dictates otherwise. See Chapter 18, "Equal Access." The school district is bound to maintain a "wholesome neutrality" that "neither advances nor inhibits" the free exercise of religion.

Prayers at commencement exercises are likewise prohibited where school officials mandate or organize the prayer. It makes no difference whether the exercise is at the elementary, middle, or high school level.

The practice of school-sponsored invocations and benedictions was challenged in *Lee v. Weisman*[20] by the parents of a middle schooler who sought an injunction from inviting clergy to give prayers at future commencements. A review of the facts revealed that the principal invited a rabbi to deliver customary non-sectarian prayers by giving him a pamphlet entitled "Guidelines for Civil Occasions." The Court held the practice to be in violation of the Establishment Clause because schools are prohibited from acting in such a way as to advance religion. School officials advanced religion by directing the performance of a formal religious exercise: They decided that there would be prayer. They selected the individual that would pray. And, they provided guidelines. Furthermore, the school's supervision and control over the ceremony negated the argument that attendance was voluntary. The Court felt that students were essentially not free to be absent in any real sense of the term voluntary because of subtle public and peer pressure.

Schools have since made an effort to circumvent the Supreme Court's prohibition against prayer at commencement exercises. A number of school districts have enacted policies where students are permitted to deliver voluntary, non-proselytizing innovations or benedictions. These efforts at student-initiated prayer have drawn inconsistent results from the Federal District Courts.

Two jurisdictions stand apart from the rest. The Supreme Court has declined to hear appeals from the Fifth and Eleventh Circuits creating a rule of law that upholds student-initiated prayer in those circuits. In the same year as *Lee, supra*, a non-proselytizing invocation at a Texas commencement exercise was upheld by the 5th Circuit.[21] The invocation was delivered by a student selected by the other members of the senior class. The court interpreted that the purpose of the invocation was to solemnize the ceremony, not endorse religion. Therefore, the students, not the school, were held to endorse a religious viewpoint by virtue of their voluntary participation.

Two years later, the Eleventh Circuit heard a case where a Florida school board responded to *Lee* by revising their graduation policy. The new policy gave the senior class the discretion to choose brief "two minutes or less" opening and closing "messages" to be delivered by a student volunteer selected by the graduating class. The Eleventh Circuit determined that the school policy had the secular purpose of safeguarding free speech and refraining from content-based regulations. It further held that such a policy did not advance or endorse religion. Moreover, the policy did not excessively entangle the school district with religion. Finally, the court reasoned that students were not coerced by school officials. The policy was neutral as to prayer and never mentioned that students should pray or deliver any message at all.[22]

The remaining jurisdictions adhere to *Lee*. The Ninth Circuit nullified an Idaho school policy. It held that state involvement and the traditional and obligatory nature of attendance at any graduation exercises made any commencement prayer unconstitutional.[23] The Court reasoned that the school district ultimately controls graduation ceremonies, and they could not relieve themselves of their constitutional duties by delegating the duties to students.

The Fourth Circuit struck down a Virginia school district policy permitting student-initiated prayer,[24] while at the same time, the Third Circuit reasoned that, despite the school board attempt's to delegate the decision to pray, "the graduation ceremony is a school-sponsored event."[25]

Legally, prayers are prayers in any form. A Texas court has noted that prayers may not be sung either.[26]

School Activities. Prayer at school functions and activities have been held to be unconstitutional in cases where school officials led prayers at band rehearsals and performances,[27] where school officials led the recitation of the Lord's Prayer before and after athletic contests,[28] and where prayers were sung at athletic contests, pep rallies, and graduation ceremonies.[29]

Student-led prayers at activities may also violate the Constitution. The Eleventh Circuit struck down the practice of reading prayers over the public address system before each varsity football game. Even though the invocations were non-sectarian and selected by the students who read them, the Establishment Clause prevailed[30] since they were a part of the activity and clearly sponsored by the school.

The Supreme Court settled the issue of school-sponsored prayer by striking down a school district policy that permitted student-led, student-initiated prayer over the public address system before football games. In *Santa Fe Independent District v. Doe*,[31] a school policy permitted speakers who were elected by the student body to deliver an invocation on school property at a school event. The Court found that the policy in question encouraged public prayer. It declared that, since attendance at football games was mandated as part of some students' extra curricular activities (i.e. athletes, band members, and cheerleaders), participation in prayer was coerced. Furthermore, the district's system of electing the student speaker "ensures that only those messages deemed 'appropriate' under the District's policy may be delivered," thereby guaranteeing "that minority candidates will never prevail and that their views will be effectively silenced." The Court's language was direct. Given the "context in which the policy arose...[the] context quells any doubt that this policy was implemented with the purpose of endorsing school prayer."

Non-School Sponsored (Personal)

Voluntary prayer, as a private activity, is permissible in public schools. There are no Constitutional restraints on an individual's right to the free exercise of religion. Accordingly, students may pray individually or in groups. They may recite prayers and read scriptures audibly or silently in classrooms, cafeterias, hallways, and lounge areas subject only to the disruption standard set forth in *Tinker*.[32] Justice O'Connor summed up the Court's attitude: "The Court does not hold that the Establishment Clause is so hostile to religion that it precludes the States from affording school children an opportunity for voluntary... prayer."[33] Voluntary school prayer that is non-disruptive is purely private speech. It is, therefore, protected by the Constitution and permitted "at any time before, during, or after the school day."[34] See Chapter 5, "Free Expression."

Released Time for Religious Instruction

The Supreme Court first addressed the question of released time for religious instruction was in 1948. A challenge was made to the practice of setting aside a portion of the school day once a week for religious instruction by inviting Protestant teachers, Catholic priests, and Jewish rabbis into the school. Released time from regular classes was provided to students who desired religious instruction. Students who did not wish religious instruction pursued their secular studies. The Supreme Court, in a series of convincing arguments, struck down the practice as unconstitutional because tax-supported facilities should not be used to disseminate religious doctrines whether aiding one or all religions.[35]

A few years later, a released time program that excused students once a week during the school day to attend religious services off school premises was upheld. The Court opined that such an action on the part of the school accommodated rather than aided religion.[36]

Taking released time one step further, a Utah State Board of Education policy allowed credit for non-denominational Bible history courses taken in parochial schools. Relying on the *Lemon* test, the Tenth Circuit invalidated the policy. The court opined that, since the grades were recorded on the student's permanent record, school officials would be required to assess the religious content of the classes. This would exceed permissible accommodation of religion and result in excessive entanglement, thereby violating the Establishment Clause.[37] In 1990, the Western District of Virginia held that a public school may not encourage or assist in the participation of a released time program for religious instruction In this instance, the court focused on "the symbolic impact created by the appearance of official involvement."[38]

Religious Activity Before or After School

Religious activity before or after school is viewed as private speech and a free exercise of religion protected by the First Amendment. The religious activity may occur before or after a regular school day, a designated school activity, an athletic event, or graduation ceremony. In at least one jurisdiction, student-initiated prayer was upheld when students took it upon themselves to recite the Lord's Prayer five minutes prior to commencement exercises. School officials knew that the students intended to pray but did not allow the prayer purposefully, intentionally, or deliberately. The court ruled that the school did not violate any law simply by its knowledge. A school's endorsement of religion requires more than mere knowledge.[39]

Even though students are permitted to participate in such religious activity without restraint, school officials acting in an official capacity are cautioned to refrain from behavior that could be interpreted as encouraging or discouraging students to participate. An individual's personal expression of faith done independently of the school is constitutionally protected.

Pledge of Allegiance

Although not a religious issue *per se*, statutes requiring the recitation of the Pledge of Allegiance were struck down as an infringement on an individual's right of the free exercise of religion.[40] Students are not compelled to participate in the recitation of the Pledge of Allegiance on religious and free speech grounds. Even though school boards may compel the ceremonial flag salute, they may not compel students to participate.

In 1992, the Seventh Circuit confirmed that any statute that compelled students to participate in the Pledge of Allegiance would be flagrantly unconstitutional. The court noted that the phrase "under God" in the Pledge of Allegiance was not government-sponsored prayer. It was, instead, a ceremonial deism without true religious significance.[41]

Implications

Teachers and Administrators:

- Review any involvement with religious activity in light of the *Lemon* test:

    1. Does the action have a secular purpose?
    2. Does it advance or inhibit religion?
    3. Would the involvement create excessive government entanglement?

- "Wholesome neutrality" in religious matters is sometimes tricky to maintain.

- Government-sponsored prayer in school or as a part of school activities is unconstitutional.

- Voluntary private prayer by individuals or groups is permissible.

- Do not portray religious material as school-sponsored.

- Students may be allowed released time for religious instruction off school premises. However, credit may not be given for such instruction on a student's permanent record. To do so would result in excessive government entanglement.

- Schools may send remedial help directly into parochial schools as long as appropriations are based on neutral criteria.

Parents and Students:

- Schools may compel the ceremonial flag salute, but they may not compel students to participate.

- Voluntary private prayer that is not disruptive is purely personal speech. Therefore, it is constitutionally protected.

- Religious activity before or after school is considered private speech beyond the school's authority to regulate.

Chapter 8 Endnotes

[1] Reynolds v. U.S., 98 U.S. 145 (1879).

[2] Cochran v. Louisiana State Board of Education, 281 U.S. 370 (1930).

[3] Board of Education of Central School District No. 1 v. Allen, 392 U.S. 236 (1968).

[4] Everson v. Board of Education of Ewing Township, 330 U.S. 1 (1947).

[5] Wolman v. Walter, 433 U.S. 229 (1977).

[6] Sloan v. Lemon, 413 U.S. 825 (1972).

[7] Meek v. Pittenger, 421 U.S. 349 (1975).

[8] Lemon v. Kurtzman, 403 U.S. 602 (1972).

[9] Id., 612-13.

[10] Washegesic v. Bloomingdale Public Schools, 813 F. Supp. 559 (W.D. Md. 1993), *certiorari* denied 115 S. Ct. 1822.

[11] Guyer v. School Board of Alachua County, 634 So.2d 806 (Fla App. 1st Dist. 1994).

[12] Helms v. Cody, 856 F. Supp. 1102 (E.D. La. 1994).

[13] Zobrest v. Catalina Foothill School District, 113 S. Ct. 2462 (1993).

[14] Agostini v. Felton, 117 S. Ct. 1997 (1997).

[15] Mitchell v. Helms, 120 S. Ct. 2530 (2000).

[16] Engle v. Vitale, 370 U.S. 421 (1962).

[17] School District of Abington Township, Pennsylvania v. Schemmp, 374 U.S. 203 (1963).

[18] Wallace v. Jaffree, 472 U.S. 38 (1985).

[19] Karcher v. May, 484 U.S. 72 (1987); Walter v. West Virginia Board of Education, 610 F. Supp. 1161 (S.D. W.Va. 1985).

[20] Lee v. Weisman, 112 S. Ct. 2649 (1992).

[21] Jones v. Clear Creek Independent School District, 977 F.2d 963 (5th Cir. 1992).

[22] Adler v. Duval County School Board, 851 F. Supp. 446 (M.D. Fla. 1994).

[23] Harris v. Joint School District No. 241, 41 F.3d 447 (9th Cir. 1994).

[24] Gearon v. Loudoun County School Board, 844 F. Supp. 1097 (E.D. Va. 1993).

[25] American Civil Liberties Union of New Jersey v. Black Horse Pike Regional Board of Education, Civil No. 93-02651.

[26] Doe v. Aldine Independent School District, 563 F. Supp. 883 (S.D. Tex. 1982).

[27] Steele v. VanBuren Public School District, 845 F.2d 1492 (8th Cir. 1988).

[28] Doe v. Duncanville Independent School District, 994 F.2d 160 (5th Cir. 1993).

[29] Aldine, *supra.*

[30] Jager v. Douglas County School District, 862 F.2d 824 (11th Cir. 1989).

[31] Santa Fe Independent District v. Doe, No. 99-62 (S. Ct. 2000).

[32] Tinker v. Des Moines Independent School District, 393 U.S. 503 (1969).

[33] Wallace, *supra.*

[34] Ibid.

[35] People of the State of Illinois *ex rel.* McCollum v. Board of Education of School District No. 71, Champaign County, 333 U.S. 203 (1948).

[36] Zorach v. Clauson, 343 U.S. 306 (1952).

[37] Lanner v. Wimmer, 662 F.2d 1349 (10th Cir. 1981).

[38] Doe v. Shenandoah County School Board, 737 F.Supp 913 (W. D. Va. 1990).

[39] Goluba v. School District of Ripon, 874 F. Supp. 242 (E.D. Wisc. 1994).

[40] West Virginia State Board of Education v. Barnette, 391 U.S. 624 (1943).

[41] Sherman v. Community Consolidated District 21, 980 F.2d 437 (7th Cir. 1992).

NOTES

Chapter 9   Student Searches

Sources:

>Fourth Amendment
>Fourteenth Amendment

Student privacy rights involving searches have roots in the constitutional guarantee against unreasonable search and seizure outlined by the Fourth Amendment. These privacy interests are balanced with the school's interests through the due process clause of the Fourteenth Amendment. In 1985, *New Jersey v. T.L.O*[1] clarified the legal standard that measures the limits of student searches. Before *T.L.O.*, schools had wide authority over students in the area of searches under the common law principle of *in loco parentis*. Gradually, more and more cases involving searches reached the courts creating the need to clarify points of law in a number of areas: justification for the search, reasonableness, scope, and liability.[2]

In *T.L.O.* a young female student was caught smoking in the girl's restroom. When brought before the assistant principal, she denied the act and was made to hand over her purse for inspection. The assistant principal noticed cigarette-rolling papers. This aroused his suspicion causing him to search further. He discovered a small amount of marijuana, some drug paraphernalia, approximately forty dollars, and a list of names of students that owed her money. After being questioned by the school authorities, the student confessed to selling marijuana and was suspended accordingly. The confiscated items were submitted to the police along with her confession. Later, the young girl was expelled from school in a proper administrative hearing that placed weight on the evidence obtained in the search. Action was brought against the school district by the parents to invalidate the search and, therefore, exclude the evidence obtained during the search.

The *T.L.O.* court opined that permissible searches of individuals by school officials must have:

1. Justification at its inception.
2. Reasonable grounds for believing that a law or school rule or regulation had been violated.

3. Reasonable scope in light of age, gender, and the nature of the infraction.

The *T.L.O.* court held that the assistant principal was justified in his search because it was reasonable for him to believe that a school rule had been violated. Furthermore, the scope of the search was held reasonable in light of the student's age (high school), gender (there was no physical intrusion), and the nature of the infraction (possession of or selling drugs).

The Court declared that the evidence was legally obtained using *in loco parentis* to justify a standard of "reasonable suspicion" as opposed to "probable cause." School officials are now held to a lower standard for personal intrusion than other state officials such as the police.

It was made clear by the *T.L.O.* court that there is a lesser expectation of privacy for students than for members of the population in general.

Justification

The justification for a student search by an administrator is to maintain discipline and order in the school system in order to preserve the educational environment and ensure the safety of students. Justification is satisfied when the one who is the object of the search has violated or is in the act of violating the law or school rules and regulations. In the words of the *T.L.O.* court:

> A search of a student by a teacher or other school official will be "justified at its inception" when there are reasonable grounds for suspecting that the search will turn up evidence that he has violated or is violating either the law or the rules of the school.

Reasonableness

The *T.L.O.* court determined reasonableness to be a hybrid of *in loco parentis* and the normal strictures imposed by the Fourth Amendment. The Court reasoned that school officials conducting a search are not acting "merely as surrogates for the parents," the essence of *in loco parentis*. They are state officers by virtue of the high Court's *dicta* in *Tinker* and *Goss*. That is to say, if public school officials have been held to be state officials with respect to the First Amendment (*Tinker* and free speech) and the Fourteenth Amendment (*Goss* and due process), it should apply in a similar fashion to the Fourth Amendment with search and seizure. Having moved away from *in loco parentis*, the Court modified the level of suspicion necessary for school officials to conduct a search. Since students are entitled to some legitimate privacy interests and since the school has the responsibility of maintaining security and order, the warrant requirement (probable cause) was deemed "unsuited to the school environment." Instead, school officials were given a "reasonable suspicion" standard in order to proceed in the search of a student. "Reasonable suspicion" gives school officials greater discretion to act and it may be triggered by a number of things. Personal observations, such as a student fleeing at the approach of a school official, turning away and clutching a pocket,[3] and exchanging plastic bags for money[4] coupled with other pertinent facts could constitute reasonable suspicion. Hearing a suspicious "thud" from a dropped book bag was also deemed reasonable.[5]

Reasonableness has been further defined in various jurisdictions to be: seeing a suspicious plastic baggie in a student's pocket,[6] observing a fidgeting middle schooler attempting to enter a restroom stall when confronted by a school security officer,[7] information from a guidance counselor concerning vials of cocaine,[8] information offered by students concerned about a weapon,[9] and entering into a known area used by students for tobacco and marijuana use.[10]

Reliable information supplied by an informer,[11] prior reputation and conduct,[12] and other factors such as age and maturity, could also give rise to reasonable suspicion.

It should be noted that police in the school setting may be held to the stricter "probable cause" standard. When asked to search a student for drugs in an alternative school setting, an officer violated the constitutional provisions of the Fourth Amendment when he grabbed a flashlight from a student who laughed at an unsuccessful search of another student. The flashlight contained an illegal substance, however, the court held that mere laughing did not constitute "probable cause" to extend the search beyond the suspected youngster.[13] In another instance, however, a police officer employed by the district observed a student behaving nervously while carrying a clear plastic bag and a wad of bills. Acting on prior reports of the student's involvement with drugs, the officer proceeded to search the student after the student stuffed the items into his pockets. The court sustained the search even though the officer had not witnessed a drug transaction.[14] The courts apparently take into consideration the degree to which the police are acting as agents of the school district. The same is true of actions by security guards.

Scope

T.L.O. described the scope of such a search to be "reasonably related to the objectives of the search" while considering the "age and sex of the student and the nature of the infraction." This standard remains essentially undefined and could lead the Court to decide the scope on a case-by-case basis.

In a Texas case, skipping school did not establish reasonable grounds for searching a locked automobile.[15] Another court upheld a school district police officer's weapons search that extended to the student's pockets because the search was reasonably related in scope to the circumstances. The officer was employed by the district, acted on information that the student had a weapon in her possession, and the administrator initiated the search. Later, city police arrived and completed the search that revealed additional contraband.[16]

Lockers and desks are generally considered school property and, as such, school officials retain a right of access.[17] However, sweeping searches lacking specific purpose have been held to be unreasonable.[18] It is safe to say that although a student has a legitimate expectation of privacy with respect to a school locker, it is not absolute.[19] Recent tendencies of the courts indicate that individualized suspicion may not be necessary if the district has established guidelines and a proven high rate of violence.

Sniffing dogs may be used to search lockers, however, the contraband that they reveal can scarcely be used in a prosecution. Students readily deny knowledge of the presence of illegal substances or paraphernalia in their lockers. It is even more difficult to obtain an admission of ownership. Unless the school can confirm that the illicit material yielded from such a search actually belongs to the accused, the dog search simply alerts the students and community that the school is serious in its efforts to prohibit the presence of illicit substances in the school.

A 1998 Pennsylvania decision has upheld general locker searches by drug sniffing dogs. The court reasoned that even though students may expect some privacy in school, it is balanced against the need for a safe, secure learning environment where a lesser level of suspicion is justified.

In simple terms, the constitutional validity of such a search must be viewed on an individual basis where the search is motivated by a school district interest that outweighs the personal intrusion on students' privacy.[20]

Personal searches must satisfy the reasonable suspicion standard.[21] Thus, even an agitated student clutching a book bag when confronted by an adult was held to be reasonable.[22]

Strip searches are generally held to be an invasion of privacy[23] even when conducted to investigate the theft of $100 from a teacher[24] or based upon a suspicion of drug dealing by Junior High students.[25]

There have been at least two significant instances where strip searches have been upheld. One high school student who acted "sluggish," displayed lethargy, and smelled of marijuana was asked, in private, to lower his pants to permit security guards to observe if he was concealing drugs. The search produced no evidence of drugs and the student sued. A federal appeals court dismissed the student's action based on T.L.O., namely, there were reasonable grounds to believe that a law or school rule had been violated and the scope of the search was reasonable in light of the age, gender, and nature of the infraction.[26]

Another federal appeals court, relying on T.L.O., held that repeatedly observing bulges in a student's pants created justification for suspecting that a law or school policy had been violated. Furthermore, having the student change into gym clothes while same-sex observers stood at a distance did not exceed the scope of the search. The fact that no drugs were found did not deter the court from affirming the lower court's summary judgment for the school district.[27]

Reasonable suspicion is also applicable to automobile searches. Objects in plain view in an automobile create no expectation of privacy and, as such, are subject to action by school officials or police.[28] In Pennsylvania, police have been held to act within their rights when examining a homicide suspect's tire tread in a school parking lot without consent.[29] The search of an automobile based on observations that led administrators to suspect that a student was drinking was upheld.[30] Furthermore, information on marijuana possession reported to the administration was substantial enough to extend a search beyond the student and his locker to a locked automobile.[31]

Although the courts have a spotted history in the area of drug testing, random drug testing of athletes has been upheld in the federal court system and the United States Supreme Court. In an Indiana school district, two students sued the school to bar them from implementing a random urinalysis drug testing policy. The school's policy required that the student and parent sign a consent form before participation would be allowed. Affirming that the school's action constitutes a search under the meaning of the Fourth Amendment, the court declared that the school was within its authority to require consent for random drug testing in order to maintain the health and safety of its students.[32]

Most recently, the Supreme court put the issue to rest in *Vernonia v. Acton* where a seventh-grade student objected to random testing by refusing to sign a consent form agreeing to the testing. Although the student had no history of any form of drug abuse, the issue was pressed to ascertain the extent to which a school district may intrude on an individual student's privacy. The court sustained the school district's policy based on the special need to deter drug use among athletes as evidenced by the existence of a serious drug problem causing numerous sports injuries that were linked to drug use.[33] More recently, the Seventh Circuit upheld a medical assessment (including taking the student's blood pressure and pulse) and search of a student suspected of being under the influence of marijuana even though a drug screening test conducted the following day proved negative.[34]

In a number of subsequent cases, schools were cautioned not to extend the scope of drug testing beyond the special need exception of *Vernonia*. In *Joy v. Penn-Harris-Madison School Corporation*,[35] suspicionless drug testing was upheld based on *Vernonia* and *Todd v. Rush County Schools*.[36] However, while schools may exercise a degree of intrusion into students' privacy, students still retain a legitimate expectation of privacy. *Joy* cited the Seventh Circuit where a policy of suspicionless testing was struck down because the district had not tried a less intrusive procedure. The court acknowledged a genuine need to deter drug use among a select group of students, but the school did not first test those reasonably suspected of drug use.[37]

Liability

Because *Wood v. Strickland*[38] established that civil rights actions under 42 U.S.C. Section 1983 enjoy "good faith" immunity from prosecution for public school officials and *T.L.O.* established that school officials are agents of the government, liability for wrongful action in search and seizure becomes a possibility.   One area might be incurred through the application of the exclusionary rule to school officials if they act beyond their authority and conduct or participate in an illegal search with the police.   In such cases, the remedy would be to exclude such information from prosecution.[39]

Liability might also arise from the school's stated responsibility to maintain order and control. The school could conceivably be held liable for failing to conduct searches, triggering the possibility for tort action in negligence. To date, the courts have not established grounds for such tort liability.

Implications

<u>Teachers and Administrators:</u>

- Well-publicized school search policies can avoid litigation, even when applied to students on field trips.[40]

- The courts have given schools wider discretion to initiate a search. Since school officials have been granted more power, police should rarely be called in to do the initial search.

- School officials do not have to provide Miranda warnings to students[41] unless police are involved in an investigation.[42]

- Surveillance in areas normally open to inspection, such as schoolyards, restrooms, and classrooms, are generally held to be permissible.[43]

- Suggested Guidelines:

  1. School officials should conduct the initial search.
  2. The search should focus on a specific individual, if possible.
  3. There should be reasonable grounds for conducting the search.
  4. The violation of a law or school policy must be imminent.
  5. The scope of the search should take into consideration the student's age and gender as well as the nature of the infraction

- Sweeping searches by persons or animals yield little that a school district can act on. It does, however, make a public statement with respect to the school's stance on substance abuse.

- Materials discovered in students' lockers without the acknowledgment of ownership/possession have no legal nexus for prosecution.

- If a locker search is deemed necessary, the Pennsylvania State Board of Education regulations indicate that unless there is a threat to the "health, welfare, and safety of students," the student in question should be afforded prior notice of the search and be given the opportunity to be present during the search.[44] However, the use of dogs to sniff individuals in a sweeping search without a warrant may be upheld if there is a policy in place and the situation dictates that such a search is based upon a legitimate need to maintain a safe school environment.[45] The school district should communicate the limitation of a student's expectation of locker privacy in writing.

- Probable cause, not reasonable suspicion, is required to support a canine sniff of a person or property attached thereto.[46]

- Strip searches are nearly always held to be an intrusion on a student's privacy.

Parents and Students:

- Minors are entitled to some constitutional protections.[47]

- Individual suspicion has long been a criteria for determining reasonableness; however, the Supreme Court recently upheld random drug testing of a student wishing to participate in interscholastic sports.[48]

- Students should be made aware that they have a lesser expectation of privacy than members of the population in general.

- Since lockers are the property of the school district, school officials have greater access to their contents.

- The more personal the location of the search, the higher degree of privacy. Hence, book bags are more private than lockers but are less private than pockets.

Chapter 9 Endnotes

[1] New Jersey v. T.L.O., 469 U.S. 325, 105 S.C.L. 733, 83 L.Ed.2d 720 (1985).

[2] Comm. v. Phillips, 366 A.2d 306, 244 Pa. Super 42 (1976); Comm. v. Mangini, 386 A.2d 482, 478 Pa. 147 (1978); In the Interest of Guy Dumas, 515 A.2d 984 (Pa. Super. 1986).

[3] Interest of L.L. v. Circuit Court, 280 N.W. 2d 343 (WI S. Ct. App. 1979).

[4] Tarter v. Raybuck, 742 F.2d 977 (6th Cir. 1984).

[5] In re the Matter of Gregory M., 82 N.Y.2d 588 (1993).

[6] State of Arizona v. Serna, 860 P.2d 1320 (Ariz. App. Div. 1 1993).

[7] In re S.K., 647 A.2d 952 (Pa. Super. 1994).

[8] State v. Moore, 603 A.2d 513 (N.J. Super. A.D. 1992).

[9] Comm. v. Carey, 554 N.E.2d 1199 (Mass. 1990).

[10] In Interest of Doe, 887 P.2d 645 (Hawaii 1994).

[11] Illinois v. Gates, 462 U.S. 213 (1983).

[12] Interest of L.L., *supra*; Rowe v. Daviess County, 655 S.W.2d 28 (Ky. Ct. App. 1983).

[13] People v. Dillworth, 640 N.E.2d 1009 (Ill App. 3d Dist. 1994).

[14] In Interest of S.F., 607 A.2d 793 (Pa. Super. 1992).

[15] Coronado v. State, 835 S.W.2d 636 (Tex. Crim. App. 1992).

[16] Wilcher v. State of Texas, 876 S.W.2d 466 (Tex. App. 1994).

[17] S.C. v. State, 583 So.2d 188 (Miss. 1991); Zamora v. Pomeroy, 639 F.2d 662 (10th Cir. 1981).

[18] Doe v. Renfrow, 451 U.S. 1022 (1981); Horton v. Goose Creek Independent School District, 677 2d 482 (5th Cir. 1982).

[19] Dumas, *supra*.

[20] Comm. v. Cass, 709 A.2d 350 (1998).

[21] Tarter, *supra*.

[22] Coffman v. State, 782 S.W.2d 249 (Tex. App. 1989).

[23] Doe, *supra*.

[24] Galford v. Mark Anthony B., 433 S.E.2d 41 (W.Va. 1993).

[25] Tipper v. New Castle Area School District, (W.D. Pa. 1994).

[26] Widener v. Frye, 809 F. Supp. 35 (S.D. Ohio 1992).

[27] Cornfield by Lewis v. Consolidated H.S. District No. 230, 991 F.2d 1316 (7th Cir. 1993).

[28] State v. D.T.W., 425 So.2d 1383 (Fla. Dist. Ct. App. 1983).

[29] Mangini, *supra*.

[30] Shamberg v. State, 762 P.2d 488 (Alaska App. 1988).

[31] People in the Interest of P.E.A., 754 P.2d 382 (Colo. 1988); State v. Slattery, 787 P.2d. 932 (Wash. App. 1990).

[32] Schaill *ex rel* Kross v. Tippecanoe County School Corporation, 679 F. Supp. 833 (N.D. Ind. 1988).

[33] Vernonia School District 47J v. Acton, 115 S. Ct. 2386 (1995).

[34] Bridgeman v. New Trier High School, 128 F.3d 1146 (7th Cir. 1997).

[35] Joy v. Penn-Harris-Madison School Corporation, 212 F.3d 1052 (7th Cir. 2000).

[36] Todd v. Rush County Schools, 133 F.3d 984 (7th Cir. 1998).

[37] Earls v. Board of Education of Tecumseh Public School District, No. 00-6128 (6th Cir. 2001); Willis v. Anderson Community School Corporation, 158 F.3d 415 (7th Cir. 1998).

[38] Wood v. Strickland, 420 U.S. 308 (1975).

[39] Dillworth, *supra*.

[40] Desilets v. Clearview Regional Board of Education, 627 A.2d 667 (N.J. Super. A. D. 1995).

[40] Todd v. Rush County Schools, 133 F.3d 984 (7th Cir. 1998).

[41] Comm. v. Snyder, 597 N.E.2d 1363 (Mass. 1992); Boynton v. Casey, 543 F. Supp. 995 (D. Me. 1982).

[42] F.P. v. State, 528 So.2d 1253 (Fla. App. 1st Dist. 1988).

[43] Stern v. New Haven Community Schools, 529 F. Supp. 31 (E.D. Mich. 1981).

[44] 22 Pa. Code, Section 12.14.

[45] Cass, *supra*.

[46] Comm. v. Martin, 626 A.2d 556, 534 Pa. 136 (1993).

[47] In re Gault, 387 U.S. 1 (1967).

[48] Vernonia, *supra*.

Chapter 10   Transportation

Sources:

> First Amendment
> Fourteenth Amendment

I t is no secret that transporting students can be a major undertaking by a school district. Most districts assign transportation duties to a person (or persons) on a full-time basis. In addition to the complex task of arranging to transport a scattered population, financial considerations demand efficiency while meeting the diverse needs of the student population. Who should be transported? When should a district transport? Indeed, should a district assume the responsibility to transport its students at all?

While there is a tendency for the courts to interpret transportation statutes narrowly, each school district has been granted broad discretionary powers to address its own particular needs. Given this type of flexibility, school districts are cautioned by the courts not to act in an arbitrary fashion[1] or violate proper procedure.[2]

School districts have the right to assign pupils to a particular school and to transport them. Sometimes this creates the need to transport students where none existed before. Schools are empowered to reorganize schools and transport students to achieve racial balance.[3] Additionally, if the atmosphere of the new school is not harmful to a student's health and general welfare and sustains an atmosphere that is conducive to learning, the decision to consolidate and assign certain pupils to another building resides solely with the school district.[4] The issue is not one of convenience; it is one of appropriateness within the context of the administrative power of the district to provide an education.

Decision to Transport

Sometimes the public school code does not require a school district to furnish free transportation.[5] The operative language in the various public school codes is generally expressed as "may" provide free transportation. The district may discontinue all or part of bus service as long as curtailment of bus service complies with statutory provisions of distance and does not interfere with basic Constitutional rights.[6] A district may decide to transport a portion of its students, i.e. exclude secondary students from transportation while providing the service to kindergarten and elementary students. A district may choose not to transport students at all. In either case, no private right exists to sue the school district based on its failure to provide free transportation.[7]

If a public school district exercises its discretion not to transport students, parents are required to provide the child's transportation. Transportation to a public school outside the district as an alternative is not required.[8] However, once a district has elected to transport its students, it must do so "to and from" the schools, including kindergarten.[9]

Although transportation usually refers to busing, such is not always the case. Schools may employ a variety of conveyances such as "rail, private carrier, [or] other common carriers."[10] Transportation can take the form of bus, trolley, or subway passes and, in certain instances, taxicab service.

Who may be Transported

The law is clear that resident students may be transported. Resident students may attend public or non-public schools. Various school codes specifically address transportation to non-public schools. Since transporting children "involves an activity without religious significance," it is well established in case law that such activity violates neither the establishment clause of the First Amendment nor the due process clause of the Fourteenth Amendment.[11] Therefore, non-public school students must be provided transportation the same as public school students within statutory limits. These statutory limits include restrictions on distance and time. Even in emergency situations, a school district that makes emergency provisions for its own public school students must do the same for non-public school students.[12]

The law is equally clear with respect to non-resident students. Whenever non-resident children attend public schools, they shall be furnished appropriate transportation similar to that provided for resident children. See Chapter 2, "Attendance," for the definition of non-resident students entitled to a free and appropriate education.

In the case of exceptional children, the school district must provide transportation when an appropriate placement has been determined.[13] The appropriate placement may be 1.) in a regular school setting, 2.) at a school within the school district boundaries, 3.) at a school located more than ten (10) miles beyond the school district boundaries, or 4.) at a school in another state. If such a placement is proscribed by the multi-disciplinary team (MDT) and included in the individualized educational program (IEP), transportation must be provided. However, the district maintains discretion over the means of conveyance. Even a change in method of transportation for a severely retarded child is not considered a change in educational placement unless the alteration significantly affects the child's learning experience.[14]   If transportation is not feasible to a place where an appropriate education can be provided to an exceptional child, suitable board and lodging for any such child may be required.

When to Transport

The authorization to transport includes kindergarten, elementary schools or secondary schools located within the school boundaries. Once a school district decides to transport students, it is not required to transport all of them. A school district does not have to transport any student who lives within one and one half miles of the school.[15] The district may, for efficiency sake, require those in private residential developments to have their children picked up at the main entrance of the development.[16] Furthermore, school district transportation policy will often reflect the statutory reimbursement limits that apply to elementary students. For example, Pennsylvania includes elementary students who live further than one and one-half (1 1/2) miles from school and secondary students who live further than two (2) miles from school (24 P.S. Code 2541).

Even within the one and one-half (1 1/2) mile limit, transportation must be provided when walking conditions are such that they pose a safety hazard to a child. When claiming a need for transportation as an exception to the distance requirements, a road or walkway must be adjudicated as hazardous by the Department of Transportation before a duty arises for the school district to provide transportation.[17] Neither a school official nor a bus employee may make that determination. However, a school district has recourse to appeal a Department of Transportation decision on the matter.[18]

Since it has been established that a district may elect to transport its own students and the right to transportation extends to non-public school students, what responsibility does a public school district have to non-public school children? A school code will establish the limits for providing transportation to such schools that are non-profit (non-public) "at a distance not exceeding ten miles by the nearest public highway."[19] The non-public school must fall within the statutory limit of ten miles. If the non-public school is more than ten miles beyond the district boundary, the school district is not required to transport the non-public student. Furthermore, the district is not required to provide transportation for part of the distance to the non-public school (i.e. up to ten (10) miles) even if the child agrees to complete the trip independently.

Transportation to non-public schools may be provided during regular school hours on such dates and periods that the non-public school is in regular session.

It stands to reason that if transportation is provided for one class of student, it must be provided for the others. If modifications are made for one class of student, they must be made for the others. If an exception is made for one class of student, it must be made for the others. If not, the policy will not stand the test of equity. An example of this is where the courts have declared it improper for school districts to require non-public students to walk to the nearest public school or to a point at or near their home to receive service, when an identical provision for public school students does not exist.[20]

Liability for injury

Acknowledging the need for safety and recognizing the issue of liability, different laws set forth a number of requirements. School districts that transport students must conduct emergency evacuation drills. School law usually requires the district superintendent to certify the evacuations to the Department of Public Instruction. Pursuant to the Motor Vehicle Code, school buses must be inspected at regular intervals. Buses are usually subject to random inspection by the State Police. Administrators should refer to their specific school codes for particulars.

All private motor vehicles employed in transporting pupils shall be adequately covered by public liability insurance. The amount of coverage is to be determined by the board of school directors.

The question of liability under the law arising from injury to children on a school bus is another matter. Generally speaking, the school district is liable for injury to children when negligence can be proven consistent with the qualified immunity provisions under the states' political subdivisions tort claims acts. Specific liability is enumerated in the acts with respect to damages caused by the operation of motor vehicles. See Chapter 16, "Negligence and Tort Liability."

Implications

<u>Teachers and Administrators:</u>

- Transporting students to and from school in not mandatory. If a school district chooses to transport, it must transport all resident students according to state code, including those that attend private schools within 10 miles of the resident district.

- Transporting students may take many forms: schools may engage buses, bus passes, rail transportation, and even taxicabs.

<u>Parents and Students:</u>

- Although a district may elect to transport its students, the right to be transported is not absolute.

- In a district that transports students, certain conditions might justify transporting students who otherwise would not receive transportation under the State Code. For example, hazardous walking conditions might dictate the need to transport. The decision, however, is not the parent's or the school's. The power to grant transportation privileges in an instance like this resides with the state Department of Transportation.

Chapter 10 Endnotes

[1] Trainer v. Chichester School District, 455 A.2d 1270, Beegle v. Greencastle-Antrim School District, 401 A.2d 374, 41 Pa. Cmwlth. 605 (1975); Alman v. Fox Chapel School District, 4 D. & C.3d 288 (1977).

[2] Save Our School v. Colonial School District, 1993 W. L. 243861.

[3] Hoots v. Commonwealth of Pennsylvania, 672 F.2d 1107 (1982), *certiorari* denied 459 U.S. 824, 103 S. Ct. 55 (1982); Balsbaugh v. Rowland, 290 A.2d 85, 447 Pa. 423 (1972).

[4] School District of City of Pittsburgh v. Zebra, 325 A.2d 330, 15 Pa. Cmwlth. 203 (1974); School District of Pittsburgh v. City of Pittsburgh, 352 A.2d 223, 23 Pa. Cmwlth. 405 (1976).

[5] Landeman v. Churchill Area School District, 200 A.2d 20, 414 Pa. 530 (1964); Alman v. Fox Chapel Area School District, 4 D. & C.3d 288 (Pa. 1977).

[6] Landeman, *supra.*; Shaffer v. Board of School Directors of Albert Gallatin Area School District, 570 F. Supp. 698 (Pa. 1983), reversed 730 F.2d 910 (Pa. 1984).

[7] Greenwald v. McKeesport Area School District, 19 D. & C.3d 79 (Pa. 1980).

[8] Babcock School District v. Potocki, 466 A.2d 616, 502 Pa. 349 (1983).

[9] Shaffer, *supra.*

[10] Rawdin v. Bristol Township School District, 44 D. & C.2d 713 (Pa. 1968).

[11] Springfield School District, Delaware County v. Department of Education, 397 A.2d 1154, 483 Pa. 539 (1979) appeal dismissed; Pequea Valley School District v. Pennsylvania Department of Education, 99 S. Ct. 3901, 443 U.S. 901, (1979); School District of Pittsburgh v. Pennsylvania Department of Education, 99 S. Ct. 3091, 443 U.S. 901, 61 L.Ed.2d 869 (1979); Bennett v Kline, 486 F. Supp. 36, affirmed 633 F.2d 109 (D.C. Pa. 1980); Rhoades v. Abington Township School District, 226 A.2d 53, 424 Pa. 202 (1967); Everson v. Board of Education of Ewing Township, 330 U.S. 1, 67 S. Ct. 504 (1947).

[12] Williams v. Duquesne School District, 131 P.L.J. 325 (C.P. Allegheny Co. Pa. 1983).

[13] Pires by Pires v. Comm., Department of Education, 467 A.2d 79, 78 Pa. Cmwlth. 127 (1983).

[14] DeLeon v. Susquehanna Community School District, 747 F.2d 149 (3rd Cir. 1984).

140

[15] Human Relations Commission v. Chester School District, 233 A.2d 290, 427 Pa. 157 (1967).

[16] Abrahams v. Wallenpaupak Area School District, 422 A.2d 1201, 54 Pa. Cmwlth 637 (1980).

[17] Id.

[18] Coladonato v. South Columbia Area School Board, 5 D. & C.3d 101 (Pa. 1977).

[19] School District of Pittsburgh v. Comm., Department of Education, 382 A.2d 772, 33 Pa. Cmwlth. 535 (1978).

[20] Persi v. Aliquippa Borough School District, 15 D. & C.3d 52 (Pa. 1979).

Chapter 11   General Employment Considerations

Sources:

> Public Employee Relations Act (PERA), Act 195, Section 702
> Pennsylvania Public School Code, 24 P.S. 11
> Title IX, 34 C.F.R. Part 106
> Title VII, 20 U.S.C. 1681 et.seq.
> Americans with Disabilities Act, 42 U.S.C. 12208
> Section 504 of the Rehabilitation Act of 1973, 34 C.F.R. Part 104

This chapter addresses a number of employment issues that directly involve the building principal.   While not responsible for engineering the terms and conditions of employment, the building administrator is entrusted with preserving teacher rights and responsibilities under the professional employees contract and state law.   The principal faces a great number of personal decisions.   Eight areas of Pennsylvania school law have been selected for discussion: hiring practices, qualifications, certification, employment classifications, contract, salaries, tenure, and assignment/transfer.

Hiring Practices

Each school district has a duty to employ the necessary number of qualified "professional employees, substitutes, and temporary professional employees to keep the public schools open." (24 P.S. Code 1106).   Since employment is a constitutionally protected property right, [1] certain categories of rights should be kept in mind during the hiring process.   Hiring involves preserving the potential employee's right to fair treatment by ensuring equal employment opportunities.

Discrimination exists in many forms.   Race, gender, and disability are most commonly encountered.   Practices affecting these other classifications of individuals are prohibited not only as overt acts but also in practices that appear to be fair in form but discriminatory in operation.   For example, charges of racial discrimination may claim that prerequisites for employment eliminate a class of individuals from consideration.   Clearly, overt criteria resulting in eliminating certain individuals from employment would be discriminatory based on federal law.   However, it is not so clear with regard to policies that, on their face, are neutral with respect to discrimination. These kinds of policies must be found to have disparate impact [2] or discriminatory treatment [3] before requiring the employer to prove that the policy is justified. If the hiring criteria do not bear a rational relationship to a legitimate government goal, the burden of proof hinges on the plaintiff's ability to prove intent.

Like racial discrimination, federal [4] statutes prohibit gender discrimination. However, any claim of gender discrimination requires proof of intent on the part of the employer. Most sex discrimination claims are based on Title IX of the Educational Amendments of 1972 and Title VII of the Civil Rights Act of 1964. Notwithstanding, gender is not scrutinized as closely as race by the courts. More recently, the courts have taken a stand to ensure equal treatment of male and female applicants in face of earlier decisions to the contrary.

Section 504 of the Rehabilitation Act of 1973 protects handicapped individuals from being "excluded from participation in, be denied benefits of, or be subjected to discrimination under any program or activity receiving Federal financial assistance." School districts are not required to make "substantial adjustments" to working conditions or hire a person that is not qualified.[5] However, if the disabled individual is not hired, the disability cannot be the sole cause for exclusion. The applicant must be "able to meet all of the program's requirements in spite of the handicap."[6] Therefore, given the fundamental nature of the teaching activity, if the disabled individual cannot perform the essential function of the job with a reasonable accommodation, the individual would be deemed unqualified. Even so, there can be no presumption of a disabled individual's ability to do the job. The courts have even rejected the presumption that blindness[7] or prior mental problems[8] provide *prima facie* grounds for exclusion.

Qualifications

Teachers must be persons of good moral character, at least eighteen (18) years of age, and citizens of the United States. However, citizenship may be waived for non-permanent exchange teachers and teachers employed for the express purpose of teaching a foreign language. The citizenship requirement may also be waived in the event that foreign language instruction is necessary to ease the transition of immigrant students residing in a school district (24 P.S. Code 1109).

All teachers must have a criminal background clearance, child abuse clearance, as well as the appropriate state certification. Criminal acts that would deny a person the right to teach in the Commonwealth are found in Section 111 of the School Code. They are: criminal homicide, aggravated assault, kidnapping, unlawful restraint, rape, statutory rape, involuntary deviate sexual intercourse, indecent assault, indecent exposure, concealing the death of a child born out of wedlock, endangering the welfare of children, prostitution or other related offenses, obscenity, corruption of minors, sexual abuse of children, and felonies under the "Controlled Substance, Drug, Device, and Cosmetic Act." Added to these by Act 30 of 1997 are: stalking, sexual assault, incest, and sexual performances.

Certification

Certification signifies technical or legal competence. It is a license to teach, and, once the requirements are met, the license cannot be arbitrarily refused. Licensing requirements vary from state to state and standards may change up to the time of applying to the Department of Education. Once obtained, certification becomes a property right. However, of itself, it is not a contract.

Certification is important in the hiring process. Failure of an applicant to possess the necessary certification means that (s)he is not able to contract for services. Schools that employ improperly certified individuals might be required to forfeit a portion of the school's state subsidy. Where no certified applicant exists for a teaching position, temporary emergency certification may be obtained. However, emergency certification may not be issued for an indefinite period of time, usually for a period of one year.

If a teacher with established tenure allows certification to expire by failing to obtain the required number of credit hours within the statutory time period, certification expires. The teacher who is not certified ceases to be a professional employee, losing substantive and procedural protection under the law.[9] Beginning July 1, 2000, Act 48 of 1999 requires all Pennsylvania public school certificate holders to complete continuing education requirements every five years in order to maintain certified status. This translates into at least six collegiate credits or 180 hours of continuing education as approved by the Act 48 plan on file with the Department of Education. Educators with inactive certification may serve as a substitute teacher for up to 90 days per school year.

Employment Classifications

In the Commonwealth of Pennsylvania, employees must demonstrate that at least 50% of their time directly involves educational activities to be considered a teacher.[10] Acting in an extracurricular capacity is not considered "educational" under the definition of the law. Therefore, unless the employee performs some teaching function, extracurricular sponsorship does not qualify one as a teacher with attendant due process rights.[11] The same conclusion has been reached for a teacher who was hired by a school district on a temporary basis as a result of available funds under state or federal programs.[12]

There are three types of teachers defined in the Pennsylvania Public School Code: professional employees, temporary professional employees, and substitutes. Professional employees are certificated teachers, counselors, nurses, supervisors, principals, assistant principals, home and school visitors, dental hygienists, and librarians, among others (24 P.S. Code 1101). They must have obtained tenure[13] by virtue of occupying a vacancy, that is, a permanent position for which another teacher is not expected to return.

Temporary professional employees describe individuals who are employed to perform the duties of a newly-created position or the duties "of a regular professional employee whose services have been terminated by death, resignation, suspension, or removal." One who fills a legitimate vacancy acquires the property rights inherent in the position and is considered a temporary professional employee under the law. They become professional employees upon securing tenure at the end of three (3) years of satisfactory performance. If there is no vacancy, the position cannot be filled by a temporary professional employee. Rather, it must be filled by a substitute.[14]

Substitutes are hired to perform the duties of regular professional employees or temporary professional employees during the predetermined period of time that the employees are legitimately absent.[15] This means that substitutes fill positions having temporal limits. If a legitimate vacancy exists, calling the person who fills such a position a substitute will not make it so.[16]

Substitutes may also be hired to temporarily replace a teacher who has resigned while a permanent replacement is sought and, as such, have no claim to the vacancy or hearing rights upon the termination of employment.[17]

Contract

Although any number of persons may be involved in hiring, only the board of education can hire. The act of hiring may not be delegated to the superintendent or any individual board member. Only the majority of all the members of the board of school directors may "appoint" a teacher to a position in the schools.[18]

Boards may adopt such rules and regulations that they deem necessary, as long as they are not contrary to state law or violate basic constitutional rights. Even so, any rules or regulations must be reasonable in terms of their purpose within the legitimate government interest.

The form and manner of executing teacher contracts is specifically enumerated in the School Code.[19] The contract carries with it rights, responsibilities, and causes for termination. The responsibilities may include duties reasonably related to the subject matter.[20] Termination of the teaching contract must be within the statutory bounds of the School Code. See Chapter 13, "Teacher Dismissal, Causes for Termination."

Salaries

The minimum salary paid to full-time teachers is set forth in the Pennsylvania Public School Code at $18,500. Local boards may or may not grant credit for experience outside the system and new teachers to a school district are entitled only to the minimum compensation set by law. Placement at any other compensation level may be done at the discretion of the board on an individual basis, according to fixed rules, or by other methods. Whatever method used, it must not be made on personal, subjective standards. Such action on the part of a school district would be discriminatory.

Tenure

A temporary professional employee acquires tenure after satisfactory teaching performance for the statutorily designated time period.[21] The statutory length of time in the Commonwealth of Pennsylvania is three (3) years. Tenure is automatic as long as performance is satisfactory. However, it may not be granted prior to the statutory probationary period.[22] The board of school directors shall enter into contracts, in writing, with each professional employee who has completed three (3) years of satisfactory service.[23]

Disqualification for tenure of temporary professional employees is valid upon a single unsatisfactory rating.[24] Any temporary professional employee who is not tendered a regular contract for employment at the end of the three (3) years probationary period shall be given a written statement signed by the president and secretary of the school board stating the reasons for refusal.[25] A simple declaration by the board at a regular board meeting is insufficient. The notice must be in writing.

Tenure was enacted to protect qualified, competent teachers. It was not designed to shield the incompetent. The Tenure Act (and the court cases that interpret it) provides guidelines for the discipline or discharge of professional employees.

Assignment and Transfer

Since teachers' obligations are not satisfied by closing the classroom door at the conclusion of a class,[26] it stands to reason that a school district may reassign teachers at their discretion absent contract language to the contrary. A professional employee does not acquire a vested right to teach in any particular class or in any particular school. In *Olson v. Methacton*,[27] the court reasoned that as long as the professional is duly certified, a school board acted within its power in making reasonable rules and regulations, reassignments or other steps necessary for proper administration.

The professional employee must be tenured by operation of law to be afforded all procedural rights associated with faculty assignments.[28]

While a negotiated agreement may have some bearing on reassignment, the power may not be delegated to any other entity. The power to transfer and assign comes from the recognized managerial prerogative of a school district to run the school system. This includes seeking a teacher's approval prior to such reassignment.[29] As such, it is not negotiable but it may be arbitrable through normal grievance procedures.[30]

Even though there is no common law right to a specific building assignment, all such moves must be within areas of certification and must not be used as a tool for discipline.[31]

Administrative reassignment poses its own problems. A Pennsylvania court made it clear that the professional employee categories in the Public School Code are not equivalent or interchangeable. In one specific case, a coordinator of instruction and curriculum who was reassigned to the position of supervisor of staff development was not a "professional employee." As such, he was not entitled to procedural protection of the school code case a hearing prior to reassignment.[32] The term professional is specific, and one cannot assume that any title or category is automatically included in its legal definition.

Principals, however, are professional employees under the school code and are entitled to procedural protections. For example, reassigning an elementary principal to the position of classroom teacher requires application of Section 1125.1 of the School Code.[33]

As a final note, if the reassignment or transfer is a product of reduction in force, all such moves must be made on the basis of seniority in accordance with Section 1125.1(c) of the Code as long as the move provides students with adequate instruction.[34] Seniority is the sole determinant, absent contractual terms that dictate otherwise.[35]

Implications

<u>Teachers and Administrators</u>:

- Be aware of the different employee classifications as well as the substantive and procedural due process associated with each.

- Charges of racial discrimination will be sustained for practices that result in the exclusion of a class of individuals from employment. Policies that on their face appear neutral but result in discriminatory treatment, require proof of intent.

- Sexual discrimination requires proof of intent in all cases.

- Exclusion of the handicapped from employment cannot be based solely on the disability. If the applicant is able to meet all of a program's requirements despite the handicap, (s)he must be hired.

- There is no vested right to teach in any certain class or school, barring contract language to the contrary.

Chapter 11 Endnotes

[1] Vail v. Board of Education,706 F.2d 1435 (7th Cir. 1988) affirmed 104 S. Ct. 2144 (1984); Valentine v. Joliet High School District, 802 F.2d 981 (7th Cir. (1986).

[2] Connecticut v. Teal, 651 F.2d 222 (4th Cir. 1981).

[3] McDonnell Douglas v. Green, 411 U.S. 792 (1983).

[4] Personnel Administrator of Massachusetts v. Feeney, 442 U.S. 256 (1979).

[5] Pittsburgh Federation of Teachers, Local 400 v. Langer, 546 F. Supp. 434 (W.D. Pa. 1982).

[6] Southeastern Community College v. Davis, 442 U.S. 397, 406 (1979).

[7] Gurmakin v. Costanza, 411 F. Supp. 982 (E.D. Pa. 1976) affirmed 556 F.2d 184 (3rd Cir. 1977 affirmed in part, vacated and remanded in part 626 F.2d 1115 (3rd Cir. 1980) *certiorari* denied 450 U.S. 923 (1981).

[8] Doe v. Syracuse School District, 508 F. Supp. 333 (N.D. N.Y. 1981).

[9] Moiles v. Marple-Newton School District, 37 SLIE No. 33 (Pa. Secretary of Education 2000).

[10] McCracken v. Central Susquahanna Intermediate Unit, 382 A.2d 1293 (Pa. Cmwlth. 1978).

[11] Moriarta v. State College Area School District, 601 A.2d 872 (Pa. Cmwlth. 1992); Bravo v. Board of Directors of the Wellsboro Area School District, 504 A.2d 418 (Pa. Cmwlth. 1986).

[12] Anthony v. Conemaugh Township Area School District, 29 Som. 309 (Pa. 1974).

[13] Scott v. Philadelphia Parking Authority, 166 A.2d 278 (1960).

[14] Gorski v. Dickson City Borough School District, 113 A.2d 334 (1955).

[15] Waslo v. North Allegheny School District, 549 A.2d 1359 (Pa. Cmwlth. (1988).

[16] Weiss v. Scranton School District, 537 A.2d 910 (1988), affirmed 521 Pa. 528 (1988).

[17] Pottsville Area School District v. Marteslo, 423 A.2d 1336 (Pa. Cmwth. 1980).

[18] 24 P.S. 508.

150

---

[19] 24 P.S. 1121.

[20] Pease v. Milcreek Township School District, 195 A.2d 104 (Pa. 1963).

[21] Pookman v. Upper St. Clair School District, 483 A.2d 1371 (Pa. 1984).

[22] George v. Department of Education, 325 A.2d 819 (Pa. Cmwlth. 1984).

[23] 24 P.S. 1121(b)(2).

[24] Homan v. Blue Ridge School District, 405 A.2d 572 (Pa. Cmwlth. 1979).

[25] 24 P.S. 1108(3)(c)(2).

[26] Pease, *supra*.

[27] Olson v. Board of School Directors, Methacton S.D., 478 A.2d 954, 84 Pa. Cmwlth. 189 (1984).

[28] Pookman, *supra*.

[29] Newkirk et. al. v. School District of Philadelphia, 261 A.2d 305, 437 Pa. 114 (1968).

[30] West Shore Education Association v. West Shore S.D., 456 A.2d 715 (Pa. Cmwlth. 1983).

[31] Genco v. Bristol Borough School District, 423 A.2d 36, 55 Pa. Cmwlth. 78 (1980).

[32] School District of Philadelphia v. Brockington, 511 A.2d 944 (Pa. Cmwlth. 1986).

[33] In re Appeal of Cowden, 486 A.2d 1014 (Pa. Cmwlth. 1985); Shestack v. General Braddock Area School District, 437 A.2d 1059 (Pa. Cmwlth. 1981).

[34] Proch v. New Castle Area School District, 430 A.2d 1034, 60 Pa. Cmwlth. 111 (1981).

[35] Duncan v. Rochester Area School District, 529 A.2d 48 (Pa. Cmwlth. 1987).

Chapter 12   Grievances and Arbitration

Sources:

> Pennsylvania Public Employee Relations Act, Act 195, Section 903
> Uniform Arbitration Act, 42 Pa.C.S.A. Section 1701 *et seq.*

The grievance process is an important part of a collective bargaining agreement. What happens in the grievance process can critically affect the original contract through interpretation and precedents. When coupled with arbitration, grievances can, and often do, make available things that were not originally intended at the bargaining table. It is no wonder that, in a state that offers collective bargaining such as Pennsylvania, at least one court felt that the less judicial participation, the better.[1] Notwithstanding, there is a significant body of case law in the area of grievances.

The grievance procedure is a mechanism in the collective bargaining agreement that allows the parties to interpret provisions of the contract that are unclear or do not specifically cover unforeseen situations. This is important because Section 903 of Pennsylvania's Act 195 requires that "arbitration of disputes or grievances arising out of the interpretation of the provisions of a collective bargaining agreement is mandatory." An arbitrator has long been considered competent to sort out differences between the parties of a contract.[2] Indeed, grievance arbitration is preferred to litigation.[3] Some courts presume that grievances should go to arbitration and reserve court action to determining whether the parties actually agreed to arbitrate the issue in question.[4] The arbitrator's decision is binding under the law so it is important that grievances be handled carefully.

Procedures

A grievance procedure should contain the definition of a grievance, and at least three steps: Level I, the building principal or other first line administrator, Level II, a central office administrator, and Level III, the board of school directors. Some school districts designate the assistant superintendent as the Level II administrator and add the superintendent as Level III, thus creating a fourth step when considering the hearing by the school board. The grievance procedure must then include the option for binding arbitration should the matter fail to be resolved within the school district. It is important, too, that specific times be set for notice and hearing in each step. Such matters are usually set by contract and each contract should be consulted for specific details. It is an accepted fact that the greatest percentage of grievances fail to reach the courts. However, those that do must pass through the arbitration process set by the Uniform Arbitration Act (UAA) and Act 195.

Procedurally, the arbitration process begins with the selection of an arbitrator by mutual agreement, by contract, or through the Bureau of Mediation (Act 195, Section 903 (i)). A succinct outline is provided as an overview of the entire process:

Notice and Hearing (UAA Section 7301)

A. If no agreement is reached by the involved parties, resolution must be determined by mutual agreement, contract language, or through an arbitrator (UAA Section 7303(a)).

The notice should be:
1. Served personally or by registered or certified mail.
2. Appearance at the hearing constitutes waiver of notice.
3. Hearing may proceed after notice if the duly notified party fails to appear at the hearing.

B. A stenographic record must be provided to the party requesting it for a fee, UAA Section 7303 (b).

C. The teacher may not waive the right to counsel (Section 7301).

D. Subpoenas may be issued for witnesses and documents; depositions are permitted for use as evidence.

The award of the arbitrator must be written, signed and delivered.

Scope

With the grievance and arbitration processes in place, the Commonwealth Court's scope of inquiry is limited to whether or not the arbitrator's award drew its essence from the collective bargaining agreement.[5] This is viewed in light of the contract language, context and any other indication of the parties' intent.[6] It is called the "essence test" and under the "essence test," if the terms of the collective bargaining agreement encompass the subject matter of the dispute, the court's inquiry ends.[7]

If the arbitrator's interpretation is reasonable, it shall stand even in matters of credit reimbursement,[8] sabbatical leave policy,[9] extra-curricular appointments and compensation,[10] additional duties,[11] continuance of past practice[12] and employee dismissal where grievance arbitration was within the scope of the procedure as set forth in the collective bargaining agreement.[13]

Matters subject to the arbitration process are numerous; however, if express provisions exist in a collective bargaining agreement, excluding a class of questions from arbitration, they shall not be arbitrable.[14] Those questions that are arbitrable include the following:

1. Work assignments, working conditions and classification, i.e., removal of an athletic director's position,[15] assignment to extra classes,[16] assignment to extra-curricular duties with compensation,[17] meeting with union field representatives at lunch period,[18] full-time substitutes as members of the bargaining unit,[19] hiring new teachers at less than provided by the collective bargaining agreement,[20] establishment of a "preferred substitute teacher" category.[21]

2. Discharge, lay-off, or suspension of employees, i.e., dismissal within the term job security,[22] abolishing the position of department head,[23] discharge for non-payment of union dues,[24] suspension due to declining enrollment.[25]

3. Seniority rights, i.e., date of determining seniority,[26] filling vacancies according to seniority.[27]

4. Wages and hours, i.e., salary increments for graduate credits,[28] credit reimbursement for education courses,[29] payment of sick leave,[30] salary increases not in line with state-mandated minimums,[31] payment of full year's salary for a half year's sabbatical leave,[32] sabbatical leave,[33] salary for teachers and teacher aides.[34]

However, dismissal couched in "discipline" terminology in the contract,[35] and a membership clause in the contract[36] were deemed not arbitrable, and decisions made by an arbitrator were invalid since the public school code contained provisions which superseded contract language. It must be noted that, if such language does not create an explicit, definitive conflict with statutory provisions, it may be subject to an arbitrator's scope of authority.[37]

The arbitrator may consider evidence that consists of more than what has been reduced in writing in the collective bargaining agreement. The arbitrator may look to past practice to clarify ambiguous language, to modify language, to amend unambiguous language and to create or prove a separate condition of employment that cannot be derived from the language of the contract.[38]

Arbitration awards are intended to apply to all members of the bargaining unit, not just the grievant. Narrow application of an arbitrator's awards would open the door to multiple filings on behalf of others.[39]

With respect to remedy, an arbitrator has flexibility and latitude, even when awarding monetary damages.[40] And, according to law, the decision is binding.[41] However, courts may review arbitrator's decisions on the basis that the remedy was impermissible,[42] that the arbitrator exceeded authority,[43] or that the award was completely irrational.[44]

Implications

Teachers and Administrators:

- Grievances that proceed to arbitration often make things available that were not originally foreseen and/or intended at the bargaining table.

- The scope of the court's inquiry in the grievance and arbitration process is limited to whether the arbitrator's decision drew its essence from the bargaining agreement consistent with due process.

- If language in the contract is explicitly in conflict with a statutory provision, the statute takes precedence over the contract language.

- In considering evidence, an arbitrator may draw on past practice as well as contract language.

- Arbitration awards apply to all members of a bargaining unit, not just to the grievant.

Chapter 12 Endnotes

[1] Scranton Federation of Teachers, Local 1147, AFT v. Scranton School District, 444 A.2d 1144 (Pa. Cmwlth. 1982).

[2] Board Of Education v. Associated Teachers of Huntington, 30 N.Y.S.2d 122 (N.Y. 1972).

[3] Donellan v. Mt. Lebanon School District, 377 A.2d 1054 (Pa. Cmwlth. 1977).

[4] Board of Education v. Frey, 392 A.2d 392 (Conn. 1978).

[5] Wilson Area Education Association v. Wilson Area School District, 494 A.2d 506 (Pa. Cmwlth. 1985); Ridley School District v. Ridley Education Association, 479 A.2d 641, 84 Pa. Cmwlth. 117 (1984); Petition of Wellsboro Area School District, 467 A.2d 1197, 78 A.D.2d 467 (1983); Neshaminy Federation of Teachers v. Neshaminy School District, 462 A.2d 629 (Pa. Cmwlth. 1983); and many others.

[6] Stein v. Philadephia Federation of Teachers Local 3, AFT, AFL-CIO, 464 A.2d 606 (Pa. Cmwlth. 1983); Pittston Area School District v. Pittston Area Federation of Teachers, Local 1590, 456 A.2d 1148 (Pa. Cmwlth. 1983).

[7] Northwest Tri-County Intermediate Unit No. 5 Education Assocation v. Northwest Tri-County Intermediate Unit No. 5, 465 A.2d 89 (Pa. Cmwlth. 1983); Central Susquehanna Intermediate Unit Education Association v. Central Susquehanna Intermediate Unit No. 6, 459 A.2d 889 (Pa. Cmwlth. 1983); West Shore Education Association v. West Shore School District, 456 A.2d 715 (Pa. Cmwlth. 1983); and many others.

[8] Central Susquehanna, *supra*; Appeal of Rose Tree Media School District, 442 A.2d 23 (Pa. Cmwlth. 1982).

[9] School District of City of Erie v. Erie Education Association, 447 A.2d 686 (Pa. Cmwlth. 1982).

[10] Pittston, *supra*.

[11] Wellsboro, *supra*.

[12] Greater Johnstown Area Vocational-Technical School v. Greater Johnstown Area Vocational-Technical Education Association, 489 A.2d 945, 88 Pa. Cmwlth. 141 (1985); Harborcreek School District v. Harborcreek Education Association, 441 A.2d 807 (Pa. Cmwlth. 1982).

[13] Wilson, *supra*.

[14] East Pennsboro Area School District v. Commonwealth, Pennsylvania Labor Relations Board, 467 A.2d 1356, 78 Pa. Cmwlth. 301 (1983).

[15] West Shore, *supra.*

[16] Wellsboro, *supra.*

[17] Pittston, *supra.*

[18] Greater Johnstown Area Vocational-Technical School, *supra.*

[19] Northwest Tri-County Intermediate Unit No. 5 Education Association, *supra.*

[20] Fairview School District v. Fairview Education Association, 368 A.2d 842, 28 Pa. Cmwlth. 366 (1977); Leechburg Area School District v. Leechburg Education Association, 380 A.2d 1203, 475 Pa. 413 (1977).

[21] Richland Education Association v. Richland School District, 418 A.2d 787, 53 Pa. Cmwlth. 367 (1980).

[22] Wilson, *supra.*

[23] Scranton School Board v. Scranton Federation of Teachers, Local 1147, A.F.T., 365 A.2d 1339, 17 Pa. Cmwlth. 152 (1976).

[24] Appeal of Jones, 375 A.2d 1341 (Pa. Cmwlth. 1977).

[25] Ridley, *supra.*

[26] Stein, *supra.*

[27] Scranton Federation of Teachers v. Scranton School District, 445 A.2d 260 (Pa. Cmwlth. 1982).

[28] West Chester Area School District v. West Chester Area Education Association, 449 A.2d 824 (Pa. Cmwlth. 1982).

[29] Central Susquehanna, *supra.*

[30] Pennsylvania State Education Association v. Baldwin Whitehall School District, 372 A.2d 960, 30 Pa. Cmwlth. 149 (1977).

[31] Robinson v. Abington Education Association, 423 A.2d 1014, 492 Pa. 218 (1980).

[32] Allegheny Valley School District v. Allegheny Valley Education Association, 360 A.2d 762 (Pa. Cmwlth. 1976).

[33] Ridley, *supra*; Erie, *supra.*

[34] Pennsylvania State Education Association v. Appalachia Intermediate Unit No. 8, 460 A.2d 1234 (Pa. Cmwlth. 1983).

158

[35] Neshaminy, *supra*.

[36] Commonwealth, Labor Relations Board v. Uniontown Area School District, 367 A.2d 738, 18 Pa. Cmwlth. 61 (1977).

[37] Greater Johnstown Area Vocational-Technical School, *supra*.

[38] Id.; Wyoming Valley West Education Association v. Wyoming Valley West School District, 500 A.2d 907, 92 Pa. Cmwlth. 365 (1985); and others.

[39] Appalachia Intermediate Unit #8 Education Association v. Appalachia Intermediate Unit #8, PLRB Case No. PERA-C-88-406W.

[40] Danville Education Association v. Danville Area School District, 467 A.2d 644, 78 Pa. Cmwlth. 238 (1983).

[41] Norwin School District v. Belan, 507 A.2d 373, 510 Pa. 255 (1986).

[42] Board of Education v. Middle Island Teachers Association, 407 N.E.2d 411 (N.Y. 1980).

[43] Trinity Area School District v. Trinity Area Education Association, 412 A.2d 167 (Pa. Cmwlth. 1980).

[44] Port Jefferson Station Teachers Association v. Brookhaven Comswogue Union Free School District, 383 N.E. 553 (N.Y. 1978).

Chapter 13   Teacher Dismissal

Sources:

>   Pennsylvania Public School Code, 24 P.S. 1, 5, 11
>   Pennsylvania Loyalty Act, 65 P.S. 211 *et seq.*
>   Local Agency Law, 2 Pa. C.S.A. 105, 553
>   Uniform Arbitration Act, 42 Pa. C.S.A. 7301 et seq.
>   First Amendment
>   Fourteenth Amendment

The Commonwealth of Pennsylvania established teacher tenure with the passage of the Teacher Tenure Act in 1937. The reasons for granting tenure are varied. Tenure provides security for teachers by protecting them from removal from their teaching positions without cause. Tenure laws are also designed to prevent capricious interference on the part of the board of school directors.

By setting requirements for attaining tenure, the Pennsylvania legislature established a property right to employment in the public schools. Thus, a teacher's position is assured under normal circumstances. Early case law has established that the tenure provisions were not intended to pose limitations on the power of school districts to dismiss teachers. Rather, tenure was intended to provide a framework whereby the local boards might exercise their discretionary powers to insure a better education for children. Although school board actions are presumed to be made in good faith, the burden of proof lies with the board in matters of dismissal, which can only be pursued for reasons set forth in the School Code.[1]

The School Code gives the board of school directors the authority to terminate the services of a teacher at retirement age (age 65) or the age where the employee is entitled to receive full benefits under the Federal Social Security Act. However, the Age Discrimination in Employment Act of 1967 makes it unlawful for government agencies to discriminate against persons over the age of forty. Mandatory retirement is no longer a legitimate reason for dismissal.

There are also administrative justifications for reducing staff that are decided by central office rather than building administrators. When a district has to reduce its number of employees, it may do so only as a result of declining pupil enrollment, curtailment or alteration of the educational program, consolidation of schools, or redistricting (24 P.S. Code 1124). These reasons are set apart from considerations predicated on unfitness to teach.

The Public School Code lists twelve (12) grounds for terminating a teacher's contract. These reasons are found in three separate parts of the Code: Section 527(a) addressing drug dealing and possession; Section 527(b) listing criminal convictions of designated crimes; and Section 1122 stating ten (10) grounds for the disciplinary dismissal of teachers.

As a rule, if the reason for terminating a teaching contract does not fall within statutory guidelines, the dismissal will be overturned. For example, a teacher certified in mental retardation who refused a transfer to teach General Educational Development (GED) mathematics on the secondary level where she had neither experience nor training could not be dismissed since refusal to accept a transfer based on her reasons was not found to be within the causes for termination set forth in the Public School Code.[2]

If a teacher's behavior is so offensive that it impairs the teacher's ability to teach even tenure will not prevent dismissal. Even though statutory language has been constitutionally challenged as indefinite and vague, the courts have sustained behavior standards that include such general terms as immorality, incompetence, intemperance, and cruelty.[3]

Since there are multiple grounds for dismissing a professional employee, teacher dismissals often involve multiple charges that may or may not all be substantiable. However, if multiple charges are brought against an employee and only one is proven, dismissal will be upheld.

Causes for the Termination of a Teaching Contract

A brief review of the causes for disciplinary dismissal in the Commonwealth of Pennsylvania follows:

Immorality

Cause of action for immorality is not confined to sexual matters. Immorality is a course of conduct that is offensive to the morals of the community and serves as a bad example to the students. Community standards need not be enumerated or published;[4] however, the standards must be the community's and not an individual's. This means that conduct merely consisting of school board disapproval is insufficient cause for dismissal.[5]

Single incidents of immoral behavior may support dismissal in some cases,[6] while more than one incident of minor indiscretions may be necessary in others.[7]

Guilty verdicts relative to charges of criminal conduct will support findings of immorality,[8] even if such criminal behavior is the result of physical and emotional stress. In a situation where a professional employee brought forth temporary mental instability caused by stress as a mitigating circumstance in a shoplifting incident, the court found that shoplifting *per se* falls within the judicial and statutory definition of immorality.[9] Corrupting minors,[10] illegal gambling,[11] and criminal harassment[12] may suffice as well.

Immorality is not confined to actions alone. What a teacher says may also be construed as immoral. A case in point involves a teacher who maintained a string of unexcused absences. Her misrepresentations as to the reasons for the absences were sufficient to find her conduct immoral, thereby justifying dismissal.[13] The Pennsylvania courts are traditionally intolerant of lying and view it as a cause for dismissal under immorality.[14] Recently, two teachers were dismissed for not being honest about their absence from work to go on a ski trip.[15]

In one instance, calling a 14 year-old student a "slut" and a "prostitute" constitutes immorality. It is not considered free speech protected under the First Amendment.[16] In another, an elementary teacher overheard his 11 and 12 year-old students using slang words with sexual connotations. After telling a class consisting of both sexes that he disapproved of such talk, he requested the class to provide him with the definitions of the words if they knew them. Although the court found that this was offensive to the moral standards of the community, no encouragement was evident to have the children use the words. The court did not find the teacher's conduct to amount to immorality.[17]

Simply admitting sexual fantasies is insufficient on its face to constitute immorality under the School Code; however, a male teacher engaging in sexual discussions with two female students outside the context of the classroom does offend the morals of the community and set a bad example for students.[18] This same case involved two unrelated incidents of spanking that was perceived as sexual in nature; one was a "disciplinary" action against a 15 year-old sophomore and the other was a proposed "birthday spanking" of a 17 year old senior. These two incidents were held to fall within the statutory definition of immorality.

Sexually oriented remarks that students find embarrassing are likewise prohibited.[19] It does not matter that the person making the remark(s) intended otherwise.

Amorous relationships with or without a sexual relationship may also constitute cause for dismissal based on immorality.[20] Similarly, seeking the affections of a 16 year-old without provocation or encouragement when told to stop will have the same result.[21]

Dismissal based on grounds of immorality includes other things such as vulgar and profane language,[22] vulgar and profane writing,[23] and circulating hate jokes.[24] Dismissal has been upheld even when it was discovered that sexual intercourse occurred during the summer after graduation (*Sertik*, *supra*).

Incompetence

Incompetence may take many forms. A professional employee may lack the scholastic knowledge or may be unfit to meet the demands of the position. One interpretation of incompetence involved a professional employee judged unfit to meet the demands of his position. In this case, the employee was an administrator who held membership in several employee organizations (i.e. NEA and PSEA) precluding him from performing all of the duties associated with his position, namely, handling grievances. He was dismissed. However, the Commonwealth Court appeal held that such membership did not render a first-level supervisor incompetent.[25] When fitness to meet the demands of the position is satisfied, incompetence charges will not be supported. This applies where the employee is physically and mentally able to resume teaching duties as well.[26]

Incompetence charges were sustained where a school psychologist was dismissed upon evidence that insufficient and improper testing was conducted, various tests were improperly scored, and placement recommendations were inappropriate. Ratings showed indifference to correcting the shortcomings when called to her attention.[27]

As long as rules are reasonable and their application is consistent, lengthy records of a series of incidents may be used to terminate a contract on the basis of incompetence.[28] These behaviors include deficiencies in personality, composure, judgment and attitude that impair teacher effectiveness. Where a second-grade teacher was a disruptive influence at her school, was unable to control her students, failed to maintain composure in front of students and staff and made unfounded accusations, complaints and threats to professional and unprofessional staff alike, she was found to be incompetent and was, therefore, dismissed.[29]

Generally speaking, dereliction in the performance of any number of teaching duties will sustain dismissal. Things such as deficient reports, failure to test properly, and deficient student records and lesson plans have been grounds for teacher dismissal.[30]

In order to sustain dismissal on grounds of incompetence, facts must be stated and documented in specific (not broad) terms. An administrator must be able to objectively state violations in terms of citing the rules and offer assistance for the teacher's improvement.

Unsatisfactory Teaching Performance

Unsatisfactory teaching performance was formerly considered as incompetence until recent amendments to the School Code made it a separate category. Unsatisfactory teaching performance is based on two (2) consecutive unsatisfactory ratings of the employee's teaching. The consecutive ratings shall not be less than four months apart and shall include classroom observations (24 P.S. Code 1122). A teacher may be determined unsatisfactory in accordance with an approved evaluation criteria.

It is well established in law that one (1) unsatisfactory rating justifies the dismissal of a temporary professional employee,[31] even if another is issued a year apart.[32] However, one is insufficient to dismiss a tenured professional employee.[33] When a dismissal is pursued, it must fall within the substantive and procedural guidelines set forth in the School Code.

Given procedural guidelines where classroom observations are made by qualified observers, they shall hold in a court of law.[34] And, the district's rating is generally presumed valid.[35]

General qualities properly observed and noted could serve as grounds for dismissal. In a 1977 case, evidence supported the Secretary of Education's decision affirming dismissal of a teacher who allegedly failed to maintain proper pace to insure that the scheduled program for the year would be completed. This teacher did not maintain lesson plans and keep her presentation organized. Her method of instruction was unvaried, "teacher-dominated," and she did not create the atmosphere conducive to learning.[36]

Unsatisfactory teaching performance may be inferred from a teacher's inability to control a classroom. Classroom control has warranted unsatisfactory ratings that result in dismissal. This has been upheld where a teacher was unable to maintain proper relationship with her students and was unable to conduct class satisfactorily.[37] Such dismissals have been sustained even when lack of control was evaluated on a form different from the Commonwealth's standard (or approved alternative) evaluation form.[38]

Intemperance

Intemperance implies, but is not limited to, the use of intoxicants. Loss of self-control or excessive actions without due restraint are also considered intemperate. In *Belasco v Board of Public Education*, the court held that, in the use of corporal punishment, the use of excessive force against a student is a main element of intemperance as defined in the Public School Code.[39] Intemperance was, likewise, sustained when a teacher shouted at the vice principal in the hallway while students were present.[40] Furthermore, the use of racial slurs has been held to presume intemperance.[41]

Cruelty

Cruelty involves the infliction of suffering and abusive treatment. The suffering may be physical as a result of a teacher assaulting a student[42] or paddling in an unacceptable fashion.[43] Abusive language might also inflict trauma, pain, or embarrassment.[44] In either case, charges of cruelty are usually accompanied by charges of intemperance.

Persistent Negligence in Performance of Duties

Persistent negligence involves acts or omissions committed or omitted in a series, that is, "a series of acts or omissions or a single act carried on for a substantial period of time."[45]   Unsatisfactory ratings are not necessarily required to create cause of action for dismissal for persistent negligence.[46]

The non-filing of lesson plans may not be sufficient grounds for persistent negligence in a regular classroom;[47] however, failing to keep proper student records, properly updating individualized educational programs (IEP's), properly supervising students, following policies of Intermediate Units, following directions of supervisors, giving notice of absences and reporting for duty on time in a special education context are sufficient.[48]

Chronic lateness, failure to supervise students properly and failing to conduct the classroom properly after being directed to by superiors is sufficient to justify dismissal in a regular classroom setting.[49]   In one recent case, chronic lateness was adjudged sufficient, of itself, to sustain the claim of persistent negligence.[50]

Failure to manage school funds properly has also resulted in dismissal for persistent negligence. Failure to deposit money as indicated by ledger entries and negligently handling funds such that missing money could not be accounted for in an audit, is an example.[51]

Physical or Mental Disability

Physical or mental disability must be documented by competent medical evidence. Furthermore, it must be such that, after reasonable accommodation of the disability as required by law, the disability substantially interferes with the employee's ability to perform the essential functions of employment (24 P.S. Code 1122). There are few dismissals on record based on physical or mental disability. This portion of the School Code was amended in 1996 extending the original statutory language covering "mental derangement" to include physical impediments to satisfactory teaching. Under the old language, a psychiatrist's report was sufficient to establish mental incapacity to teach.[52] It would most likely be sustained under the new statutory language as well.

Advocation of or Participation in Un-American or Subversive Doctrines

The Pennsylvania Loyalty Act authorizes the termination of the contract of a professional employee for advocating or participating in un-American or subversive doctrines (Section 16). The Pennsylvania School

Code does the same (24 P.S. Code 1122). The question arises as to whether a school district should elect to pursue a dismissal based on the School Code or the Loyalty Act. Case law favors dismissal based on the School Code, since dismissal based on the Loyalty Act requires a "fair preponderance of the evidence."

The issue was addressed in a mass dismissal involving 16 teachers. The Philadelphia School District handed out unsatisfactory ratings based on the teachers' refusal to answer questions asked by the superintendent or a subcommittee of the House of Representatives on grounds of self-incrimination. The appeal of several of these cases held that the school board should have followed the procedure set forth in the Loyalty Act, not the School Code. This decision was reversed by the Pennsylvania Supreme Court and affirmed by the United States Supreme Court.[53] Since the dismissal was based upon insubordination and lack of candor and not upon disloyalty, the dismissal was proper under the School Code for incompetence.

Willful Neglect of Duties

Willful neglect of duties is a category added recently to the Pennsylvania Public School Code. Teachers may be dismissed for willful neglect of duties; however, to date, the courts have not interpreted the new statutory language. It would stand to reason that, as long as state and local school laws or regulations are reasonable and applied in a consistent manner,[54] a professional employee may be held accountable.

The term "willful" suggests the presence of intention and at least some power of choice.[55] Simply denying intent does not make it so.[56]

Proving intent is not easy in the face of denials by the accused. However, the employee's actions in and of themselves may support intent.[57] Furthermore, the court may consider the employee's range of personal and professional experience as well.[58]

Willful and Persistent Violation of School Laws

Language in the School Code addresses the "persistent and willful violation of or failure to comply with school laws of this Commonwealth (including directives and established policy of the board of directors)." As mentioned above, a willful act implies intent. This includes what a teacher "should have known" in terms of school district policy.[59] Even so, willfulness should not be presumed when the facts do not support such a conclusion.[60]

Persistent has been defined as a series of acts or omissions or a single act performed over a period of time. Single incidents are not interpreted as persistent.[61]

There are many examples of willful and persistent violation of school laws. Administering corporal punishment to fourth and sixth graders as well as isolation of students in an unsupervised closet in direct contravention of school district regulations have justified the dismissal of a teacher.[62] Teachers have been dismissed for absences in excess of sick leave policy and failure to report absences as stipulated by school policy.[63]

Even intemperate behavior is seen to be in violation of this provision of the School Code, since intemperate behavior is usually a violation of school board regulations.[64]

Willful and persistent violation of school laws may take many forms. In one case, conducting religious exercises on a daily basis while ignoring the superintendent's directives to cease was justification to dismiss an elementary teacher.[65] In another, a teacher was ordered to cease pursuing a relationship and the affection of a sixteen-year-old student. The teacher disobeyed orders, continued advancements, and was summarily dismissed as a result of persistent and willful violations of school law even though dismissal was proper on immorality grounds as well.[66] There are numerous other examples: giving wine to students,[67] repeated lateness,[68] violating a school district residency requirement,[69] refusing to report to assignments,[70] and leaving the classroom during portions of scheduled classes.[71]

If a directive from the district is unlawful or violative of constitutionally protected conduct, failure to comply with it may not be used as grounds for dismissal. (For example, a district cannot require an employee to discriminate on the basis of sex or race.) It should be noted that unless the request is clearly unlawful or immoral, the employee should comply with the request before initiating a procedural remedy such as filing a grievance.

Drug Possession and Dealing

Section 527 of the Pennsylvania Public School Code addresses the provisions in The Drug Free Workplace Act of 1988 (41 U.S.C. 701 *et seq.*) and the Controlled Substance, Drug, Device, and Cosmetic Act (P.L. 233, No. 64). The law states that school district employees who are convicted of delivery of or possession of a controlled substance with the intent to deliver shall be terminated from their employment (24 P.S. Code 527(a).

Conviction of Certain Crimes

The School Code further states that public or private school employees convicted of any of the offenses listed in Section 527(b) shall lose their positions. These convictions mirror the offenses that preclude the issuance of certification outlined in Section 111 of the School Code. The following is a comprehensive list of the offenses:

1. Criminal homicide;
2. Aggravated assault;
3. Kidnapping;
4. Unlawful restraint;
5. Rape;
6. Statutory rape;
7. Involuntary deviate sexual intercourse;
8. Indecent assault;
9. Indecent exposure;
10. Concealing the death of a child born out of wedlock;
11. Endangering the welfare of children;
12. Dealing in infant children;
13. Prostitution and related offenses;
14. Offenses involving obscene and other sexual materials;
15. Corruption of minors;
16. Sexual abuse of children;
17. Offenses designated as a felony under the Controlled Substances, Drug, Device and Cosmetic Act;
18. Out-of-state or federal offenses similar to those listed above.

Recently added to this list was: stalking, sexual assault, incest, indecent assault, and sexual performance.

Any loss of employment for the reasons stated shall be immediate within statutory and procedural guidelines regardless of whether or not the criminal conduct occurred on or off school premises.

Procedures

A great number of teacher dismissal cases involve due process where the letter of the law was not followed with regard to specific procedural guidelines. Substantively, professional employees are entitled to due process in defense of liberty or property interests guaranteed by the Fourteenth Amendment. A teacher's right to employment is always balanced against society's interest in educating its children and preventing harassment of those children by persons entrusted to their care.[72]

Once rights are secured under the Fourteenth Amendment, procedural due process kicks in. Just what the procedural standards are and to what degree they must apply, depends upon the circumstances of each case. There are basic elements to consider.

Generally speaking, tenured professional employees cannot be dismissed without full compliance with the requirements of the Public School Code.[73] You must, however, be a teacher to receive procedural protection. If one's position has not been acted upon by the school board and a teacher reports to work subject to the board's action on the superintendent's recommendation, the teacher is not a professional employee to whom the board must apply statutory procedures.[74] No contract means no procedural safeguards in dismissal. Similarly, if teaching certification expires, a teacher ceases to be a professional employee entitled to procedural protection.[75]

Since only the board has the authority to hire, only the board can dismiss. Termination of contract solely by the superintendent is not adjudication under Local Agency Law.[76] However, a superintendent may suspend the teacher without pay for misconduct, pending the outcome of a board hearing.[77] Suspension without pay was placed into perspective when a Pennsylvania court noted that the primary purpose for the existence of the public schools is for the education of the children and not the "incidental financial benefit of those participation therein."[78]

Tenured Teacher

For the tenured teacher, the substantive provisions of the Fourteenth Amendment require the following procedural due process provisions:

1. Sufficient notice of charges;
2. A hearing whereby a written record is kept, proof of guilt is established beyond a reasonable doubt, and a decision is rendered based on the evidence presented;
3. A right of appeal.

Formal school board action need not be taken to authorize the initiation of charges against a professional employee.[79] The action may be initiated by the superintendent. According to the School Code, notice must contain a "detailed written statement of charges" upon which dismissal is based as well as the time, date, and place for a hearing. The charges must conform to the causes for termination of contract set forth in Section 1122 of the Code. A professional employee may not be dismissed prior to written notice stating the charges and giving an opportunity for a hearing.[80] If a professional employee is discharged without having had the required notice, the employee will be reinstated.[81]

A hearing must not start "sooner than (10) days nor later than (15) days after such written notice" (24 P.S. Code 1127). Such a hearing must be impartial and provide the constitutional guarantees of counsel, the right to present evidence, the right to cross-examine witnesses and the right to avoid self-incrimination.

A written record must be kept in accordance with the Code and the hearing should be fair and impartial. Several cases provide guidelines on impartiality. *Barndt v Wissahickon* established that due process was not violated simply because the school board had pecuniary interest as an employer as well as decision maker.[82]

The principle that the same person may not simultaneously prosecute and adjudicate was affirmed in *Blascovich*.[83] However, in other court cases courts have held that a board solicitor may prosecute and/or different lawyers from the same office may prosecute as long as their functions are not mixed or become involved in board deliberations.[84] The mixed rulings were put to rest when a 1995 Commonwealth Court decision confirmed that a school district solicitor might act as prosecutor despite the contention that there was a continuing relationship that gave the appearance of an impropriety.[85]

In the hearing, the burden of proof lies with the school board and, although only a quorum need be present at the hearing, their decision must be rendered by a two-thirds vote of all board members (24 P.S. Code 1129). Failure to attain a two-thirds vote will result in the retention of the teacher. If such a vote is taken and the required two-thirds is not obtained after nearly a year of suspension, the complaint against the teacher can be dismissed.[86]

In the hearing, the most significant element is presentation of the evidence.   Evidence where an employee possessed knowledge of appropriate procedures justifies dismissal.[87] Where only two individuals knew what occurred and their testimony was in conflict, it was the duty of the board to weigh testimony and determine which version it will accept.[88] Often it is not so difficult to establish questionable behavior. Unsatisfactory ratings supported by qualified observers including the assistant principal for instruction, the social studies chairperson, the dean of the grade level and the principal establish a sufficient case for dismissal.[89] Similarly, two unsatisfactory ratings along with voluminous testimony by students, supervisors, superintendent and principal were considered substantial.[90] Indeed, unsatisfactory ratings may not necessarily contain numerical scores but if they have accompanying anecdotal records, they will be held to be substantial.[91] It follows then that, given the importance of a rating, if a year-end rating is not included in the record, dismissal may be reversed.[92]

The courts have held that a plea of *nolo contendere* to federal charges of operating illegal gambling are admissible as evidence of guilt in proceedings based on a charge of immorality.[93] Later, Pennsylvania's Commonwealth Court held that such a plea was not admissible where the record had been expunged and where no judgment had been entered.[94]

If a dismissal hearing considers an unsatisfactory rating based in part on hearsay evidence, such evidence is admissible.[95] As a general rule, evidence must be relevant to the matter at hand, well documented to the point of being considered substantial and it must be careful not to be violative of any constitutional rights. The board must send written notice of the discharge "within (10) days after such hearing is actually concluded" (24 P.S. Code 1130).

Non-Tenured Teacher

Like a tenured teacher, non-tenured charges may be initiated without board action. Reasonable, timely notice is required.[96] Although a stenographic record is not necessary, it may be provided at a cost to the requesting party.

A fair and impartial hearing must be granted to the non-tenured professional. Even so, a single unsatisfactory rating may constitute a *prima facie* case for dismissal.[97] When the board votes, a simple majority rather than two-thirds vote is required to sustain dismissal. Written notice is also required (2 Pa.C.S. 555).

Grievance Arbitration

In accord with Section 1133 of the School Code, an employee may elect arbitration to satisfy due process requirements in a dismissal case.[98] Procedures must follow the Uniform Arbitration Act, 42 Pa. C.S.A. 7301 *et seq.*

Appeals

Depending upon which due process vehicle is chosen, a certified teacher has a right of appellate review. If an appeal is taken from a dismissal hearing under the School Code, it may go to the Secretary of Education (24 P.S. Code 1131) who may only affirm or reverse the board's decision[99] even though there is broad authority to consider new evidence.[100] The Secretary of Education is the ultimate fact finder with the power to determine a.) credibility of witnesses, b.) the weight of testimony, and c.) inferences drawn from testimony.[101]

On the one hand, appeals may be taken to the Court of Common Pleas where reversal can be based on violation of constitutional rights or where findings of fact are unsupported by substantial evidence.[102] Commonwealth Court may also hear appeals in the event of an abuse of discretion or error of law, according to Section 1132 of the Public School Code.

Arbitration hearings, on the other hand, may be appealed to the Court of Common Pleas or Commonwealth Court where reversal is possible only through interpretation of the collective bargaining agreement.[103] Of course, if a constitutional issue is present, the appeal may proceed directly to the appropriate federal court.

Reporting

Pennsylvania's Professional Education Discipline Act, Act 123 of 2000, took effect in February of 2001. It requires a superintendent or assistant superintendent to report the dismissal of a certified employee for cause or conduct that results in a criminal indictment or conviction of a crime set forth in the Public School Code. These acts must be reported within 30 days of the administrative decision. They must also report information that gives reason to believe that a certified employee has caused physical injury to a student or child as a result of negligence or malice or has committed sexual abuse or exploitation involving a student or child. This report must be filed within 60 days of receipt of the information. In either case, failure to comply may result in disciplinary action.

Implications

Teachers and Administrators:

- A teacher may only be dismissed according to law. The School Code lists the reasons. There are no other grounds for dismissal.

- Note that, in Pennsylvania, insubordination is not a valid ground for dismissal. However, couched in statutory language, i.e., willful neglect of duties or persistent negligence, a teacher's "insubordinate" actions may be cause for dismissal.

- Likewise, improper supervision *per se* is not a valid reason for teacher dismissal in Pennsylvania.

- Unless an act is immoral or illegal, teachers should do it first, then grieve. The administrator's word is law.

- Two consecutive unsatisfactory ratings are sufficient to dismiss a teacher, even if they occur a year apart.

- Even with tenure, the statutory grounds for dismissing a teacher will prevail as long the charge is substantiable and procedural guidelines are followed.

- Charges against a teacher must comply fully with statutory and collective bargaining guidelines.

- Any dismissal of a professional employee should be accompanied by detailed anecdotal records.

- If a school district pursues action for dismissal, the statement of charges will usually contain as many infractions as possible. However, the board needs only prove one of them to succeed.

- The same types of behavior may be used to substantiate more than one statutory infraction.[104]

- A disciplinary dismissal (as opposed to an administrative reduction in force) requires a total of six (6) votes, a two-thirds vote of the entire board, not just a quorum.

- Board dismissals in Pennsylvania are generally appealed to the State Secretary of Education before resorting to the Court of Common Pleas or Commonwealth Court. If a Constitutional issue is raised, the case can be heard in the court of the appropriate federal jurisdiction.

Chapter 13 Endnotes

[1] West Shore School District v. Bowman, 409 A.2d 474, 48 Pa. Cmwlth. 104 (1979); Neshaminy Federation of Teachers v. Neshaminy School District, 462 A.2d 629 (1983).

[2] Allegheny Intermediate Unit v. Jarvis, 410 A.2d 389, 48 Pa. Cmwlth. 636 (1980).

[3] Bovino v. Board of School Directors of Indiana Area School District, 377 A.2d 1284, 32 Pa. Cmwlth. 105 (1977).

[4] Covert v. Bensalem Township School District, 104 Pa. Cmwlth. 441 (1987).

[5] Baker v. School District of Allentown, 371 A.2d 1028, 29 Pa. Cmwlth. 458 (1977).

[6] West Chester School Board v. West Chester Area Educational Association, 28 SLIE 16 (CP Chester 1991).

[7] Shoup v. Forest Area School District, 30 SLIE 84 (1993).

[8] Neshaminy Federation of Teachers v. Neshaminy School District, 428 A.2d 1023, 59 Pa. Cmwlth. 63 (1981).

[9] Lesley v. Oxford Area School District, 420 A.2d 764, 54 Pa. Cmwlth. 120 (1980).

[10] Jacobs v. State College Area School District, 26 SLIE 91 (1989); Morgan v. Altoona Area School District, 17 SLIE 13 (1980).

[11] Baker v. Allentown School District, 29 Pa. Cmwlth 453 (1977).

[12] Covert, *supra*.; Horton v. Jefferson County DuBois Area Vocational Technical School, 157 Pa. Cmwlth 424 (1993).

[13] Bethel Park School District v. Krall, 445 A.2d 1377 (Pa. Cmwlth. 1982).

[14] Balog v. McKeesport Area School District, 484 A.2d 198, 86 Pa. Cmwlth. 132 (1984).

[15] Riverview School District Riverview Education Association, 639 A.2d 974 (Pa. Cmwlth. 1994).

[16] Bovino, *supra*.

[17] Central York School District v. Ehrhart, 387 A.2d 1006, 36 Pa. Cmwlth. 278 (1978).

[18] Penn-Delco School District v. Urso, 382 A.2d 162, 33 Pa. Cmwlth. 501 (1978).

[19] Jeffery v. Marple-Newton School District, 23 SLIE 88 (1986).

[20] Sertik v. Pittsburgh School District, 136 Pa. Cmwlth. 594 (1990).

[21] Keating v. Board of School Directors of Riverside School District, 99 Pa. Cmwlth. 337 (1986) appeal denied 514 Pa. 626.

[22] Lenker v. East Pennsboro School District, 632 A.2d 969 (Pa, Cmwlth. 1993).

[23] Dohanic v. Department of Education, 111 Pa. Cmwlth. 193 (1987).

[24] West Chester, *supra.*; Reitmeyer v. Unemployment Compensation Board of Review, 602 A.2d 505 (Pa. Cmwlth. 1991).

[25] Ellwood City Area School District v. Secretary of Education, 9 Pa. Cmwlth 477 (1973).

[26] Board of School Directors of Fox Chapel Area School District v. Rossetti, 387 A.2d 957, 36 Pa. Cmwlth. 105 (1978).

[27] Grant v. Board of School Directors of Centennial School District, 471 A.2d 1291, 80 Pa. Cmwlth. 481 (1984).

[28] Bruckner v. Lancaster Area Vocational-Technical Joint School Operating Committee, 453 A.2d 384 (Pa. Cmwlth. 1982).

[29] Hamburg v. North Penn School District, 484 A.2d 867, 86 Pa. Cmwlth. 371 (1984).

[30] Homan v. Blue Ridge School District, 405 A.2d 572 (Pa. Cmwlth. 1979).

[31] Kudasik v. Board of Directors, Port Allegany School District, 455 A.2d 261 (Pa. Cmwlth. 1983).

[32] Bohenik v. Valley View School District, 25 SLIE 45 (1988).

[33] New Castle Area School District v. Bair, 368 A.2d 345, 28 Pa. Cmwlth. 240 (1977).

[34] In re Feldman, 395 A.2d 602, 38 Pa. Cmwlth. 634 (1978); Barndt v. Board of School Directors of Wissahickon School District, 368 A.2d 1355, 28 Pa. Cmwlth. 482 (1977).

[35] Travis v. Teter, 370 Pa. 326 (1952).

[36] Rosso v. Board of School Directors of Owen J. Roberts School District, 380 A.2d 1328, 33 Pa. Cmwlth. 175 (1977).

[37] Barndt, *supra.*

[38] Stefen v. Board of Directors of South Middletown Township School District, 377 A.2d 1381, 32 Pa. Cmwlth. 187 (1977).

178

[39] Belasco v. Board of Public Education of School District of Pittsburgh, 486 A.2d 538, 87 Pa. Cmwlth. 5 (1985).

[40] Bond v. Philadelphia School District, 27 SLIE 87 (1990).

[41] Casilli v. Board of Public Education of the School District of Pittsburgh, 23 SLIE 7 (1985).

[42] Caffas v. Upper Dauphin Area School Board of School Directors, 23 Pa. Cmwlth. 578 (1976); Landi v. West Chester School District, 23 Pa. Cmwlth. 586 (1976).

[43] Belasco, *supra*, Blascovich v. Board of School Directors of Shamokin Area School District, 410 A.2d 407, 49 Pa. Cmwlth. 131 (1980).

[44] Bovino, *supra*, Lenker v. East Pennsboro School District, 159 Pa. Cmwlth. 18 (1993),

[45] Gobla v. Board of School Directors of Crestwood School District, 414 A.2d 772, 51 Pa. Cmwlth. 539 (1980); Lucciola v. Commonwealth, Secretary of Education, 360 A.2d 310, 25 Pa. Cmwlth. 419 (1976).

[46] Clairton School District v. Strinich, 431 A.2d 267, 494 Pa. 297 (1981).

[47] Board of School Directors of Eastern York School District v. Fasnacht, 441 A.2d 481, 64 Pa. Cmwlth. 571 (1982).

[48] Harrison v. Capital Area Intermediate Unit, 479 A.2d 62, 84 Pa. Cmwlth. 344 (1984).

[49] Hoffman v. West Chester Area School District School Board, 397 A.2d 482, 40 Pa. Cmwlth. 374 (1979).

[50] Marinaro v. Cheltenham Township School District Board, Teacher Tenure Appeal, No.7-88.

[51] Boehm v. Board of Education of School District of Pittsburgh, 373 A.2d 1372, 30 Pa. Cmwlth. 468 (1977).

[52] Clark v. Colonial School District, 387 A.2d 1027, 36 Pa. Cmwlth. 419 (1978).

[53] Philadelphia School District Board of Public Education v. Beilan, 386 Pa. 82 (1956), affirmed 357U.S. 1414 (1958), rehearing denied 358 U.S. 858 (1958).

[54] Blascovich, *supra*.

[55] Lucciola, *supra*.

[56] Phillips v. Trinity Area School District, 29 SLIE 40 (1992).

[57] Ross v. Blue Mountain School District Board of School Directors, 21 SLIE 21 (1985).

[58] Rhodes v. Laurel Highlands School District, 118 Pa. Cmwlth. 119 (1988).

[59] Landi, *supra*.

[60] Visco v. Cheltenham Township School District, 27 SLIE 17 (1990).

[61] Belasco, *supra*.

[62] Harris, *supra*.

[63] Ward v. Board of Education of School District of Philadelphia, 496 A.2d 1352 (Pa. Cmwlth. 1985).

[64] Strinich, *supra*.

[65] Fink v. Board of Education of Warren County School District, 442 A.2d 837 (Pa. Cmwlth. 1982).

[66] Keating v. Board of School Directors, Riverside School District, 513 A.2d 547 (Pa. Cmwlth. 1986).

[67] Jacobs v. State College Area School District, 26 SLIE 91 (1989).

[68] Marinaro, *supra*.

[69] Walton v. Pittsburgh School District, 28 SLIE 86 (1991).

[70] Strinich, *supra*; Johnson v. United School District Joint School Board, 201 Pa. Super. 375 (1963).

[71] Bond, *supra*.

[72] Keating v. Board of School Directors Riverside School District, 513 A.2d 547 (Pa. Cmwlth. 1986).

[73] Board of School Directors of Centennial School District v. Secretary of Education, 376 A.2d 302, 31 Pa. Cmwlth. 307 (1977); New Castle Area School District v. Bair, 368 A.2d 345, 28 Pa. Cmwlth. 240 (1977).

[74] McCorkle v. Bellefonte Area Board of School Directors, 401 A.2d 371, 41 Pa. Cmwlth. 581 (1979).

[75] Occhipinti v. Board of School Directors of Old Forge School District, 464 A.2d 631 (1983).

[76] Olson v. Warren County School District, 11 D. & C.3d 243 (1978).

[77] Kaplan v. Philadephia School District, 388 Pa. 213 (1957); Board of School Directors of Eastern York School District v. Fasnacht, 441 A.2d 481, 64 Pa. Cmwlth. 571 (1982).

180

[78] Philadelphia School District Board of Education v. Kushner, 109 Pa. Cmwlth. 120 (1987).

[79] Clark v. Colonial School District, 387 A.2d 1027, 36 Pa. Cmwlth. 419 (1978).

[80] Bruckner v. Lancaster County Area Vocational-Technical Joint School Operating Committee, 467 A.2d 432, 78 Pa. Cmwlth. 314 (1983).

[81] West Shore School District v. Bowman, 409 A.2d 474 (Pa. Cmwlth. (1979).

[82] Barndt v. Wissahickon School District,368 A.2d 1355 (Pa. Cmwlth. 1977).

[83] Blascovich v. Board of Directors of Shamokin Area School District, 410 A.2d 407, 49 Pa. Cmwlth. 131 (1980).

[84] Commonwealth v. Feeser, 364 A.2d 1324, 469 Pa. 173 (1976); Boehm v. Board of Education of School District of Pittsburgh, 373 A.2d 1372, 30 Pa. Cmwlth. 468 (1977); In re Feldman, 395 A.2d 602, 38 Pa. Cmwlth. 634 (1978).

[85] Harmon v. Mifflin County School District, 32 SLIE 1 (1995).

[86] Rike v. Commonwealth, Secretary of Education, 465 A.2d 720 (Pa. Cmwlth. 1983).

[87] Foderaro v. School District of Philadelphia, 531 A.2d 570 (Pa. Cmwlth. 1987) appeal denied 518 Pa. 644.

[88] Wissahickon School District v. McKown, 400 A.2d 899, 42 Pa. Cmwlth. 169 (1979).

[89] In re Feldman, *supra*.

[90] Steffen v. Board of Directors of South Middletown Township School District, 377 A.2d 1381, 32 Pa. Cmwlth. 187 (1977).

[91] Hamburg v. North Penn School District, 484 A.2d 867, 86 Pa. Cmwlth. (1984); Penn-Delco School District v. Urso, 382 A.2d 162, 33 Pa. Cmwlth. 501 (1978).

[92] Hamburg v. Commonwealth, Department of Education, 458 A.2d 288 (Pa. Cmwlth. 1983); New Castle v. Bair, *supra*.

[93] Baker v. School District of Allentown, 371 A.2d 1028, 29 Pa. Cmwlth. 458 (1977).

[94] Warren County School District of Warren County v. Carlson, 418 A.2d 810, 53 Pa. Cmwlth. 458 (1980).

[95] Board of Public Education of School District of Pittsburgh v. Pyle, 390 A.2d 904, 37 Pa. Cmwlth. 386 (1978).

[96] Husted v. Canton Area School District, 458 A.2d 1037 (Pa. Cmwlth. 1983); see 2 Pa. C.S.A. Sec. 553.

[97] Kudasik v. Board of Directors, Port Allegany School District, 455 A.2d 261 (Pa. Cmwlth. 1983).

[98] Pedersen v. South Williamsport Area School District, 667 F.2d 312 (3rd Cir. 1982).

[99] Commonwealth v. Oxford Area School District, 356 A.2d 857 (Pa. Cmwlth. 1976).

[100] Clairton v. Strinich, 431 A.2d 267, 494 Pa. 297 (1981).

[101] Carmichaels Area School District v. Harr, 492 A.2d 126 (Pa. Cmwlth. 1981).

[102] Nagy v. Belle Vernon Area School District, 412 A.2d 172, 49 Pa. Cmwlth. 452 (1980).

[103] Leechburg Area School District v. Dale, 424 A.2d 1309, 492 Pa. 515 (1981).

[104] Bassion v. Northeast Bradford School District, 31 SLIE 88 (1994).

NOTES

Chapter 14   Confidentiality

Sources:

> Family Educational Rights and Privacy Act of 1974 (FERPA),
>   20 U.S.C.A. Section 1232g
> Health and Human Services Regulations, 42 C.F.R. Part 2
> Freedom of Information Act, 5 U.S.C. 552

Confidentiality and the dissemination of information from governmental agencies receiving federal funds are addressed in several state and federal laws. There are two important pieces of legislation directly affecting the public schools. The first is the Family Educational Rights and Privacy Act (FERPA), [1] which covers written educational records. The second is a body of laws called Health and Human Services Regulations, [2] which regulates the sharing of written or oral information concerning drugs and alcohol, mental health, and at-risk information. While FERPA is school-specific, Health and Human Services Regulations are agency specific. Most schools, however, deal with community service agencies on a regular basis to provide support for students who need help. Added to this, schools now have their academic responsibilities joined by social and psychological responsibilities in the form of Student Assistance Programs (S.A.P.'s). To be sure, record keeping has grown more complex over the years.

It is important to note that confidentiality is not the same as privileged communication. Privileged communication is reserved for attorneys, physicians, psychiatrists, and the clergy. The courts may not require information that is held in privileged communication to be disclosed. Confidentiality; however, is regulated by laws that define the limits of disclosure.

Student Records

Family Educational Rights and Privacy Act

Student records must be compiled, maintained, and accessed according to law. Fortunately, the Family Educational Rights and Privacy Act (FERPA) sets forth clear guidelines to accomplish these ends. Problems arising from collecting, maintaining, and accessing school records can be avoided by adhering to FERPA guidelines that have been adopted in some form by the individual states.[3]

FERPA addresses the exchange of student information via written educational records. The key term is "written" meaning that much educational information may be exchanged orally as long as access is not provided to the actual written documents. The term "educational records" refers to all of the documents housed and maintained by the school including written records on file from outside agencies, mental health professionals, or law enforcement agencies. Once a document comes to rest in a school, the information becomes an "educational record" and access is determined by the type or classification of the information as proscribed by law.

Plan. Every school district is required to adopt a plan with respect to student records. This plan must be submitted to the State Department of Education and must be made available to the Department of Education upon request.

Collecting data. School authorities are urged to operate on the principle that no information should be collected from students without prior consent from the parents. This consent can be individual, specific to the data gathering, or representational, via elected representatives such as the Board of School Directors. On the one hand, data within the ordinary purview of the public school curriculum such as aptitudes, achievement and skill outcomes in subject matter areas require representational consent. On the other hand, personality testing, psychological evaluation, behavior probing or other non-scholastic and non-aptitude testing requires individual consent and prior notice. Under the Hatch Act, consent is required in testing, surveys, analyses, or evaluative devices that reveal information such as political affiliation, psychological problems, sexual behavior and attitudes, and information concerning self-incriminating behavior. In either case, no consent should be binding unless freely given with prior knowledge. Where individual consent is required, the student's consent should also be obtained if the student is reasonably competent to understand the situation. In all situations, however, the student must not be led to feel duress or experience psychological harm.[4] Prior consent usually comes from the parent or guardian; however, it may come from the student if the student is an emancipated minor.

If data is gathered for non-school purposes, anonymity does not secure the right to gather information. Individual consent, in writing, is necessary.

Classification, Maintenance, and Security. There are three classifications of student personnel data that lie on a continuum from least intrusive (objective and impersonal) to more intrusive (subjective and personal). Each category requires different arrangements for maintenance and security. The least intrusive and most objective of the classifications is Category "A" Data, commonly referred to as directory information. This classification contains:

> ...the minimum personal data necessary for operating the school system...identifying data (including names and addresses of parents or guardian), birth data, academic work completed, level of achievement (grades, standardized achievement test scores), and attendance data.

Recently the United States Department of Education amended FERPA by redefining directory information to include the student's email address and photograph.

Directory information is commonly encountered in the public schools as permanent record cards or transcripts. They must be maintained for a period of one hundred (100) years with a designated professional person(s) responsible for maintenance and access including provisions for challenging the validity of any information. This is the reason that schools microfilm and electronically duplicate permanent records for long-term storage.

Student records should be maintained under lock and key at all times. Security for information contained in computer data banks should include providing external locking mechanisms and limiting access by creating codes to protect the data from intrusion by unauthorized personnel.

Category "B" Data is slightly more subjective than Category A Data. It consists of important, but not absolutely necessary, information that the school can use to help a child or protect others. Category B data deals with:

> ...scores on standardized intelligence and aptitude tests, interest inventory results, health data, family background

information, systematically gathered teacher or counselor ratings or observations.

As schools regularly accumulate data in folders or through electronic record keeping, they generally create Category B files. Guidance folders are examples of Category B data. Student Assistance Program records also qualify as Category B data, since much of the data is systematically gathered by behavioral checklists. Discipline reports are Category B as long as they contain unambiguously described verified reports of behavior patterns.

Category B data must be accurate. Any unnecessary information should be eliminated at periodic intervals. This usually occurs when a student moves from one administrative level to another (elementary to middle school/junior high school, to high school). Furthermore, this information should be kept under lock and key by the designated professional person(s) responsible for maintaining such records.

Category "C" Data is the most subjective. It includes:

...potentially useful information but not yet verified or clearly needed beyond the immediate present: for example, legal or clinical findings including certain personality test results, and unevaluated reports of teachers, counselors and others which may be needed in ongoing investigations and disciplinary or counseling actions.

Category C data includes notes from disciplinary investigations, anecdotal records maintained by school personnel, and results obtained from tests administered by the school psychologist. This information should be reviewed annually and either destroyed or re-categorized as Category B data as long as there is continuing usefulness for such information and the data's validity has been established. In the latter instance parents should be notified of the re-categorization and have the nature of the information explained to them. The same security provisions should be followed with Category C data as with A and B.

Confidential files of outside professionals in the school should be maintained consistent with the above rules and any rules dictated by professional ethics. If outside counselors or social workers wish to maintain personal records of student contacts, they should store clients' records in their own offices as opposed to the school. Records housed in the school become educational records governed by FERPA.

Access. Most problems in the area of pupil records occur when there is unauthorized access and dissemination. Pennsylvania courts have held that lists of names of high school students can be inspected by a photographer[5] or inspected for the purpose of providing the basis for placement in a particular school building, room, session, and for the purpose of transportation.[6]

Names, addresses and other minimal personal data are category A (directory information). Category A data is accessible to the child, parent, guardian, or legal representative as well as persons who have a legitimate interest in the child.

Specific consent is required for the release of any data in Category B with the following exceptions: Schools may release a student's permanent record file which may include both Category A and Category B data to: (a) other school officials and teachers with a legitimate educational interest; (b) the state superintendent when within specified duties; and (c) officials of other school districts in which the student intends to enroll.

Even though parents or guardians have access to Category B data as well as minor students with parental permission, permission to access school information must be obtained from graduates over 18 years of age. Furthermore, emancipated minors retain their right to control access to their records regardless of their age.

In a situation where the parents of a student are divorced or separated, the non-custodial parent has access unless a court order, statute, or legally binding document says otherwise. If the school district releases information to a non-custodial parent, it is advisable to notify the custodial parent.

An adoptive parent has full rights to access, while the natural parent loses all previous rights. The adoption has the same effect as a court order.

Category C data may be released only in compliance with a judicial order or orders of administrative agencies with subpoena powers. When a court requests the data, compliance is mandatory. Refusal to yield the appropriate information could result in a contempt citation accompanied by a jail term. One case in point held that a student victimized in a sexual assault was entitled to a disclosure of the school district's psychological assessment of the perpetrator.[7]

Confidential personal files of professionals in the school are the personal property of the professional and not the school. As such they are subject to the terms of employment, ethical considerations, and any agreements made between the professional and the parents of the students. In one case where a teacher abused fourth-grade students, a group of parents and the school administrator agreed to have the children evaluated by a psychologist who would share "all information gathered" with the parents. When the psychologist refused to disclose counseling notes made for personal use in treatment, a Pennsylvania court held that disclosure was subject to the prior agreement and parent access to the information was upheld.[8]

Disclosure is mandatory when school personnel have reason to believe that child abuse occurred. Suspected abuse must be reported; however, no liability exists for erroneous reporting as long as the disclosure is made in good faith. Such disclosure is protected as long as the information is released to an appropriate agency for a legally definable purpose.[9] In the August 2000 amendments, school entities were given permission to "disclose student records to a court without consent and without a court order or subpoena if a parent or student over 18 years of age initiates legal action against a school entity.[10]

A recent decision has raised concerns over what can or cannot be shared in the classroom. The United States Court of Appeals for the Tenth Circuit has held that the common practice of allowing students to grade their classmates' work and announce the results aloud violates FERPA.[11] The Appeals Court reaffirmed an earlier three-judge panel decision. While not binding in other jurisdictions, teachers would do well to reevaluate some grading practices to ensure students' privacy rights.

Special education. Maintenance and security requirements for special needs students are similar to those of regular students. However, more stringent access regulations are in effect because of the sensitive nature of special education placement. Directory information (Category A) still requires representational consent. However, the educational record (consisting of Category A and Category B information) requires specific consent. When the consent is legitimate for special situations, records of who accessed the information must be kept: a record of each party, including date of access and purpose for access. No record of access is required for authorized employees of the school district (or agency), parents, or anyone already having consent to the educational records.

Parents, guardians or other legal representatives have the same access rights to special education records as they would have with regular education students. Furthermore, such access must be provided within 30 days. A copy may be requested accompanied by a reasonable charge for copies or records. When a student has attained the age of majority (18 years) or is attending post-secondary education, consent to disseminate or to provide access shall be accorded to and required only of that student.

Health and Human Services Regulations

With the increasing need to deal with at-risk student issues, exchanging information becomes more complicated. Schools encounter substance abuse, suicide, and mental health issues in student assistance programs that link education with community service agencies, rehabilitation facilities, and private mental health professionals. The nature of the school information and how it is shared is a growing problem. With the creation of student support teams in many states, an individual's privacy may be assaulted by another individual's professional right to know. Bound by a different set of regulations, non-school agencies and mental health professionals are held to a higher degree of confidentiality in both written and spoken word than FERPA dictates.

Health and Human Services Regulations [12] apply to programs, especially alternative schools or programs that focus on a particular disorder. The operative term is "program," and it is defined as any person or organization, in whole or part, that provides diagnosis, treatment, or referral for treatment for drug and alcohol, mental health, or at-risk issues. Schools are not in the business of diagnosing, treating, or referring for treatment, yet they are required by law to deal with the educational disruption that manifests deeper social and psychological dysfunction. As long as the schools do not operate as providers of individualized services, they are bound only by FERPA. Still, schools must deal with individualized service providers, creating the need for them to know the law and understand the limitations that the law sets forth.

Unlike FERPA, the Health and Human Services (HHS) regulations make no distinction between classifications of data to determine accessibility. If a program fits the definition set forth in HHS regulations, confidentiality must be maintained by all personnel, full or part-time, paid or volunteer. As a general rule, the program may not disclose any information orally or in writing. The program may not directly or indirectly identify a person under treatment. Indeed, it may not even acknowledge presence.

Although there are nine (9) exceptions to this strict confidentiality,[13] the one that merits discussion is proper consent in the form proscribed by law. Schools commonly exchange information using consent forms. When sharing or requesting information of the kind generated by programs described in the HHS regulations, the proper consent form should contain eight (8) elements:

1. Client's name
2. Name of the program making the disclosure
3. Name of the person or organization to which the disclosure is to be made
4. Nature of the information
5. Purpose of the disclosure
6. Revocation statement
7. Signature of the client or parent/guardian if the client is under age (In Pennsylvania, the age is fourteen (14) years)
8. Date.

A written notice of prohibition on re-disclosure must accompany the release of confidential information under HHS regulations. A prohibition on re-disclosure expressly forbids releasing information to any other party without the written permission of the person to whom it pertains.

The existence of two federal laws governing the disclosure of confidential information coupled with the operation of Student Assistance Programs (S.A.P.) in schools has caused confusion in some educational circles. Teachers become impatient with agencies who are legally bound to withhold information, and S.A.P. teams sometimes operate in a counselor rather than a student assistance mode.

Some S.A.P. teams appear to function like a "program... providing diagnosis, treatment and or referral for treatment" by providing what appears to be individualized services. As such, it is conceivable that they may be held to stricter confidentiality limits than FERPA. Yet a number of student assistance teams continue to freely share information between and among persons or agencies that may have no right to the information by law. It is not unusual to find language in school-based S.A.P. policies that describe an S.A.P. team's role in terms of diagnosis, counseling (treatment), or referral as part of interventions and aftercare.

The question is: "Which federal law controls in a situation where student support services operate as an individualized service provider?" This is an area for potential litigation.   Should S.A.P. teams that offer "individualized services" be held to the stricter confidentiality guidelines of the Health and Human Services regulations barring any oral or written disclosure?   Should they be governed by the less stringent FERPA guidelines permitting oral disclosure in what the law describes as "classroom situations?"   Refer to the Confidentiality Comparison chart on page 198.

Juvenile Services Records

With the increasing threat of violence in our schools, Pennsylvania has recently enacted legislation requiring Juvenile Services to apprise schools of the criminal activities of their students.[14] This information is not to be used to prevent students from entering a school. Rather, it is intended to protect other students and teachers from danger. The law provides that Juvenile Services disclose the name, address and date of birth of the young perpetrator. The substantiated charge, adjudication date, disposition date, description of the incident and disposition are also a part of the report. If the juvenile has been adjudicated delinquent for an act or acts which, if committed as an adult, would be classified as a felony, additional information contained in the probation or treatment report would be included. The report would contain prior delinquent history and the supervision plan of the delinquent juvenile.

Actual adjudication is required before the report can be generated. Since many students are on probation by consent decree as a result of lesser criminal activity, no actual adjudication occurs. Therefore, no exchange of information occurs. Only adjudication resulting in formal or intense probation will require disclosure.

The information must be signed by the juvenile probation officer and must be maintained separately from the juvenile's official school record. This information may only be disseminated to protect school personnel and students from danger or to arrange appropriate counseling and education for the child.

If the commission of the crime occurred on or within 1,500 feet of the school, the information may be used to ascertain whether the child should face disciplinary action or be admitted to the regular school setting.

Employee Records

The fact that a public employee's records are in the possession of a public institution or agency does not automatically make them public records. The nature of the records and the purpose for which they were created determines whether they are public. Personnel files apply to particular individuals and, even under the Freedom of Information Act, they are generally not accessible to the public at large. With few exceptions, they are exempt from intrusion because access "would constitute a clearly unwarranted invasion of personal privacy."[15]

A five-part test on disclosure of employee information to the public was developed by the West Virginia courts. It may be of persuasive value in other jurisdictions. The steps are briefly outlined:

1. Would the disclosure result in a substantial invasion of privacy? If so, how serious?[16]
2. To what extent are the value of public interest and the purpose (objective) of those seeking disclosure?[17]
3. Is the information available for any other source(s)?[18]
4. Is the information granted with the expectation of confidentiality?[19]
5. Is it possible to limit the disclosure so as to limit the invasion of privacy?[20]

Privacy rights are rarely conceded in personnel matters. Even so, when a certain personnel official became concerned about an employee's fitness to teach, a complete medical examination was ordered, including a psychiatric exam. The school district was held to be within its right to request such an exam, since the decision to order the exam was not done arbitrarily or capriciously. The school's access to the medical records did not violate the teacher's right to privacy.[21] Here there was a compelling interest to affirm that the teacher was fit to teach, thus assuring that no harm would come to students. That is not always the case. If there is no legitimate concern to override an employee's privacy, the courts will not sustain the intrusion.

Implications

<u>Teachers and Administrators</u>:

- Confidentiality is not the same as privileged communication. Access to written confidential records is possible under the Federal Educational Rights and Privacy Act (FERPA).

- Under FERPA there are three categories of data along with maintenance requirements and access criteria.

- FERPA only governs written information. Much information can be shared in schools as long as it is done orally.

- Records from outside agencies that are kept in schools are considered educational records. The question is what type of educational records are they?

- In Pennsylvania, schools must maintain juvenile service records that move from district to district with the student.

- Prior written consent must be obtained if schools require students to take Department of Education funded surveys that ask them to reveal personal information.

- Student Assistance Programs create a nexus for Health and Human Services regulations and FERPA. It is important to know what can be shared between school-based support programs and community service agencies.

- Although the federal Freedom of Information Act does not apply to student records, sometimes a school receives requests for specific information that might compromise confidentiality. Keep in mind that the Freedom of Information Act does not apply to state and local governments; however, the Pennsylvania Right to Know Act does. Even so, when a citizen of Pennsylvania invokes the law, a district's only obligation is to permit inspection or copying of certain documents. Schools are not required to prepare new documents or compile information in different formats or lists.

Parents and Students:

- School district personnel have great latitude in sharing oral information about students.

- Students are not required to disclose personal information in Department of Education funded surveys without written parental consent.

- Student Assistance Program (S.A.P.) records are educational records and are accessible to parents under FERPA guidelines.

- Proper consent in the form proscribed by law is required by law in order to disclose information from Health and Human Services (HHS) programs.

- In Pennsylvania, students fourteen years of age and older are required to sign consent forms for data disclosure from community service agencies.

Family Educational Rights and Privacy Act, FERPA

20 U.S.C. Section 1232g

I.   Addresses the release of written "educational records" other than directory information from institutions receiving federal funds

II.   **Classification of Data**

Category "A" (Directory Information): "... minimum personal data necessary for operating the school system...identifying data (including names and addresses of parent or guardian), birth data, academic work completed, level of achievement (grades, standardized achievement test scores), and attendance data " as well as a student's email address and photograph.

Category "B": Important but not absolutely necessary information the school can use to help the child such as "...scores on standardized intelligence and aptitude tests, interest inventory results...family background, Student Assistance records, systematically gathered teacher or counselor ratings or observations."

Category "C": "...includes potentially useful information but not yet verified or clearly needed beyond the immediate present: for example, legal or clinical findings including personality test results, and unevaluated reports of teachers, counselors and others that may be needed in ongoing investigations and disciplinary or counseling actions."

III.   **Maintenance**

> **Category "A" Data** (Directory Information) must be maintained for 100 years.

> **Category "B" Data** should be eliminated at intervals such as a student's movement within a district from one administrative unit to another.

> **Category "C" Data** should be reviewed annually and may become Category "B" data.

IV.   **Access**

Category "A" Data (Directory Information)

1. Child, parent, guardian, or legal representative
2. School officials within the district, including teachers, having a legitimate educational interest
3. Officials of other schools for the purpose of enrollment (parents notified; right to challenge content)
4. Other third parties with routine consent

Category "B" Data

1. Student over 18 years of age and no longer attending high school
2. Married student regardless of age
3. Parent
4. Student with parent permission
5. School officials within the district, including teachers, having a legitimate educational interest
6. Officials of other schools for the purpose of enrollment (parents notified; right to challenge content)
7. Other third parties with specific consent

Category "C" Data

1. Judicial order
2. Agencies with the power of subpoena

U. S. Department of Health
and Human Services Regulations
42 C.F.R. Part 2

I.   Applies to programs, especially alternative schools or programs directly or indirectly receiving federal funds, that focus on a particular disorder

II. **Program:** Any person or organization, in whole or part, that provides alcohol or drug abuse **diagnosis**, **treatment**, or **referral for treatment**

A. Not exclusive to drug and alcohol services; applies to at risk issues as well
B. Applies to all personnel, full or part time, paid or volunteer
C. Limited to individualized services, not classroom situations

III. **General Rule:** The program may not disclose any information <u>verbally or in writing</u>:

A. Cannot directly or indirectly identify a student as a drug or alcohol abuser
B. Cannot acknowledge presence
B. Exceptions to the rule:

1. Proper consent in the form proscribed by law
2. Internal communications between or among those with a legitimate interest
3. No patient identifying information
4. Medical emergency requiring assistance
5. Research or audit of program or service
6. Crime on premises involving drug use or mental condition
7. Child abuse
8. Court order
9. Qualified Service Organization Agreement (QSOA)

CONFIDENTIALITY COMPARISON

FERPA	**Health and Human Services Regulations**
20 U.S.C. Section 12.32g	**42 CFR, Part 2**
1. Governmental Relationship	Governmental Relationship
2. Written Information	Written or Oral Information
3. Educational Records	Drug and Alcohol, Mental Health, or At-Risk Information
4. Category of Information, determines the nature of consent	Any information requires proper consent
5. Classroom Situations (School)	Individualized Services (Agency or Professional Care)
6. Client: Student	Client: Patient
7. Student Assistance Team Model	Counselor Model
Relevant Legislation:	**Relevant Legislation:**
Student Rights and Responsibilities: Pupil Records	Federal Consent Laws
Special Education Regulations on Confidentiality	Right to Know Law

Chapter 14 Endnotes

[1] 20 U.S.C.A. 1232g.

[2] 42 C.F.R. Part 2.

[3] 22 Pa. Code 12.31 *et. seq.*

[4] Trachtman v. Anker, 563 F.2d 512 (2nd Cir. 1977) *certiorari* denied, 435 U.S. 925 (1978).

[5] MacKnight v. Beaver Area School District, (C.P. Beaver Co. 1982).

[6] Young v. Armstrong School District, 21 Pa. Cmwlth. 203 (1975).

[7] J.N. by and through Hager v. Bellingham School District No. 501, 871 P.2d 1106 (Wash. App. Div. 1 1994).

[8] Parents Against Abuse v. Williamsport, 594 A.2d 796 (Pa. Cmwlth. 1991).

[9] Roman v. Appleby, 558 F. Supp. 449 (E.D. Pa. 1983).

[10] 34 C.F.R. Sec. 99.31 (a)(9)(iii).

[11] Falvo v. Owasso Independent School District, 2000 U.S. App. Lexis (10th Cir. 2000).

[12] 42 C.F.R. Part 2

[13] The nine exceptions are:

1. Proper consent in the form proscribed by law
2. Internal communications
3. No patient identifying information
4. Medical emergency
5. Research or audit
6. Crime on premises
7. Child abuse
8. Court order, and
9. Qualified Service Organization Agreement (QSOA).

[14] 42 Pa.C.S. 6301 *et seq.*

[15] 5 U.S.C. 552; 43 P.S. 1321-24.

[16] Tennessean Newspapers, Inc. v. Levi, 403 F. Supp. 1318, (M.D. Tenn. 1975).

[17] Campbell v. U. S. Civil Service Commission, 539 F.2d 58, (10th Cir. 1976).

[18] Wooster Republican Printing Co. v. City of Wooster, 383 N.E.2d 124, 56 Ohio St. 2d 126 (1978).

[19] Judiciary Committee v. Freedom of Information Commission, 473 A.2d 1248, 39 Conn. Sup. 176 (1983).

[20] Rural Housing Alliance v. U. S. Department of Agriculture, 498 F.2d 73 (D.C. Cir. 1974).

[21] Murray v. Pittsburgh Board of Education, 759 F. Supp. 1178 (W.D. Pa. 1991).

Chapter 15   Educational Malpractice

Sources:

>   Negligence Theory
>   Contract Law

To date, the courts have been reluctant to support claims of educational malpractice. Educational malpractice is the attempt to hold educators liable to provide a certain level of quality education to their students. Educational malpractice claims are based on harm or injury that some students experience as a result of the failure of schools to engage in appropriate instruction, testing, placement or counseling. These claims have increased and litigation has become a very real possibility.

Educational malpractice is a form of negligence, thus, each element of negligence must be proven for it to be sustained in a court of law: duty, failure to live up to a standard of care, actual injury, and proof that the failure to meet the standard of care caused the injury (proximate cause). Proving these elements is difficult under normal circumstances. To do so in the context of public education is even more challenging.

The issue of educational malpractice can be traced in a series of cases beginning with *Peter W. v. San Francisco Unified School District*.[1] *Peter W.* was granted a high school diploma from the San Francisco public schools. However, he graduated at a fifth-grade reading level. Since California state law requires a student to read at an eighth-grade level to graduate, his parents sued the school district for failing to teach him the necessary skills and graduating him without those skills. The California Court of Appeals reversed a lower court decision and refused to recognize an actionable duty of care:

> Unlike the activity of the highway or the marketplace, classroom methodology affords no readily acceptable standards of care, or cause, or injury. The science of pedagogy itself is fraught with different and conflicting theories of how or what a child should be taught, and any layman might -- and commonly does -- have his own emphatic views on the subject.[2]

The court reasoned further that public policy considerations precluded recovery of damages. "To hold [schools] to an actionable 'duty of care' in the discharge of their academic functions, would expose them to tort claims -- real or imagined -- of disaffected students and parents in countless numbers." The court went on to state "the ultimate consequences, in terms of public time and money, would burden them - and society - beyond calculation."

A series of litigation in regular and special education followed, most notably in the state of New York. In *Donahue v. Copiague*, an illiterate high school graduate was denied relief.[3] In *Hoffman v. Board of Education*, a student with a severe speech defect, diagnosed in kindergarten as mentally retarded, who graduated after failing to receive a recommended two-year reevaluation, was likewise denied relief.[4] In the latter case, the New York Court of Appeals reversed the Appellate Division on public policy grounds. The court did not accept reasoning that attempted to make a distinction between misfeasance (by not reevaluating) and nonfeasance (alleging that children were not learning).

Courts have been reluctant to accept educational malpractice as a basis for relief in tort or contract.[5] However, in one case, *Doe v. Board of Education of Montgomery County*, even though relief was not granted, the Court noted a distinction between instructional malpractice versus placement malpractice in a strong dissent opinion.[6]

A significant ruling was rendered in *Snow v. New York* where the precedents of *Peter W.*, *Donohue* and *Hoffman* were not controlling. Here, damages were based on medical malpractice rather educational malpractice. A deaf child had been institutionalized as retarded based on an IQ test designed for those with hearing ability. Despite teachers' recommendations, the school failed to retest upon discovering the hearing disorder.[7] Damages were awarded for the resulting educational deprivation caused by inadequate treatment, testing, and the failure to educate.

Curiously, on the same day that *Snow* was decided, *Torres*[8] was denied recovery in a nearly identical set of circumstances. *Snow* involved hearing impairment; *Torres* involved inability to speak English. The court appeared willing to permit a claim based on a more traditional cause of action (i.e. medical malpractice) that does not imply review of educational policy. Quantifying a person's auditory ability is less complex an issue than determining a person's language skills.

In Pennsylvania only a few cases have been argued on educational malpractice grounds. Two are offered for discussion. *Aubrey v. School District of Philadelphia*[9] addressed regular education and *Lindsey v. Thomas*[10] addressed special education. While both were denied recovery based on the reasoning of *Peter W.*, *Aubrey* added that not permitting a senior to graduate until fulfilling a state required course of studies does not amount to a gross violation of public school policy.

The court summarized its position on educational malpractice in *Rich v. Kentucky Country Day, Inc.*[11] Citing *Peter W.*, the Kentucky Court of Appeals found no clear standard of care with which to measure the conduct of an educator. Likewise, it found no clear duty based on the evidence of standards associated with the profession.

Rich further found it difficult to determine the nature of damages. The court acknowledged that there are factors outside the school's control that influence the success or failure of students. These factors are things like "attitude, motivation, temperament, past experience, and home environment."[12] Given the existence of such intervening variables, the problem becomes one of determining how to quantify the harm done to a particular student.

Still, the strongest argument against educational malpractice lies in public policy considerations. Schools would be subject to a flood of litigation resulting in an undue burden on public resources. "The ultimate consequences, in terms of public time and money, would burden [the schools] -- and society -- beyond calculation."[13] Furthermore, embracing a cause of action for educational malpractice would force the courts to interfere with the daily operations of the public schools. Historically, the courts are reluctant to do so.[14]

Given the courts' reluctance to sustain charges of educational malpractice, cause of action still exists in intentional torts, medical malpractice and gross violations "that the court would be obliged to recognize and correct."[15]

Implications

<u>Teachers and Administrators:</u>

- There is no common law duty, by virtue of professional standards, against which damages may be sought by students who have failed to learn in school. Failure to achieve academically is not characterized as an "injury" within the meaning of tort law.[16]

- Public policy considerations preclude recovery under educational malpractice.

- Recovery is barred for educational malpractice based on negligence and contract law (with the possible exception of a contract for specified medical services).

<u>Parents and Students:</u>

- The fact that schools are financed with public monies does not give the taxpayer a right to dictate to the educational system under the threat of action for educational malpractice.[17]

- Even if a law establishes standards for special education testing and evaluation, no common law duty exists under educational malpractice upon which damages can be awarded. Damages must be sought elsewhere under a different cause of action.[18]

Chapter 15 Endnotes

[1] Peter W. v. San Francisco Unified School District, 60 Cal. App. 3d 814, 131 Cal. Rptr. 854 (1976).

[2] Id., 131 Cal. Rptr. at 86l.

[3] Donohue v. Copiague Union Free School District, 47 N.Y. 2d 440, 418 N.Y.S.2d 375, 391 N.E.2d 1352 (1979).

[4] Hoffman v. Board of Education, 64 A.D.2d 369, 410 N.Y.S. 2d 99 (1978) reversed 49 N.Y.2d 121, 400 N.E.2d 317, 424 N.Y.S.2d 376 (1979).

[5] Paladino v. Adelphi University, 89 A.D.2d 85, 454 N.Y.S.2d 868 (1982).

[6] Doe v. Board of Education of Montgomery County, 453 A.2d 814, 295 Md. 67 (1982).

[7] Snow v. State of New York, 98 A.D.2d 442, 469 N.Y.S.2d 959, (Sup. Ct. App. Div. 1983) affirmed 61 N.Y.2d 608, 475 N.Y.S.2d 1026, 468 N.E.2d 1004 (1984).

[8] Torres v. Little Flower Children's Services, 64 N.Y.2d 119, 485 N.Y.S.2d 15, 474 N.E.2d 223 (1984).

[9] Aubrey v. School District, 437 A.2d 1306 (Pa. Cmwlth. 1981).

[10] Lindsey v. Thomas, 465 A.2d 122, 77 Pa. Cmwlth. 171 (1983).

[11] Rich v. Kentucky Country Day, Inc., 793 S.W.2d 832 (Ky. App. 1990).

[12] Id.

[13] Peter W., *supra*.

[14] Poe v. Hamilton, 565 N.E.2d 887 (Ohio App. 1990).

[15] Donohue, *supra*.

[16] Peter W., *supra*.

[17] Rich, *supra*.

[18] Johnson v. Clark, 418 N.W.2d 466 (Mich. App. 1987).

NOTES

Chapter 16   Negligence and Tort Liability

Sources:

>   Negligence Theory in Tort Law
>   Political Subdivisions Tort Claims Act, 42 Pa. C.S.A. 850, 854 *et seq.*
>   Civil Rights Act, 42 U.S.C. 1983
>   Pennsylvania Child Protective Services Act, 11 P.S. 2201-2224
>   Recreation Use of Land and Water Act, 68 P.S. 477

Governmental agencies, such as public schools, have historically been granted immunity from prosecution under tort law. The logic behind this "sovereign immunity" was justified in simple terms, "the king can do no wrong." The monarch derived power from God as a "divine right;" therefore, suing the lord of the manor was tantamount to bringing suit against the Almighty. The net result was that there was no recourse in law for persons to recover damages from the government or its agencies. The practical consequence for many years was that schools were immune from prosecution in the performance of their governmental function, namely, education.

Over the years, the law has evolved considerably. Until 1959, schools were protected from lawsuits based on negligence. In 1959, *Molitor v. Kaneland Community Unit School District No. 302*[1] succeeded in breaking the barrier of sovereign immunity for school districts in the state of Illinois. However, for a number of years thereafter, other state courts clung to the concept of immunity. Pennsylvania was one of them.

During the period following *Molitor*, school district liability in Pennsylvania hinged on the distinction between governmental acts and proprietary acts. Governmental acts were considered a part of the school's public agency function. Accordingly, schools were immune from prosecution. Proprietary acts were considered beyond the school's public agency function. They were, therefore, liable. This distinction ended in 1973.

In 1973, a Pennsylvania student was injured in an industrial arts class. The ensuing litigation, *Ayala v. Philadelphia Board of Education*,[2] redefined immunity for public schools in the Commonwealth making schools liable for certain actions of negligence in the same manner as individuals and private corporations.

Negligence

To understand negligence, one must become familiar with tort law. A tort is the commission or omission of an act whereby another is directly or indirectly injured in person, property, or reputation. It is an offense against an *individual* for which civil actions may be taken in a court of law to recover damages for the injury received from a wrongdoer. Although torts sometime resemble crimes, they are not. A crime is an offense against *society* where criminal laws exist to protect the community at large.

Torts may be intentional or unintentional. Intentional torts are willful acts such as assault, battery, slander, libel, and trespass, to mention a few. Intentional torts are always actionable because they are positive conscious acts having the purpose of injuring another. Unintentional torts are negative, heedless acts resulting in injury to another person. Negligence falls into the category of unintentional torts.

Negligence may involve injury as a result of doing something (an act) that a reasonable person would not do, or failing to do something (an omission) that a reasonable person guided by ordinary considerations would do. These acts and omissions must contain certain elements before liability can be established and damages can be awarded. There must be: 1.) a duty to protect others, 2.) failure to meet an appropriate standard of care, 3.) actual injury or loss, and 4.) proof that the failure to meet the standard of care caused the injury (proximate cause). If any of these four elements, is missing, the charge of negligence will not be sustained against individuals or institutions, public or private.

Tort Liability

As various jurisdictions opened the door to governmental liability, corresponding state legislatures had no alternative but to define the limits of tort liability for schools and other governmental agencies. Fearing a flood of litigation, they established qualified immunity by enacting numerous Tort Claims Acts.

In 1978, Pennsylvania passed its own Political Subdivisions Tort Claims Act. By listing eight (8) permissible areas of tort liability for governmental agencies, the legislature both acknowledged and limited one's right to sue a school district. As a result, cause of action for negligence may only be brought against a school district under one of the following categories:

1. Damages caused by operation of Motor Vehicles.

2. Damages to Personal Property, belonging to others in the care, custody and control of the school district.

3. Damage to person or property caused by condition of Real Estate under the care, custody and control of the school district.

4. Harm caused by the dangerous condition of Traffic Controls, Street Lights, or Trees in the care, custody and control of the school district.

5. Harm caused by the dangerous condition of Utilities owned by the school district.

6. Harm caused by the dangerous conditions of Streets owned by the school district.

7. Harm caused by the dangerous condition of Sidewalks within the right of way of streets owned by the school district.

8. Harm caused by Animals in the care, custody and control of school districts.

The courts have consistently turned away routine litigation that does not fall under the eight (8) exceptions to immunity listed in the Tort Claims Act. Moreover, the burden of proof lies with the plaintiff to show cause of action.[3] Under the Tort Claims Act, Pennsylvania defines a school district as a "local agency" for purpose of governmental immunity.[4] This has been determined to be a constitutional,[5] valid exercise of power.[6]

Note that the Tort Claims Act creates no exception to immunity for willful tortious conduct.[7] This does not mean that immunity exists for intentional torts. Crime, fraud, willful misconduct, or conduct motivated by malice always incurs liability. However, to recover damages, willful misconduct must be mentioned in the original complaint,[8] not in the amended complaint.[9]

Schools, then, are liable for their negligent actions in eight (8) areas as defined by the Political Subdivisions Tort Claims Act. They are held to the same theoretical liability as other entities with respect to establishing the four elements of negligence. When a question of liability arises, the proper jurisdiction is the Court of Common Pleas. This held true even when a plaintiff attempted to invoke provisions of the Health Care Services Malpractice Act to send an injury case to arbitration. The court did not permit enjoining the school district in a law suit with a hospital and the physicians who treated the injuries sustained by a student in a fall from the "still rings" in physical education class.[10]

All of the conditions listed in Pennsylvania's Tort Claims Act apply to all governmental agencies but, not all apply directly to school districts. For the most part, schools have been challenged in the area of motor vehicles, traffic controls, as well as care, custody, and control of real property (including streets and sidewalks).

<u>Motor Vehicles</u>

Two conditions, possession or control of motor vehicles and actual operation, must be satisfied to incur liability. A school district is liable when the motor vehicle is operated by a school district employee. The issue of liability rests on how one operates the vehicle and whether the person should be driving the vehicle in the first place. Therefore, students who take a joy ride in an automobile being worked on in auto shop class[11] and injuries caused by a student driving from one school to another[12] do not fall under the "motor vehicle" exception. However, a van operated by school officials is a "motor vehicle" for purposes of liability.[13] Schools are not held liable where actual operation of a vehicle is absent, i.e., getting in and out of a vehicle while it is at rest.[14]

<u>Traffic Controls</u>

Generally speaking, schools do not erect and maintain traffic controls or signals. The local municipality has this responsibility. In at least one instance, however, the courts were faced with clarifying what constitutes a traffic control or signal when a child was injured due to faulty flashing lights on a school bus. The court held that a school bus stopped with lights flashing is not a "traffic control" under the meaning of the Act.[15] Hence, the district was not liable.

Care, Custody, and Control of Real Property

The vast majority of cases involve the question of "care, custody and control" in the area of real property, including dangerous conditions in the buildings or premises. Liability will exist when there is negligence that makes the school property unsafe for activities for which it is regularly used, for which it is intended to be used, or for which it may be reasonably foreseen to be used.[16]

Control involves possession. Consequently, liability may not be sustained if possession is absent. For instance, a visiting team's school district was not held liable for injuries suffered by an infant struck in the head by a baseball because it could not be shown that the defendant "possessed" the field under the Tort Claims Act.[17]

In establishing liability, determining what constitutes real property is not always easy. It must be "real property," i.e., real estate, not an object such as a piano or vaulting horse.[18] And it cannot be an improperly lit hotel swimming pool on a field trip since the school district would not be considered the owner or caretaker of the facility.[19]

Gore v. Bethlehem Area School District established the standard for determining the difference between real property and personal property:

1. The manner in which it is physically attached or installed.
2. The extent to which it is essential to the permanent use of the building.
3. The intention of the parties who attached or installed it.[20]

This standard is used specifically in assessing the limits of liability when gym and shop equipment are involved in injuries. Generally, such equipment is considered personal property and not real property.[21] However, originally installed and secured equipment bolted to the floor or secured in concrete may be interpreted as real property.[22]

Once the issue of real property or actual real estate that is proper to the school district is established, "condition" becomes the focus. Dangerous conditions have been interpreted as conditions that compromise safety as a result of failing to comply with statutory standards. Such was the case when a handicapped individual fell off a curb and sustained injuries because a school failed to install curb cuts as proscribed by law.[23]

Injuries must result from the condition of the property itself not from a condition incidental to the property. Foreign substances, such as snow or ice, on top of a sidewalk or affixed to real property may not incur liability unless the condition of the property created the unnatural accumulation that caused the injury.[24] The same result was reached when an individual slipped on a wet floor.[25] In another case, failure to supervise a school employee that pulled a table out from under a spectator while attending a wrestling match was not a failure to correct a dangerous condition. The employee's act alone caused the injury; therefore, it did not fall under the Tort Claims Act.[26]

Supervision

The courts have held that "condition" and "care, custody or control" implies physical defect, not supervision.[27] Liability, therefore, does not exist where an injury occurs as a result of faulty supervision or instruction.[28] Even failing to show up for cheerleading practice where injuries were sustained by a student in a school parking lot was held to be exempt from liability.[29] Similar decisions were handed down in incidents where a student was stabbed to death by another student in study hall,[30] where a student sustained an eye injury by another student while a teacher was momentarily absent from a fifth-grade classroom to monitor the return of a class from recess;[31] where a student was injured at the hands of another student;[32] and where a student was stuck in the eye by a pencil thrown by another student.[33] School districts were not precluded from raising immunity as an issue where a middle-school student was injured when she fell down steps while blindfolded due to an Iranian hostage simulation exercise. Since the injury was not due to unsafe conditions relative to the steps, but rather the teacher's supervision, immunity was upheld.[34] In another case, when a chemistry teacher failed to take proper safety precautions and dropped a chemical beaker that splashed flaming fluid on a student's face, immunity also precluded recovery![35]

Recent cases involving extra-curricular activities reveal the same results. A student hit in the head by a line drive off the bat of the coach while rounding the bases was not interpreted as falling under the real property exception of the Tort Claims Act. The accident was not due to care, custody or control of real property but rather the action of the coach.[36] Likewise, recovery was not permitted for injuries sustained in a district-sponsored race because the negligence was related to the conduct of the district employee supervising the race and not a defect of the land itself.[37]

Even the drowning of a mentally retarded youngster in an unsupervised swimming pool yielded no recovery for the plaintiff.[38]

Foreseeability

Another element of care, custody and control of school grounds is foreseeability.[39] Generally, schools are not liable for unforeseen violent criminal acts by persons from the outside or from within the school.

Injuries perpetrated by outsiders are difficult to foresee. One school district was immune from prosecution where it failed to prevent a trespasser from entering the school and raping a mentally retarded minor in the rest-room.[40] Another school's failure to provide police protection was not sufficient to establish liability even when a student was fatally stabbed in the hallway.[41] Recently, litigation involving an employee's attempt to recover damages had the same result. Even action brought forth by an assistant principal who was sexually assaulted in an unlocked room by an unknown assailant was dismissed citing governmental immunity.[42]

Recovery for damages caused by perpetrators from within the school has been similarly interpreted. School officials were held immune from prosecution when a fifteen (15) year-old student died from injuries suffered in a beating that occurred in the hallway between classes.[43] And, since there is no custodial relationship creating an affirmative constitutional duty to protect students from other students, schools are not liable for unforeseen assaults and harassment[44] or sexual molestation.[45] Arguably, since *T.L.O. v. New Jersey* extended students' rights to privacy citing the school's responsibility to maintain control and discipline, an avenue may be left open to incur liability for supervision or lack of it. Recent cases involving sexual harassment reflect a softening by the courts in this area.

The element of foreseeability has been established in a number of cases. A school was held liable when a student was cut by a circular saw in Industrial Arts class because the guard had been removed from the saw earlier in the semester.[46] The saw was anchored and the injury was deemed foreseeable since the instructor and the school were aware of the lack of a safety guard. Although a vaulting horse is not considered real property, the landing surface around a vaulting horse is. Since adequate matting is a necessary element to the hardwood floor of a gymnasium, injuries sustained as a result of a failure to provide it are foreseeable making the school liable.[47] Finally an 11-year-old elementary student who sustained an injury while playing hockey by receiving a blow to the mouth by another student's hockey stick recovered damages. The school was held liable because the physical education instructor was aware of such dangers and had made repeated requests for safety equipment, all of which went unfulfilled.[48]

Additional Concerns

State-Created Danger

Case law has taken a turn in recent years to ascribe liability to school districts for what has been called "state-created danger" based on an affirmative duty to protect students from harm. Cause of action under the state-created danger theory is different from tort law where proof of the elements of negligence is required: duty, standard of care, injury and proximate cause. The concept took form in 1989 in *Deshaney v. Winnebago County Department of Social Services*[49] where the United States Supreme Court addressed an interesting set of facts. The Winnebago County Department of Social Services failed to remove a child from the custody of his father who repeatedly physically abused him. When the child was rendered permanently brain damaged and profoundly retarded after a severe beating, the mother sued the agency for violating the child's Fourteenth Amendment substantive due process rights. The *Deshaney* court decided that there was no affirmative duty on the part of the state to prevent private attacks; however, "while the state may have been aware of the dangers...*it played no part in their creation* (my italics)." This suggestion gave birth to the state-created danger theory.

The United States Supreme Court has yet to hear a case based on state-created danger. However, personal injury under the theory of state-created danger has been sustained as a cause of action using two lines of reasoning. The first line of reasoning was offered by the Third Circuit in the form of a four-part test.[50] For a state-created danger to exist:

1.) The harm must be foreseeable and direct. This may include such things as equipment in need of repair, students with a known propensity for aggression, failure to get a background check, hazing, and allowing unsafe conditions to exist.

2.) The "state" must act with willful disregard for the safety of the plaintiff. This implies that some knowledge was present, yet the condition was ignored.

3.) A relationship must exist between the "state" and the plaintiff. This does not necessarily mean a full custodial relationship. Just being a student or an employee would suffice.

4.) The "state" must create an opportunity for the third party crime to occur. This means that the injury could not have occurred without it.

The facts in two recent cases speak for themselves. In *Maxwell v. The School District of Philadelphia*,[51] a special education student was assaulted and raped in the classroom behind a chalkboard while the classroom was locked and a teacher was present. The teacher knew that the same assailants attacked the girl earlier yet told students that she didn't care what they did as long as they didn't bother her. While not as shocking as *Maxwell*, *Sciotto v. Marple-Newton School District*[52] addressed a spinal cord injury that resulted in paralysis when a student wrestled an alumnus who was heavier and more experienced creating foreseeable harm. Furthermore, the coaches displayed deliberate indifference with respect to the mismatch by creating the opportunity for danger by condoning a tradition of alumni matches.[53]

The second basis for claims under the state-created danger theory was identified in the Tenth Circuit. In two cases that survived preliminary motions to dismiss by the defendants, the courts took the four elements developed in the Third Circuit and added a fifth, namely, that the conduct of the state must be so ill conceived as to shock the conscience. Both cases involved students with disabilities. In *Armijo v. Wayon Mound Public Schools*[54], the school was found to have acted in conscious disregard when it suspended a student who had known suicidal tendencies and, without parental notification, drove him to an empty house where he had access to weapons. In *Sutton v. Utah State School for the Blind*,[55] a blind student was repeatedly sexually assaulted. The principal's failure to take any action was construed as deliberate indifference at a level that would shock the conscience.

While there is no clear conclusion to be drawn from the few cases that have been brought under the state-created danger theory, schools should be aware of the potential liability that may exist.

Civil Rights, Section 1983

In addition to the Political Subdivision Tort Claims Act, there are a number of other legal avenues establishing liability. Liability for a school district's actions may be sought under 42 U.S.C. Section 1983. Under Section 1983, liability exists for government officials whose actions deprive persons of "any rights, privileges, or immunities secured by the Constitution." Until recently, recovery for a violation of one's civil rights in personal security under Section 1983 seemed unlikely.[56] However, recent court decisions involving sexual abuse illustrate a new trend. In New York, affirmative duty to protect students was established by a state law requiring schools to supervise activities. Since this law created liability for "foreseeable injuries" due to a lack of supervision, recovery was granted to a third grader who was sexually assaulted by two older students who were previously involved in other incidents.[57]

The United States Supreme Court has also dealt a blow to the "good faith" immunity under Section 1983 for school (government) officials. *Crawford-El v. Briton*[58] rejected the "clear and convincing evidence" rule adopted by the District of Columbia federal appeals court. This will make it more difficult for public officials to have lawsuits thrown out on the basis of qualified immunity.

The number of sexual abuse charges in public schools has grown in recent years. Chapter 17, "Sexual Harassment," addresses the problem more completely in the context of Section 1983 and Title IX.

Child Abuse

Child abuse is another area of potential liability for educators. In Pennsylvania, the law mandates the reporting of child abuse cases by certain professionals, including teachers. Additionally, there are criminal penalties provided for failure to report suspected abuse. However, immunity is granted from criminal and civil liability for those who, in good faith, erroneously report instances of abuse. A case in point involved a high school counselor and social worker that reported child abuse. Good faith was presumed under the Pennsylvania Child Protective Services Law and since they were acting within the scope of their professional duties, they were entitled to qualified immunity.[59] Not only do teachers enjoy "good faith" immunity from erroneous reports, they do not fall under the definition of "a person responsible for a child's welfare" under the Child Protective Services Law except where the abuse is sexual in nature. Unless sexual abuse is charged, remedy must be sought in civil tort law or teacher dismissal proceedings.[60]

Recreational Facilities

Various state laws such as Pennsylvania's Recreation Use of Land and Water Act (RULWA), have resolved questions concerning the public's unsupervised access and use of school grounds during off-school hours. Liability may exist for school districts that negligently maintain land, buildings, structures, and other things on the premises of playgrounds, ball fields, or other recreational facilities. RULWA limits the school's duty to protect those who use the land free of charge from potential hazards. Liability exists only when there is "willful or malicious failure to guard or warn about a dangerous condition, use, structure, or activity.[61]

RULWA has been applied to softball fields and bleachers,[62] playgrounds and sliding boards,[63] and lacrosse fields.[64] As recreational access to school property has increased, schools have had to pay particular attention to maintaining and securing their facilities from hazardous use.

Consent Forms

Consent forms may or may not be a valid release of a school district's liability. Some jurisdictions have upheld the contractual nature of such forms,[65] while others have not.[66] The nature of the activity and the wording on the consent form determines the validity of the form in those jurisdictions that release the school district from liability. Title, content and appearance must be such that informed consent results from its use. That is, the consent form must provide sufficient information to permit the person signing the form to make a legitimately free choice. The signer must be competent and fully understand the nature of the action.[67] Students are generally not considered legally competent to give consent.

Some jurisdictions have held that consent forms violate public policy because schools owe a duty to the public for the safety and well being of the children under their care. A Washington state court established a six-factor test to determine whether an exception exists.[68] The greater the number of factors that apply in any given situation increases the likelihood that the consent form will be rendered invalid:

218

1. The agreement involves an activity generally accepted as suitable for public regulation.

2. The party released from liability is performing a service of great public importance.

3. The activity is held open to any member of the public (within certain established standards).

4. The party seeking release from liability has decisive bargaining advantage. The consent form is standardized such that it makes no provision for accommodating individual circumstances.

6. The person signing the consent form is placed under the control of the party seeking release from liability.

Even where consent forms are not supported in law, the act of signing one may be used to ascertain the signer's assumption of the risk,[69] one of the legal defenses to the claim of negligence.[70]

Implications

<u>Teachers and Administrators</u>:

- Teachers who drive students in their own vehicles are personally liable. The school is not.

- To avoid the potential liability for unsupervised access to school district recreation facilities, districts must inspect, maintain, and promptly repair hazardous conditions that appear.

- School districts have qualified immunity under the law. In order to establish liability, cause of action must fall within the eight categories outlined in the Political Subdivisions Tort Claims Act or other relevant legislation.

- Once a cause of action is established, all of the elements of negligence must be proved. If any of the elements are missing, the charge of negligence will not be sustained by the courts.

- Understand the potential for liability under the state-created danger theory. Be proactive and adopt a policy to eliminate dangers as well as train staff to recognize problems.

- Teachers enjoy "good faith" immunity from erroneous child abuse reports.

<u>Parents and Students</u>:

- It is not an easy matter to obtain recovery for injuries sustained at school as a result of negligence. Schools have limited liability. Intentional acts, however, are always actionable.

- It is difficult to establish liability for unforeseeable intentional acts by a third party, i.e. student-to-student.

- Although corporal punishment is legal in Pennsylvania, excessive corporal punishment may incur liability as a violation of Section 1983.

- Courts are more likely to support claims against teachers who perpetrate injury to students, especially when the harm is sexual.

- Schools are liable for reporting instances of sexual abuse and/or harassment by teachers. Furthermore, schools must take action to stop it or face charges of liability for their failure to do so.

Chapter 16 Endnotes

[1] Molitor v. Kaneland Community Unit School District No. 302, 163 N.E.2d 89, 18 Ill.2d 11 (1959).

[2] Ayala v. Philadelphia Board of Education, 305 A.2d 877, 453 Pa. 584 (1973).

[3] Shedrick v. William Penn School District, 654 A.2d 163 (Pa. Cmwlth. 1995).

[4] Singer by Singer v. School District of Philadelphia, 513 A.2d 1108 (Pa. Cmwlth. 1986).

[5] Knudsen v. Delaware County Regional Water Quality Control Authority, 478 A.2d 533, 84 Pa. Cmwlth. 36 (1984); Brown v. Quaker Valley School District, 486 A.2d 526, 86 Pa. Cmwlth. 496 (1984).

[6] Magill v. Appalachia Intermediate Unit 08, 646 F. Supp. 339 (W.D. Pa. 1986).

[7] Acker v. Spangler, 500 A.2d 206, 92 Pa. Cmwlth. 616 (1985).

[8] Merritt v. Board of Education of School District of Philadelphia, 513 A.2d 504 (Pa. Cmwlth. 1986).

[9] Gilbert v. School District of Philadelphia, 511 A.2d 258 (Pa. Cmwlth. 1986).

[10] Staub v. Southwest Butler County School District, 398 A.2d 204, 263 Pa. Super. 413, affirmed 413 A.2d 1082, 489 Pa. 196 (1979).

[11] Davies v. Barnes, 503 A.2d 93 (Pa. Cmwlth. 1986).

[12] Capuzzi v. Heller, 125 Pa. Cmwlth. 678 (1985).

[13] McKee v. Southeast Delco School District, 512 A.2d 28, 354 Pa. Super. 433 (1986).

[14] Love v. City of Philadelphia, 518 Pa. Cmwlth. 370 (1988); White v. School District of Philadephia, 553 Pa. 214 (1998).

[15] Aberant v. Wilkes-Barre Area School District, 492 A.2d 1186 (Pa. Cmwlth. 1985).

[16] McCloskey by McCloskey v. Abington School District, 515 A.2d 642 (Pa. Cmwlth. 1986).

[17] Lowman by and Through Lowman v. Indiana Area School District, 507 A.2d 1270 (Pa. Cmwlth. 1986).

[18] Vince by Vince v. Ringgold School District, 499 A.2d 1148, 92 Pa. Cmwlth. 598 (1985); Brown, *supra*.

[19] Davis v. School District of Philadelphia, 496 A.2d 903 (Pa. Cmwlth. 1985).

[20] Gore v. Bethlehem Area School District, 113 Pa. Cmwlth. 394 (1988).

[21] Canon-MacMillan School District v. Bioni, 127 Pa. Cmwlth. 317 (1989); Brown, *supra*.

[22] Ayala, *supra*; Norwin School District v. Cortazzo, 625 A.2d 183 (Pa. Cmwlth. 1993).

[23] Gilson v. Doe, 600 A.2d 267 (Pa. Cmwlth. 1991).

[24] Finn v. City of Philadelphia, 645 A.2d 320 (Pa. Cmwlth. 1994).

[25] Shedrick, *supra*.

[26] Acker v. Spangler, 500 A.2d 206, 92 Pa. Cmwlth. 616 (1985).

[27] Ziccardi v. School District of Philadelphia, 498 A.2d 452 (Pa. Cmwlth. 1985); Tomlinson v. Board of Education, 583 N.Y.S.2d 664 (A.D.3d Dept. 1992).

[28] McCloskey, supra; Davies, *supra*.

[29] Messina v. Blairsville-Saltsburg School District, 503 A.2d 89 (Pa. Cmwlth. 1986).

[30] Close v. Voorhees, 446 A.2d 728 (Pa. Cmwlth. 1982).

[31] Simonetti by Simonetti v. School District of Philadelphia, 454 A.2d 1038 (Pa. Super. 1982).

[32] Auerback v. Council Rock School District, 459 A.2d 1376 (Pa. Cmwlth. 1983).

[33] Robson v. Penn Hills School District, 437 A.2d 1273, 63 Pa. Cmwlth. 250 (1981).

[34] Mooney by Mooney v. North Penn School District, 493 A.2d 795 (Pa. Cmwlth. 1985).

[35] Usher v. Upper St. Clair School District, 487 A.2d 1022, 87 Pa. Cmwlth. 461 (1985).

[36] Lewis by Keller v. Hatboro-Horsham School District, 465 A.2d 1090 (Pa. Cmwlth. 1983).

[37] Farber v. Pennsbury School District, 571 A.2d 546 (Pa. Cmwlth. 1990).

[38] Nusheno v. Lock Haven University 574 A.2d 128 (Pa. Cmwlth. 1990).

[39] Vann v. Board of Education of School District of Philadelphia, 464 A.2d 684 (Pa. Cmwlth. 1983).

[40] Merritt, *supra*.

[41] Gilbert, *supra*.

[42] Portersfield v. City of New York, 573 N.Y.S.2d 681 (A.D. 1991).

[43] Guthrie v. Irons, 439 S.E.2d 732 (Ga. App. 1993).

[44] Elliott v. New Miami Board of Education, 799 F. Supp. 818 (S.D. Ohio 1992).

[45] D.R. v. Middle Bucks Area Vocational Technical School, 972 F.2d 1364 (3rd Cir. 1992).

[46] McKnight v. City of Philadelphia, 445 A.2d 778, 299 Pa. Super. 327 (1982).

[47] Singer by Singer, *supra*.

[48] Berman by Berman v. Philadelphia Board of Education, 456 A.2d 545 (Pa. Super. 1983).

[49] Deshaney v. Winnebago County Department of Social Services, 489 U.S. 189 (1989).

[50] Mark v. Borough of Hatboro, 51 F.3d 1137 (3rd Cir. 1995).

[51] Maxwell v. The School District of Philadelphia, 1999 WL 313764 (E.D. Pa. 1999).

[52] Sciotto v. Marple-Newton School District, 1999 WL 740691 (E.D. Pa. 1999).

[53] The case was settled in excess of $3 million soon after the court accepted the claim for adjudication.

[54] Armijo v. Wayon Mound Public Schools, 159 F.3d 1253 (10th Cir. 1998).

[55] Sutton v. Utah State School for the Blind, 173 F.3d 1226 (10th Cir. 1999).

[56] Davison v. Cannon, 106 S. Ct. 668 (1986).

[57] Shante D. v. City of New York, Board of Education Local School No. 5, 615 N.Y.S.2d 317 (1994).

[58] Crawford-El v. Briton, 000 U.S. 96-827023 0 (1998).

[59] Roman v. Appleby, 558 F. Supp. 449 (D.C. Pa. 1983).

[60] Pennsylvania State Educ. Assoc. v. Comm., Dept. of Public Welfare, 449 A.2d 89 (Pa. Cmwlth. 1982).

[61] 68 P.S. 477.6.

[62] Lowman v. Indiana Area School District, 96 Pa. Cmwlth. 3891 (1988).

[63] Zackhery v. Crystal Cave Co., 391 Pa. Super. 471 (1990).

[64] Seiferth v. Downingtown Area School District, 604 A.2d 757 (Pa. Cmwlth. 1992).

[65] Childress v. Madison County, No. WL-4269 (Tenn. App. 1989).

[66] Wagenblast v. Odessa School District, 758 P.2d 968 (Wash. 1988).

[67] Childress, *supra*.

[68] Wagenblast, *supra*.

[69] Tepper v. New Rochelle School District, 531 N.Y.S.2d 367 (App. Div. 1988).

[70] The defenses are:
1. Assumption of the risk
2. Act of God
3. Contributory negligence
4. Intervening variable

Chapter 17   Sexual Harassment

Sources:

> Title IX of the Educational Amendments of 1972, 20 U.S.C. 1681
> Title VII of the Civil Rights Act of 1964, 42 U.S.C. 2000(e)
> Civil Rights Act of 1871, 42 U.S.C. 1983

Sexual harassment is a form of discrimination. Even though it may be subtle, its impact is real. When sexual harassment occurs, the intent of the perpetrator is not the controlling factor. What matters is the effect that the questionable behavior has on the victim. It is judged from the victim's perspective, not from the perspective of the perpetrator.

Sexual harassment is defined by Title IX and Title VII of the Civil Rights Act of 1964, federal and state regulations, and litigation. Title VII addresses employment, while Title IX addresses discrimination on the basis of sex in educational programs and activities that benefit from federal financial assistance. Discrimination in the form of sexual harassment may range from words or actions that create uneasiness (innuendo and gestures) to direct sexual assault (forcible compliance).   The context of the misconduct is sex, but the impact on the victim is felt in degrees of intimidation. The intimidation may come from members of either sex.[1]

Sexual Harassment Defined

Sexual harassment is a verbal or physical act that is sexual in nature. It cannot be incited by the victim (unwelcome) and it must affect or alter the learning or work environment. Sexual harassment may be opposite sex or same sex harassment.[2] To be actionable in a court of law, a school district must know or should have known about the illicit behavior *and* failed to take effective action against it.

It is clearly established in law that schools may be held liable for compensatory and punitive damages arising from the sexual misconduct of its employees. In some jurisdictions this holds for student misconduct as well. Administrators should be aware that they might be personally held liable if they ignore or attempt to suppress alleged misconduct. The three components of sexual harassment are discussed below.

Sexual in Nature

Even a single incident can constitute sexual harassment. Coerced intercourse and forcible kissing are clearly sexual in nature.[3] However, treatment springing from arrogance or jealousy between members of the opposite sex may simply be construed as rudeness or ineptitude. As such, they would have no basis for a charge of sexual harassment. On one hand, calling a person a "jerk" or "jackass" is considered rude, but it would scarcely qualify as sexual. On the other hand, referring to a female as a "bitch," "sow," or "ho" would clearly have sexual overtones.

Unwelcome Behavior

Unwelcome behavior is behavior that is not instigated by the victim. In a school setting, the unwelcome behavior may be student-to-student or adult-to-student. If it is adult to student, the behavior is generally considered unwelcome due to the age and developmental difference between the two parties (even if the particular student invites or requests sexual attention).

If two students are involved, it is sometimes difficult to determine if the behavior is unwelcome. Claims of sexual harassment have fallen by the wayside when what initially appears to be objectionable was revealed to be reciprocal and invited, i.e., flirting, touching, and passing notes. Nonetheless, all claims of sexual harassment should be taken seriously.

Adverse Effects

Sexual harassment claims must have an adverse effect on the victim. In public schools, the misconduct must affect the learning environment in one of two ways: as a *quid pro quo* or by creating a "hostile environment." *Quid pro quo* literally means "something for something." This form of adverse effect exists when sexual demands are placed on an individual in return for some reward such as preferential treatment, grades, and/or some material consideration. Threatening to reveal damaging personal information can also be used to coerce compliance.

A hostile environment is created when the victim is intimidated by words or actions that interfere with his or her education. Most sexual harassment claims are the result of multiple occurrences of questionable conduct.[4] Indeed, the United States Supreme Court made it clear that a single inconsequential act or comment does not *per se* violate Title VII standards. The alleged harassment must be "so severe or pervasive as to alter the conditions of the victim's employment and create an abusive working environment.[5]

Sexual harassment may include psychological damage, even though it may not be severe.[6] Reasonableness is the rule. The Office of Civil Rights has stated that "relevant circumstances" should be considered when determining whether sexual harassment occurred. Things such as age, frequency, severity, scope, and context of the harassment are taken into consideration.

Sexual harassment manifests itself in a number of ways. It may come from teacher-to-teacher or superior-to-subordinate. An adult employee may also harass a student. Likewise, a student may sexually harass another student. For the purposes of this discussion, sexual harassment will include all three forms but will focus on the two areas that have created the most concern and controversy in public schools: employee-to-student and student-to-student. Both of these areas are fertile grounds for litigation, and the courts have granted sizable damages against a number of school districts.

Employee-to-Student

The determination of an employer's liability hinges upon whether the school knew or should have known about the existence of sexual misconduct. If, under normal circumstances, the school district was aware of sexual abuse or harassment and failed to act reasonably to curtail the misconduct, the school district will have established "a practice of custom or policy of reckless indifference."[7] In Pennsylvania, this notion was made clear in *Stoneking v. Bradford Area School District* where a female student was allegedly abused and harassed by the high school band teacher. Reckless indifference was confirmed when a pattern of events reflected previous complaints by other students, prior warnings to the teacher from the administration, and inaction on the part of the school district.[8] In *Stoneking*, the female student was made to apologize for her accusations before the entire band, whereupon, she exited in tears. The private records of the principal revealed that, on several occasions, the district instructed the teacher to remove the couch from his office and refrain from meeting alone with students. The case was settled confidentially by the school district's insurers ending litigation at the appeals level.

Liability for the sexual misconduct of an employee is not automatic. When the court could establish that a district acted promptly and efficiently where an employee was involved in sexual misconduct, the school district was not held liable.[9] Even when an appropriate, promptly conducted investigation exonerated an employee who was later found to be culpable, the court concluded that there was absence of "reckless indifference."[10] Of course, if the school district has no knowledge of misconduct, the result would be the same. In the Fifth Circuit, a second grader was repeatedly molested by a health teacher in a darkened classroom while showing films. The student told her parents, and the parents reported it to the child's homeroom teacher. Since the homeroom teacher failed to pass on the information to the school administrator, the appeals court overturned a jury verdict of $1.4 million against the school district holding that the district is responsible for employee conduct only if "management" is notified.[11]

Any kind of forced physical contact will be considered sexual harassment by the courts. Such was the case in *Franklin v. Gwinnett County Public Schools* where a teacher harassed a student by calling her at home, forcibly kissing her on the mouth, and coercing sexual intercourse.[12] Likewise, the courts will construe sexual advances, sexual comments, suggestive jokes and banter as harassment. Often, these actions are addressed under the state's Public School Code resulting in the dismissal of the employee for immorality or other statutory grounds. See Chapter 13, "Teacher Dismissal, Causes."

If the school district displays what the courts have defined as reckless or deliberate indifference, compensatory and punitive damages may be assessed under Title IX. The victim may recover against the perpetrator and/or the school district.

Punitive damages may also be available to the victim of sexual misconduct. Indeed, liability may extend to administrators who act with deliberate indifference. In *Doe v. Taylor Independent School District*, students were granted a constitutional liberty interest to be free from sexual molestation. Declaring that a "special relationship" exists between the school and the student by virtue of the state compulsory education laws, the court held that placing a child in school effectively prevents parents from acting on the child's behalf. The school, therefore, has custody. The court opined that the school owed the students an affirmative duty to protect them from the level of constitutional deprivation that results from molestation.

The *Doe* court formulated a test to determine when an administrator may personally be held liable:

1. The [administrator] learned of facts or a pattern of inappropriate sexual behavior by a subordinate indicating the subordinate was sexually abusing the student.

2. The [administrator] demonstrated deliberate indifference toward the student's constitutional rights by failing to take necessary actions to prevent or stop the abuse; and

3. Such failure caused a constitutional injury to the student.[13]

Actual notice to the school district is necessary to obtain damages under Title IX. The Supreme Court made it clear that damages require that an official must ..."at a minimum [have] authority to address the alleged discrimination and to institute corrective measures on the recipient's behalf, [have] actual knowledge of discrimination in the recipient's programs and fail to adequately to respond..."[14]

Student-to-Student

Student-to-student sexual harassment has had mixed results in the courts. On the one hand, the notion of liability for the wrongful tortious acts of a third party precludes recovery for sexual harassment by other students. In *DeShaney v. Winnebago County Department of Social Services*, the Supreme Court held that "the state has no constitutional duty to protect its citizens from private persons" barring a custodial relationship where the person is incapable of protecting him/herself.[15] In Pennsylvania, despite mandatory attendance and the *in loco parentis* authority of the schools, students are not held to be in state custody during school hours. Here, a female high school student was sexually harassed and molested by male students. The girl was forcibly raped in the locker area of the vocational classroom. In spite of claims that the instructor was lax in discipline, the court sustained the school's contention that it was not liable.[16]

The Fifth Circuit came to the same conclusion in a different line of reasoning. The court refused recovery for damages under Title IX for student-to-student sexual misconduct reasoning that federal law applies solely to recipients of federal funds -- the school district itself or its employees -- not to peers.[17]

In some jurisdictions, however, recovery has been granted based on the belief that school administrators and school districts have an affirmative duty to protect students. Take, for example, *Doe v. Petaluma*. *Doe* involved a female student who was sexually harassed by other students for a period of two years. During this time, the girl and her father notified the school counselor who failed to inform them of the district's Title IX grievance policy or report the misconduct to the school's Title IX officer. The child was forced to transfer to a private school and the parents sued, alleging a hostile environment, bodily injury, and mental as well as emotional distress. The court reasoned that, although Title IX claims are limited to intentional discrimination, the legal principle of *respondeat superior* might be applied. This concept of Agency Law suggests that a school district may be found to discriminate when one of its agents have done so.[18]

In *Burrow by and Through Burrow*, a female student was harassed continually by other students because she identified students who attended a party at her house and had done more than $1500 damages to the premises. She endured physical and verbal assaults: she was kicked between the legs, had her life threatened, was the object of repeated obscenities such as "whore," "slut," and "bitch," and had sexual obscenities written about her on her books, locker, and on the restroom walls. The district failed to respond to the student's complaint, characterizing the harassment as "students picking on one another." No one was punished, and the student was permitted to graduate early rather than endure the hostile environment. The court upheld a claim for damages against the district based on Title IX stating that there was enough evidence from which a jury may reasonably conclude "intentional" discrimination. However, the plaintiff's Section 1983 claim that the victim's equal protection rights were violated was dismissed. The court reasoned that neither the school district nor the administrators had an affirmative duty to protect the young girl from sexual harassment by her peers.[19]

Davis v. Monroe County Board of Education clarified the question of liability in a sharply divided Supreme Court decision. The Supreme Court ruled that school districts are liable when school officials know and are deliberately indifferent to sexual harassment "so pervasive and objectively offensive that it can be said to deprive the victims of access to the educational opportunities or benefits provided by the school.[20] LaShonda Davis was a victim of prolonged harassment by a fifth-grade classmate, G. F. Vulgar statements and repeated attempts to touch her were reported to the principal on numerous occasions. Notwithstanding these reports, no disciplinary action was taken. The incidents ended when G. F.

was charged with and pleaded guilty to sexual battery. LaShonda's grades suffered. She became unable to concentrate on her studies, and at one point had written a suicide note. At no time during the months of G. F.'s reported misconduct was he disciplined, nor was any effort made to separate G. F. and LaShonda. Furthermore, the Monroe County Board of Education had not trained its personnel on sexual hof established a policy dealing with such issues. It is clear that, while schools may be held liable for student-to-student sexual harassment, the legal standard appears to be high enough to keep every hallway or playground taunt from becoming a federal case.

Employee-to-Employee

The same set of standards applies to sexual harassment between and among employees. As an employment issue, it has implications for supervision with possible action to dismiss. See Chapter 13, "Teacher Dismissal, Causes." Sexual harassment also carries with it implications for liability for administrators who engage in such behavior or fail to act when they know or should have known that harassment occurred. The courts have declared that principals must take "some affirmative action" against perpetrators. [21]   If questionable behavior is reported, it should be investigated. Clear procedures should be established and followed.

Implications

<u>Administrators</u>:

- Sexual harassment must be sexual in nature, unwanted, and have an adverse effect on the learning environment.

- Actively pursue all complaints involving sexual misconduct. Document everything.

- Failure to act on student-to-student sexual harassment may result in liability for the district and/or individual administrator. Failing to act may be construed as deliberate indifference.

- Sexual harassment should be addressed in a district-wide policy by a designated Title IX administrator.

- Educate the entire school staff on procedures and consequences resulting from sexual harassment.

<u>Teachers</u>:

- Be sensitive to actions and words that offend students. It could result in the loss of your job and criminal prosecution.

<u>Parents and Students</u>:

- Report misconduct directly to an administrator, not to a teacher. This will put the school district on notice of alleged sexual misconduct.

- Students have a legal right to be free from sexual harassment. Report suspected misconduct immediately.

- Student-to-student sexual harassment will be grounds for liability if the school displays deliberate indifference to the plight of the victim.

- Know your rights.

Investigating Charges of Sexual Harassment

Consider every charge of sexual harassment as a serious matter. Actively pursue all complaints involving sexual misconduct and *document everything*. Keep in mind the elements of sexual harassment: that it must be sexual in nature, unwelcome, and have adverse affects on the learning environment. Once you have determined who will handle the claim:

I.   INVESTIGATE

Interview the alleged victim.
1. Obtain the identity of the alleged perpetrator(s).
2. Document the details of each and every allegation including time, place, and the names of witnesses.
3. Determine the circumstances surrounding the alleged incident, including the relationship between the victim and the accused.
4. Document the victim's response(s).
5. Establish the frequency and intensity of the alleged misconduct.
6. If the alleged victim is a student, contact the parents.

Interview the alleged perpetrator.
1. Question each of the allegations and allow for a response.
2. Ask if the conduct was unwelcome.
3. Establish the relationship of the parties from the suspect's perspective.
4. Assess the extent of the adverse affect on the alleged victim.

Interview witnesses.

II.   REVIEW

Review the documentation and consider any other pertinent records that may exist.

III.   ACT

Determine whether the behavior was inappropriate. If sexual harassment was present, take prompt, corrective measures in accordance with the school's discipline code. Inaction may be construed as "deliberate indifference" resulting in liability to the principal as well as the school district.

IV.   INFORM

Follow-up with the alleged victim (and parents, if (s)he is a minor).

Chapter 17 Endnotes

[1] Nabozny v. Podlesny, et al., 92 F.3d 446 (7th Cir. 1996).

[2] Oncale v. Sundowner Offshore Service, Inc., 523 U.S. 75 (1998).

[3] Sertik v. School Board of the City of Pittsburgh, 584 A.2d 390 (Pa. Cmwlth. 1990); Franklin v. Gwinnett County Public Schools, 112 S. Ct. 1028 (1992).

[4] Karabian v. Columbia University, 14 F.3d 773 (2nd Cir. 1994).

[5] Clark Couny School District v. Breeden, No. 00-866 (S. Ct. 2001).

[6] Harris v. Forklift Systems, 114 S. Ct. 367 (1993).

[7] Monell v. New York City Department of Services, 436 U.S. 658 (1978).

[8] Stoneking v. Bradford Area School District, 882 F.2d 720 (3rd Cir. 1989).

[9] Black v. Indiana Area School District, 985 F.2d 707 (3rd Cir. 1993).

[10] Colburn v. Upper Darby, 946 F.2d 1017 (3rd Cir. 1991).

[11] Canutillo Independent School District v. Leija, 101 F.3d 393 (5th Cir. 1996).

[12] Franklin, *supra*.

[13] Doe v. Taylor Independent School District, 15 F.3d 393 (5th Cir. 1994).

[14] Gebser v. Lago Vista Independent School District, 96-1866 (1988).

[15] DeShaney v. Winnebago County Department of Social Services, 489 U.S. 189 (1989).

[16] D.R. v. Middle Bucks AVTS, 972 F.2d 1364 (3rd Cir. 1992).

[17] Rowinsky v. Bryan Independent School District, 80 F.3d 1006 (5th Cir. 1996).

[18] Doe v. Petaluma City School District, 830 F. Supp. 1560 (N.D. Cal. 1993).

[19] Burrow by and Through Burrow v. Postville Community School District, 929 F. Supp. 1193 (Iowa 1996).

[20] Davis v. Monroe County Board of Education, et al., No. 97-843 (S. Ct. 1999).

[21] Nicole M. v. Martinez United School District, 94 F. Supp. 1369 (Cal. 1997).

Chapter 18   Equal Access

Sources:

>   The Equal Access Act, 20 U.S.C. 4071-74
>   First Amendment

The Equal Access Act was designed to ensure that secondary schools do not discriminate against, deny equal access to, or fail to provide a fair opportunity to students who wish to conduct a meeting within the definition of "limited open forum" on the basis of "religious, political, philosophical or other content of the speech at such meetings."

Not every opportunity for free expression falls under the Equal Access Act (EAA). Guidelines for student speech have been established by the courts over the years. See Chapter 5, "Free Expression." The EAA deals specifically with the right to assemble as a constitutional guarantee of an individual's freedom under the law.

Assemblage under the EAA does not include distributing materials or advertisements.   For example, students who distribute religious pamphlets cannot expect unregulated freedom to do so. School districts have the right to specify the time, place, and manner for the distribution of such material.[1]

Similarly, not every opportunity to meet in a school setting is considered unlimited. Schools maintain control over their facilities in certain situations. However, if a school district chooses to establish a "public forum," it must abide by the guidelines set forth by the EAA.

Schools are deemed to have a limited open forum when they "offer an opportunity for non-curriculum related student groups to meet on school premises during non-instructional time." Non-curriculum related groups are distinguishable from curriculum-related groups.

Curriculum-related groups are under the control of the school district and may be created or dissolved as the district sees fit. Groups are curriculum related if they fall into one of three categories: 1.) a group whose participation is required for a particular course or results in academic credit (i.e., a stringed orchestra that meets after school hours but results in a grade; 2.) A group whose subject matter concerns the body of a course or courses as a whole (i.e., Civil War Club); or, 3.) a group whose subject is actually taught, or will be taught, in a regularly offered course (i.e., a foreign language club).

Non-curriculum related groups are groups that do not "directly relate to the body of courses offered by the school."[2] Chess clubs along with coin and stamp collecting clubs have been considered non-curriculum related.

Religious Groups

Religious groups are clearly non-curriculum related and, therefore, meet under the EAA guidelines. In 1981 a state university was not permitted to exclude a student religious group from using school facilities.[3] Nine years later, the ruling was applied to public high schools in *Westside v. Mergens*.

The issue in *Mergens* addressed the application of the EAA to permit a student-initiated religious group to meet at a public secondary school. Here, a student requested permission to form a Christian club having the same privileges and meeting on the same terms as other student groups with the exception of a faculty sponsor. The purpose of the club was to permit reading and discussion of the Bible, promote fellowship, and group prayer. Membership would be voluntary and open to all students regardless of religious affiliation. The school denied the student permission to form the club because the school policy required all student clubs to have a faculty sponsor. The administration felt that a religious club at the school would violate the Establishment Clause of the United States Constitution. The *Mergens* Court ended the division that existed in the lower federal courts.[4]

Mergens found many Westside student clubs to be non-curriculum related. Accordingly, the Westside Community Schools maintained a limited open forum under the EAA forbidding discrimination against the club based on its religious content. The Court opined that when a forum for free expression is created, the government (in this case a public school) is not permitted to pick and choose who speaks or what is spoken.

The impact of *Mergens* is felt in subsequent cases. One school district was forced to rent a high school auditorium to a church for the purpose of holding a baccalaureate service. Another was forced to rent school facilities to a non-profit religious organization for a Christmas dinner. In the former, the district had adopted a policy prohibiting prayer at a school function. However, since the school district had established a public forum, its disassociation from the baccalaureate service was sufficient to prevent it from violating the Establishment Clause.[5] The latter instance held that the school district's attempt to exclude the dinner was based on the content of the members' speech in a public forum.[6]

The EAA was pitted against a state constitution when a Christian club was denied the permission to meet on school property in Idaho. Even though the constitutional provision prohibited the use of public school classrooms for religious purposes, when a federal law is made pursuant to the United States Constitution and the state law is in conflict, the federal law will prevail. In this case the federal law did not merely permit access (which would allow the state to restrict the activity), it mandated access (which prohibits the state's control over the activity).[7] The Ninth Circuit concurred.[8]

Mergens was controlling in the Eighth Circuit when a school district changed its policy to exclude a nondenominational religious club that had been meeting for four years. The amended school policy was a result of complaints received from several district residents and it contained provisions to allow scouts and athletic teams to continue to use school facilities. The court held that the club was denied access under the EAA based on its religious nature. Therefore, the policy was unconstitutional because it discriminated on the basis of content.[9]

Still, the Supreme Court rejected an appeal from the Second Circuit that the schools may restrict access if they maintain reasonable guidelines establishing a limited public forum.[10] Most recently, however, the Court in *Good News Club v. Milford Central School* upheld a religious group's request to use school facilities to conduct weekly after-school meetings based on the reasoning that the district had exercised viewpoint discrimination in denying access.[11]

Non-Religious Groups

Some non-religious (secular) groups are non-curricular as well. They enjoy the same access as religious groups under the law. For example, a speaker from the Nation of Islam was permitted to speak at a school fund-raiser held at a Detroit high school despite his religious affiliation because the message was secular.[12] Indeed, "the mere disagreement...with the group's philosophy affords no reason to deny it recognition."[13] The EAA seeks to insure equal treatment, not preferred treatment. In an Illinois school district, the use of the facilities by the Boy Scouts, who affirm belief in God, did not constitute preference toward religion because school facilities were available to them. Their acknowledgment of the deity did not make them religious; furthermore, they were permitted to use school facilities because the facilities were available to all non-curriculum related groups on a first-come first-served basis.[14]

Schools may not pick and choose among student groups based on ideology. This applies to groups promoting peace[15] as well as gay and lesbian groups.[16] "Conduct may be prohibited or regulated, within broad limits. But government may not discriminate against people because it dislikes their ideas."[17]

School districts are not obliged to create limited public forums. They do so when they allow non-curriculum related groups to meet. Once established, the school district may not discriminate against any student group that elects to meet based on the content of free expression.[18]

General Considerations

The EAA describes a "fair opportunity" to meet in a public forum as a uniform guarantee of certain conditions and assurances by the school.

Conditions

Certain conditions must be met if a meeting is to be considered valid under the EAA. The first condition is that the meeting must be voluntary. This means that no coercive force can be exerted by the school or any requirement to attend be placed by the school to attend such a meeting.

The second condition is that the meeting must be student-initiated. Student-initiated means that there can be no sponsorship or faculty supervision.[19] That is to say, school employees may not participate or direct such a meeting. A school employee may be present in a "custodial," not participatory, capacity. If the school employee's presence is required under school policy, it may be only for the purpose of maintaining order and discipline.

Non-school persons may not conduct, direct, or regularly attend such meetings. And, although sponsorship guidelines are strict, using the school media to advertise such a meeting does not constitute sponsorship. Students may use the public address system, bulletin boards or school newspapers to announce the proposed meeting times and places.

The third condition is that the meeting must be held within the bounds of local control in preserving discipline and the educational environment. Disciplinary control and the school's authority to "maintain order and discipline on school premises" and "to promote the well-being of students and faculty" are permitted under EAA. The approval of other students in the school system is not necessary. Therefore, meetings that might create dangerous situations or disrupt the school may be subject to control even though some students think otherwise.

Assurances

A meeting falls within the guidelines of the Equal Access Act if certain assurances are made:

1. The school must not influence or require participation in any form of prayer.

2. The district may not expend public funds beyond "incidental costs." Congress' debate suggests that paying a teacher to monitor in a non-participatory, custodial capacity is considered incidental. Duplicating costs for advertising such meetings are also incidental.

3. If school policy requires "custodial" attendance by school employees, the employees may not be forced to do so contrary to their personal beliefs.

4. Schools may not specify the numerical size of the group that wishes to use the school facilities to restrict participation in any way. The district may only specify numerical size with respect to the facilities' capacity to handle the request for use.

5. The meeting or activity for which the school facilities are in use must not be unlawful or unconstitutional.

6. There must be a guarantee of equal treatment.

Implications

<u>Teachers and Administrators</u>:

- Schools are not obligated to create limited public forums. They elect to do so when they allow their facilities to be used by non-curricular groups.

- If non-curricular groups are permitted to use school facilities, the facilities must be made available to <u>all</u> non-curricular groups, religious or non-religious, including those that espouse unpopular ideas. To prohibit a group on the basis of the content of its free expression is unconstitutional.

- The EAA guidelines are clear. Policies should reflect the conditions and assurances required by law.

<u>Parents and Students</u>:

- Student-initiated religious groups, although non-curricular, have a right to use school facilities for their meetings.

- School employees may be present in a custodial capacity at non-curricular uses of school facilities for religious meetings if school policy requires their presence. However, non-school personnel may not conduct such meetings according to the EAA.

- Non-religious, student-initiated groups, such as gay and lesbian societies, have the same right to assemble and express their personal views as religious groups.

Chapter 18 Endnotes

[1] Thompson v. Waynesboro Area School District, 673 F. Supp. 1379 (M.D. Pa. 1987).

[2] Board of Education of Westside Community Schools v. Mergens, 493 U.S. 182 (1990).

[3] Widmer v. Vincent, 454 U.S. 263 (1981).

[4] Nartowicz v. Clayton County School Dist., 736 F.2d 646 (11th Cir. 1984); Lubbock Civil Liberties Union v. Lubbock Independent School District, 669 F.2d 1038 (5th Cir. 1982).

[5] Verbina United Methodist Church v. Chilton County Board of Education, 765 F. Supp. 704 (M.D. Ala. 1991).

[6] Grace Bible Fellowship v. Maine School Admin. Dist. No.5, 941 F.2d 45 (1st Cir. 1991).

[7] Hoppock v. Twin Falls School District, 772 F. Supp. 1160 (D. Idaho 1991).

[8] Garnett v. Renton School District No.403, 987 F.2d 641 (9th Cir. 1993).

[9] Good News/Good Sports Club v. School District of the City of Ladue, Missouri, 28 F.3d 1501 (8th Cir. 1994).

[10] Bronx Household of Faith v. New York City Bd. of Education, 127 F.3d 207 (1997).

[11] Good News Club v. Milford Central School, 121 S. Ct. 2093 (2001).

[12] S.A.F.E. v. Detroit Board of Education, 815 F. Supp. 1045 (E.D. Mich.1993).

[13] Healey v. James, 408 U.S. 169 (1972).

[14] Sherman v. Community Consolidated School District 21, 8 F.3d 1160 (7th Cir. 1993).

[15] Student Coalition for Peace v. Lower Merion School District Board, 776 F.2d 431 (3rd Cir. 1985).

[16] Gay and Lesbian Students Association v. Cohn, 850 F.2d 361 (8th Cir. 1988).

[17] Id., at 368.

[18] Lamb's Chapel v. Center Moriches School District, 770 F. Supp. 91 (A.D. N.Y. 1991).

[19] Garnett, *supra*, Bender v. Williamsport Area School District, 741 F.2d 538 (3rd Cir. 1984), vacated on other grounds 475 U.S. 534 (1986).

Chapter 19 Discrimination

Sources:

> Fourteenth Amendment
> Title VII of the Civil Rights Act of 1964, 42 U.S.C. 2000e-2
> Title IX of the Educational Amendments of 1972, 20 U.S.C. 1681-86
> U.S. Department of Education Regulations, 34 C.F.R. 106.1-106.71

Discrimination exists in many forms in the public school setting. It affects both students and teachers with respect to their age, religion, ethnicity, gender, and race. Essentially, discrimination stems from a violation of the Due Process Clause of the Fourteenth Amendment in applying specific legislation such as the Civil Rights statutes, Title VII or Title IX. The issue of hiring teachers and maintaining an equitable working environment requires a basic knowledge of fairness under the law. See Chapter 11, "General Employment Considerations." Likewise, dealing with students on a daily basis cannot be done effectively without a fundamental sense of equity. See Chapter 1, "Activities," and Chapter 17, "Sexual Harassment". This chapter solely addresses race and gender.

Race

Racial discrimination has been addressed by the courts in a variety of societal situations; however, it has been contested most often in the arena of pubic education. All students have a right to equal protection against racial discrimination through the Equal Protection Clause of the Fourteenth Amendment. Schools, as governmental entities, are prohibited from fostering discrimination as a matter of constitutional principle. Since the Fourteenth Amendment applies only to state-sponsored discrimination, legislation has been enacted to address incidents of private discrimination. This legislation exists in the form of state and federal civil rights statutes as well as specific federal legislation designed to provide equity.

Defining Equality

In 1849, the Supreme Court of Massachusetts established the "separate but equal" doctrine creating legalized racial segregation in the public schools of Boston.[1] Declaring that it did not consider the races to be unequal *per se*, a black child was compelled to attend a black elementary school far from her home even though there were other "white" schools closer. The court reasoned that there are an "infinite variety of circumstances" in society that result in the separation of the races, and, as long as available facilities were equal, segregation does not automatically result in discrimination. In spite of the fact that in 1879 it upheld the rights of African Americans to sit as equals on juries,[2] the United States Supreme Court embraced "separate but equal" in *Plessy v. Ferguson*[3] in 1896. Faced with a challenge to local laws establishing separate railroad train car facilities for blacks and whites, the Court declared that racial integration is not constitutionally mandated as long as blacks and whites were treated equally. Thus, "separate but equal " became the law of the land. In 1927, the doctrine was applied to public schools in *Gong Lum v. Rice*.[4]

Not content with what was considered by many to be "bad law," the issue of legalized segregation in the form of "separate but equal" was attacked methodically. In a series of cases intended to establish a new judicial base for overturning *Plessy*, black lawyers trained specifically for this task by Charles Houston, dean of the Howard University Law School, began their assault on legal segregation.[5]

A new wave of litigation was brought before the courts with the support of the NAACP. In 1938, the Supreme Court declared in *Gaines v. Canada* that, even under the separate but equal doctrine, a state may not deny blacks admission to a "white" law school because no separate law school existed for blacks.[6] Here, the state went so far as to offer to pay tuition to an out of state institution for blacks. Both the student and the Court declined the offer. In *Sweatt v. Painter,* separate but equal was further eroded when Texas' segregated higher education system was declared unconstitutional in both tangible and intangible ways.[7] For the first time the Court recognized the inferiority of not only the facilities but the reputation of the faculty, the traditions, and the prestige. In the same year, *McLaurin v. Oklahoma* addressed the admittance of a black student to a "white" law school where he was required to remain apart from the other students. The plaintiff was assigned to a desk in the anteroom of the classroom, had to eat separately in the cafeteria, and even was confined to a particular section in the library. The Court concluded that "such restrictions impair and inhibit the student's ability to study, engage in discussion, exchange views with other students, and in general, learn his profession."[8] This set the stage for the landmark *Brown v. Board of Education* decision.

In 1954, "separate but equal" was struck down in *Brown v. Board of Education*.[9] After hearing arguments for two years, the Supreme Court concluded that "separate educational facilities are inherently unequal." (*Brown I*) The Court perceived the intent of the Fourteenth Amendment to prohibit segregation in public schools in spite of *Plessy*.   However, segregation was so pervasive in law and society that the Court found it necessary to charge state governments and the lower courts to act "with all deliberate speed" to eliminate it.[10] (*Brown II*)

Interestingly enough, *Brown* was decided almost simultaneously with another case, *Bolling v. Sharpe*. *Bolling* successfully challenged the validity of segregation in the public schools of the District of Columbia when black students were "refused admission to a public school attended by white children solely because of their race." The Court stated that "in view of our decision that the Constitution prohibits the states from maintaining racially segregated public schools, it would be unthinkable that the same Constitution would impose a lesser duty on the Federal Government."[11]

With these decisions, segregated school districts were required to become integrated and unitary.   Unfortunately, they were not given guidelines or conditions upon which to base their transformations. Not surprisingly, integration proceeded at a slow pace. Numerous plans were concocted to forestall the inevitable. One such plan involved the Little Rock, Arkansas, Public Schools. The Court ignored Arkansas' arguments and declared that integration must proceed in spite of the potential for social unrest and the state's attempt to revive Civil War claims of nullification. Constitutional rights were "not to be sacrificed or yielded to the violence and disorder which have followed upon action of the Government and Legislature." Furthermore, the "rights of children not to be discriminated against in school admission" may not be nullified openly or "through evasive schemes for segregation."[12] Another such "evasive scheme" was struck down when the Prince Edward's County, Maryland school system closed completely. Students were given vouchers to attend the now private schools where black students were selectively denied access. The Supreme Court declared that the time for "all deliberate speed" had run out.[13]

Delays in abolishing dual systems and establishing integrated schools were judicially terminated in 1969 with the Supreme Court's decision in *Alexander v. Holmes County Board of Education.* When the

Court declared that it was "the obligation of every school district...to...operate now and hereafter only unitary schools."[14] Lower courts dictated affirmative action to ensure compliance.

Types of Segregation

The pervasive nature of segregation can be viewed in an historical perspective that includes the existence of state and local laws as well as "natural" patterns of racial separation. *Brown* and its progeny have settled the issue of legalized segregation by declaring such laws unconstitutional. However, when segregation appears to exist through no act or intent of any governmental body, the courts are posed with the difficult problem of ascertaining whether official action is really the cause of the segregation.

De Jure. *De jure* segregation arises by law. Its existence is due to governmental action that establishes a pattern of separation of the races or permits such separation to occur. Prior to *Brown I* and *II*, the law of the land supported the concept of "separate but equal" with numerous state and local laws embracing segregation. When *Brown* declared all *de jure* segregation unconstitutional, the courts became the battleground for civil rights.

Originally, Jim Crow laws of the South were the targets in the effort to dissolve segregation. They were obvious and could be attacked with predictable success. However, in the North, there were no overtly discriminatory laws to speak of. Segregation in the North thrived on state and local legislation that appeared on its face to be racially neutral. The complex nature of determining segregation under these circumstances led to considerable litigation.

The courts have identified three elements to *de jure* segregation. The first element addresses whether segregation is openly supported or permitted by government action. If it is, governmental entities and/or agencies will be held to violate the constitution as per *Brown*.

The second element addresses the intent to discriminate. Official intent or purpose must be proven to establish that *de jure* segregation exists.[15] For example, Denver was ordered to integrate a public school system that "by use of various techniques, such as the manipulation of student attendance zones, school site selection, and a neighborhood school policy, created ...segregated schools."[16] The cities of Columbus and Dayton, Ohio were also instructed to implement affirmative action to correct segregation. The racially imbalanced public schools of Dayton had certain attendance zones that made provisions for allowing white students to transfer from integrated schools, and as a further manifestation of intent, the Board of Education actually rescinded the previous Board's voluntary desegregation plan.[17] The Court found that the public schools in Columbus maintained "an enclave of separate black schools" prior to and subsequent to *Brown*. In their opinion, this represented a "cognitive omission" on the part of the school board[18] creating *prima facie* evidence of intent. The courts determine racially discriminatory purpose by examining foreseeable consequences, circumstantial evidence, historical background, and specific sequences of events.[19]

A Pennsylvania example of court ordered integration is *Hoots v. Commonwealth* where a plan for reorganizing Allegheny County's five school districts resulted in four predominantly white districts (on average, 95.6% white) and one predominantly black district (63% black). When court testimony revealed that "race, indeed, was taken into consideration" to create the new plan, intent became a matter of record.[20] The plan was reworked and the Woodland Hills School District was formed.

The third element addresses the creation of or increases in existing segregation. If by action a board creates or measurably increases segregation, the net effect will be a non-unitary educational system that violates the United States Constitution. The measure of segregation is determined by such factors as student assignment, faculty, transportation, extra-curricular activities, and facilities.[21] Only unitary systems will be viewed by the courts to "no longer discriminate between children on the basis of race."[22] Anything less is unacceptable.

These elements and the criteria used to define *de jure* segregation continue to be the basis for litigation some 40-plus years after *Brown*.

De Facto. *De facto* segregation exists when racial separation occurs without governmental action or intent. It comes about as a result of a normal course of events that produces segregation. Because it is non-purposeful, it is not unconstitutional even though it appears to be the same thing as *de jure*; namely, racial minorities comprise the majority of a given school's population.

There is no duty to correct *de facto* racial imbalance. For example, one district provided materials to reasonably correct educational inequalities in a school system that had "naturally" segregated schools. In spite of efforts to integrate through litigation, the school was not required to racially mix *per se*.[23]

Even so, school districts have the <u>power to correct</u> racial inequity. The power to correct segregation usually flows through governmental entities created by state law. Human rights commissions are one type of governmental body with the general authority to oversee matters of equity and compliance with civil rights legislation. An example of the power of such commissions to address segregation occurred when the Supreme Court of Pennsylvania upheld the Pennsylvania Human Relations Commission's (PHRC) right to order the Chester School District to initiate plans to integrate.[24] The PHRC was further permitted to develop and impose a mathematical definition of segregation on the Uniontown School District.[25]

School districts themselves may elect to correct a racial imbalance without the prodding of a governmental agency. The district's authority to correct *de facto* segregation has withstood challenges in nearly all jurisdictions. Even when an attempt was made to place state limits on the voluntary actions of a school board through a statewide voting initiative it was struck down by the United States Supreme Court.[26]

Remedies

The United States Supreme Court has issued guidelines on remedying segregation in the public schools. First, the remedy should be commensurate with the nature and the scope of the violations. Second, the remedy should restore the victims to the position they would have occupied in the absence of discrimination. Third, the remedy must "take into account the interest of state and local authorities in managing their own affairs."[27]

The most prevalent and controversial remedy to segregation has been forced busing. In 1971, *Swann v. Charlotte-Mecklenburg* held that busing "is a permissible tool…to be considered in light of the objectives sought," namely, racial balance. It sustained a District Court order as "within the court's power to provide equitable relief" and "well within the capacity of the school authority."[28]

Milliken v. Bradley held that multi-district remedies are another legitimate way to address racial imbalance, especially where a single district is unable to accomplish desegregation or where *de jure* segregation exists in each and every school district involved in the remedy.[29] Even so, the Court cautioned against casually ignoring school district lines and engaging in a monumental consolidation without first establishing that racially discriminatory acts have been a substantial cause of inter-district segregation.

Integrating the faculty has also been successfully defended in the courts.[30] In Pennsylvania, racial quotas for the faculty were upheld in a case where four white teachers lost jobs due to the Philadelphia School District's attempt to meet conditions that made the district eligible for federal funds.[31] Even seniority rights have been overturned by the lower courts to achieve a racially balanced faculty.[32]

Ordering a tax increase to fund desegregation is not an acceptable remedy for segregation; however, requiring the district to raise a levy to fund the district's portion of a desegregation plan is.[33] The significant difference is that a court may not itself increase a levy. To do so would be an abuse of judicial discretion.

Activities

The Equal Protection Clause of the Fourteenth Amendment also ensures racial equality in school activities. Racial discrimination is subject to the same strict scrutiny in activities as in educational programs.

Gender

Gender discrimination has just recently become an issue in the public schools with challenges to provide equity in academic programs, athletics, and extra-curricular activities. The Constitution grants individuals rights to fair and equitable treatment under federal and state laws. The Equal Protection Clause of the Fourteenth Amendment applies to gender in much the same manner as race with one significant difference -- gender is not held to the same constitutional status as race. Racially-based court challenges must pass "strict judicial scrutiny" where the government must demonstrate a "compelling state interest" to enact legislation affecting race. Gender discrimination does not enjoy the same degree of scrutiny by the courts. In order to pass laws affecting gender, the governmental entity needs only to demonstrate that its actions are not "arbitrary or capricious." The United States Supreme Court established this "softened" status for claims of gender discrimination in *Reed v. Reed* where one state's intestate laws gave preference to men over women as estate administrators. [34] The law maintained that "men are as a rule more conversant with business affairs than…women." Although a plurality of the Court was willing to equate the equal protection of gender with race, other justices were not.

A clearer definition of the Court's position came later in *Craig v. Boren* when it held that "classifications by gender must serve *important governmental objectives* and must be *substantially related* to achievement of those objectives. [35] This placed the standard of judicial scrutiny for claims of gender discrimination squarely between the "compelling state interest" standard for racial claims and the conventional "rational relationship" standard.

Substantial Relation Standard

In order to trigger claims of gender discrimination, inequitable treatment must exist as a matter of policy and/or practice. Once the plaintiff establishes overt discrimination or preferential treatment of one gender over another, the burden of proof shifts to the government or school whose policy is being questioned. The rule or policy that results in the unequal treatment of males and females must have an important purpose or objective and be substantially related to carrying out that purpose or objective. This is the substantial relation test, and it is used to determine the constitutionality of all legislation or policies that result in claims of gender inequity.

Legislation

Title IX of the Civil Rights Act of 1964 (as amended, 1972) states: "No person in the United States should, on the basis of sex, be excluded from participation in, be denied the benefits of, or be subjected to discrimination under any educational program or activity receiving federal financial assistance." This encompasses all educational functions including testing, activities, and financial aid. If no federal funds are involved, there is no need to comply;[36] however, if federal funds are used in any capacity by an educational institution, Title IX would apply to the entire institution. [37]

Title IX establishes equal employment opportunities stating: "It shall be an unlawful employment practice for an employer … to fail to hire or to discharge any individual, or otherwise discriminate against any individual with respect to his compensation, terms, conditions, or privileges of employment, because of such individual's race, color, religion, sex or national origin…or deprive an individual of employment opportunities or otherwise adversely affect his status as an employee because of such individual's race, color, religion, sex or national origin." See Chapter 11, "General Employment Considerations."

Remedies

Title IX is enforceable through the Office of Civil Rights (OCR) for employees as well as students.[38] Individuals may seek private remedies to enforce Title IX[39] including punitive damages for intentional violations.[40] See also Chapter 17, Sexual Harassment.

Educational Programs

According to the Code of Federal Regulations, a person may not, on the basis of sex, be excluded from participation in, be denied the benefits of, or be discriminated against in the full range of educational services.[41] The prohibition from exclusion applies to course offerings including health, physical education, industrial, business, vocational, technical, home economics, music, and adult education classes. Grouping may be made on the basis of ability as assessed by objective standards. Sometimes, however, a single standard may have an adverse effect on members of one sex. When this occurs, other non-discriminatory standards must be adopted in its place.[42] If classes are disproportionately composed of one sex, action must be taken to correct the inequity. If there are disparities in how course materials are used or counseling services are implemented, the courts will look to the substantial relation standard.[43]

Single sex public schools have been challenged by both males and females. *Varchheimer v. School District of Philadelphia*[44] challenged the constitutionality of one such sex-segregated high school. A female student wanted to attend an all-male high school where all-female high schools of comparable quality already existed. The United States Supreme Court relied on the substantial relation standard to deny her claim of discrimination based on the restrictive impact that it would have on the school board's ability to make sound educational decisions. Since Philadelphia had numerous single-sex high schools of equal quality and prestige, the Court dismissed the plaintiff's "desire to attend a specific school based on its particular appeal" because to do so would have a deleterious effect on the system as a whole, forcing the closing of all public single-sex schools. The validity of post-secondary single-sex institutions has been upheld even in the case where a male student sought admission to a female nursing school.[45]

Activities

Equal opportunity must exist for members of both sexes in activities.[46] Separate athletic teams may be provided; however, where a team exists for one sex but not for the other, the excluded sex must be allowed to try out for the team[47] unless the sport is a contact sport[48] where appropriate fair standards may be applied so as to avoid discrimination.[49]

Unequal expenditures for male and female teams do not automatically constitute non-compliance with the law. Schools must provide adequate funding for teams of either sex as necessary. For more discussion on equality in activities and athletic programs, see Chapter 1, "Activities."

Harassment

Sexual harassment is clearly an act of discrimination. It ranges from words or actions that create uneasiness in the school environment (a civil rights violation) to direct sexual assault (a criminal as well as a civil rights violation). Harassment occurs student-to-student, employee-to-student, and employee-to-employee. Actions by students against teachers are equally forbidden and are generally considered criminal behaviors. Therefore, cause of action must be brought before a criminal, not a civil, court.

Sexual harassment is unwelcome sexual behavior that adversely affects the learning or work environment. Adverse effects exist *quid pro quo* when sexual demands are placed on an individual in return for favors. It also exists in the form of a hostile environment that adversely affects the victim in school or at work. A complete discussion on sexual harassment is presented in Chapter 17, "Sexual Harassment."

Implications

Teachers and Administrators:

- Equity in matters of race and gender must be maintained.

- Although the United States Constitution addresses civil rights in its Bill of Rights, it does not provide for remedies to discriminatory actions. The state and federal civil rights statutes establish the means to procure damages for civil rights violations.

- Schools have the power to correct *de facto* segregation but are not required by law to do so.

- Gender discrimination is not held under as strict a judicial scrutiny as racial discrimination.

- Schools, though not required to do so, may provide athletic teams for both sexes.

Parents and Students

- Racial and gender discrimination is against the law. Violations of civil rights are enforceable through appropriate government agencies.

- Compensatory and punitive damages are available for sexual harassment that the school knew about or should have known about.

- If a school does not have teams for both genders, the excluded gender has a right to try out for the team.

Chapter 19 Endnotes

[1] Roberts v. City of Boston, 59 Mass. 198 (Mass. 1849).

[2] Strauder v. West Virginia, 100 U.S. 303 (1879).

[3] Plessy v. Ferguson, 163 U.S. 537, 16 S. Ct. 138 (1896).

[4] Gong Lum v. Rice, 275 U.S. 78, 48 S. Ct. 91 (1927).

[5] This group included a young Thurgood Marshall who later rose to prominence as a civil rights defender *(Brown v. Board of Education)* and a Supreme Court Justice.

[6] Missouri *ex rel.* Gaines v. Canada, 305 U.S. 337 (1938).

[7] Sweatt v. Painter, 339 U.S. 629 (1950).

[8] McLaurin v. Oklahoma State Regents, 339 U.S. 637 '1950).

[9] Brown v. Board of Education of Topeka, Shawnee County, Kansas, 347 U.S. 294, 74 S. Ct. 686 (1954).

[10] Brown v. Board of Education of Topeka, Shawnee County, Kansas, 349 U.S. 294, 75 S. Ct. 753 (1955).

[11] Bolling v. Sharpe, 347 U.S. 497 (1954).

[12] Cooper v. Aaron, 358 U.S. 1 (1958).

[13] Griffin v. County School Board of Prince Edward County, 377 U.S. 218 (1964).

[14] Alexander v. Holmes County Board of Education, 396 U.S. 19 (1969).

[15] Keyes v. School District No. 1, Denver Colorado, 413 U.S. 189 (1973).

[16] Id.

[17] Dayton Board of Education v. Brinkman, 443 U.S. 526 (1979).

[18] Columbus Board of Education v. Penick, 443 U.S. 449 (1979).

[19] Diaz v. San Jose Unified School District, 733 F.2d 660 (9th Cir. 1984), *certiorari* denied, 471 U.S. 1065 (1985).

[20] Hoots v. Commonwealth, 672 F. 2d 1107)3rd Cir. 1982).

[21] Board of Education of Oklahoma City Public Schools v. Dowell, 111 S. Ct. 630 (1991); Swann v. Charlotte-Mecklenburg Board of Education, 402 U.S. 1 (1971); Green v. County School Board of New Kent County, Virginia, 391 U.S. 430 (1968).

[22] Columbus, *supra*.

[23] Deal v. Cincinnati, 369 F.2d 55 (6th Cir. 1966).

[24] Pennsylvania Human Relations Commission v. Chester School District, 426 Pa. 360 (1967).

[25] Pennsylvania Human Relations Commission v. Uniontown School District, 445 Pa. 52 (1973).

[26] Washington v. Seattle School District No. 1, 458 U.S. 457 (1982).

[27] Milliken v. Bradley, 433 U.S. 267 (1977).

[28] Swann v. Charlotte-Mecklenburg Board of Education, 402 U.S. 1 (1971).

[29] Milliken v. Bradley, 418 U.S. 717 (1974).

[30] United States v. Montgomery County Board of Education, 395 U.S. 225 (1969).

[31] Kromnick v. School District of Philadelphia, 739 F.2d 894 (3rd Cir. 1984), *certiorari* denied, 105 S. Ct. 782 (1985).

[32] Arthur v. Nyquist, 712 F.2d 816 (2nd Cir. 1983).

[33] Missouri v. Jenkins, 495 U.S. 33 (1996).

[34] Reed v. Reed, 404 U.S. 71 (1971).

[35] Craig v. Boren, 429 U.S. 190 (1976).

[36] Grove City College v. Bell, 465 U.S. 555 (1984).

[37] Id.

[38] North Haven Board of Education v. Bell, 456 U.S. 512 (1982).

[39] Cannon v. University of Chicago, 441 U.S. 677 (1979).

[40] Franklin v. Gwinnett County Public Schools, 503 U.S. 60 (1992).

[41] 34 C.F.R. 106.31.

[42] 34 C.F.R. 106.34.

256

[43] 34 C.F.R. 106.36.

[44] Varchheimer v. School District of Philadelphia, 430 U.S. 703 (1977).

[45] Mississippi University for Women v. Hogan, 458 U.S. 718 (1982).

[46] 34 C.F.R. 106.41.

[47] Force v. Pierce City R-VI School District, 570 F. Supp. 1020 (1983).

[48] 34 C.F.R. 106.41.

[49] O'Connor v. Board of Education of School District 23, 449 U.S. 1301 (1980).

Chapter 20   Students with Disabilities

Sources:

Section 504 of the Rehabilitation Act of 1973, 29 U.S.C. 794
Americans with Disabilities Act, 42 U.S.C. 12101-12213
Individuals with Disabilities Education Act, 20 U.S.C. 1400-1485

All children, regardless of handicap or disability, are entitled to an education. As special needs students, they have protected rights to a free and appropriate education in the least restrictive environment. Early court decisions established the entitlement of education for mentally retarded children[1] and stressed the importance of due process of law prior to identifying, excluding or terminating students' educational programs.[2]   The notion of exceptionality presently includes learning disabled, social and emotionally disturbed, gifted, and physically handicapped children.

Section 504 of the Rehabilitation Act of 1973 addresses discrimination based on handicap. It details a comprehensive plan for providing services and civil rights enforcement for individuals with disabilities. Its passage in 1973 resulted in litigation that not only secures equal treatment in academic programs but also in extra-curricular programs as well.   Under Section 504, school districts are required to make "reasonable" as opposed to "substantial" modifications in programs to accommodate the handicapped.   Modifications may affect curriculum and/or related services, including accommodations to the existing physical facilities.

The Americans with Disabilities Act (ADA) was patterned after the Rehabilitation Act of 1973. It provides that no qualified individual with a disability shall, by reason of the disability, be denied the benefits, services, programs, or activities of a public entity such as schools. It guarantees equal opportunity for individuals with disabilities and assures them of their civil rights.

With the passage of the Individuals with Disabilities Education Act (IDEA), handicapped children were assured of the due process necessary to secure and sustain a free and appropriate education. It has become the primary avenue for equal protection claims.[3] And, while the right extends to public school students, under IDEA '97, an eligible child who is voluntarily enrolled in a private or parochial school does not have an entitlement to special education and related service.[4]

Although the terms "inclusion" and "mainstreaming" do not appear in the text of the relevant legislation, the language of the statute ensures that removal of special needs students from the regular school environment should occur "only when the nature or severity of the handicap is such that education in the regular classes with the use of supplementary aids and services cannot be achieved satisfactorily."[5]

Sometimes it is necessary to pull the handicapped from the regular school environment. Even with the legislative safeguards in place, discrimination will not occur automatically if a person is excluded as a result of a disability. It is possible to exclude some students if it can be established that the sole reason for exclusion is not the handicap.[6] For example, a disability that prevents one from performing the minimum tasks necessary for a specific educational program may justify exclusion. In one case, hearing impairment was justified in excluding an individual from nursing training.[7] Exclusions of this sort have been sustained even in the face of affirmative action claims.[8] The courts continue to decide whether discrimination exists for the disabled on a case-by-case basis.

This chapter addresses the key aspects pertaining to special needs students in learning support, handicapped, and, in Pennsylvania, gifted education:

1. Right to an education
2. Evaluation
3. Appropriate placement: the least restrictive environment and individualized education programs (IEP's).
4. Related services
5. Records

Right to an Education

The responsibility for providing an appropriate educational program for a handicapped school-aged child falls upon the school district of residence.[9] To this end, states like Pennsylvania have established clear procedural guidelines governing the education of exceptional children.

States may choose to extend the right to an education to any class of citizen, thereby creating a legitimate entitlement to a public education.[10]

Special education services and programs are available to students with physical, neurological, and mental impairments including emotional disturbances, developmental delays, and specific learning disabilities. The special need may be single or multiple. In Pennsylvania, "gifted and talented" students are included in the special needs category since they, too, deviate from the norm in physical, mental, emotional, or social characteristics that require special education facilities and/or services.[11] The courts have held that if a state chooses to apply these procedural safeguards to the gifted, it is constitutional and solely a matter of state law.[12] Although Pennsylvania ensures procedural rights for gifted youngsters on par with those granted to handicapped students, not all substantive rights of the handicapped apply, such as placement in an approved private school.[13]

Under the IDEA, schools are required to make every effort to locate, identify, and evaluate children who are suspected of having a disability qualifying them for special education services. This applies to all children, birth through age 21, whether they attend a public school or not. Private or parochial school students must be informed that, should their child be enrolled in a public school, the school will develop an IEP (which provides a free and appropriate public education (FAPE).[14] The home-schooled setting is dealt with differently. The United States Supreme Court recently declared that children with disabilities who are home-schooled are not entitled to special education services under IDEA.[15]

The IDEA recognizes that the right to a free and appropriate public education (FAPE) terminates when a student graduates according to the IEP, either through the accumulation of credits or by accomplishing the goals as outlined in the IEP by age 21, as long as the IEP is followed and the requirements are consistent with the school district's graduation policy. The IDEA regulations further state that graduation is a change in placement[16] and thus requires prior written notice.[17]

Section 504 of the Rehabilitation Act of 1973 recognizes disabilities such as Attention Deficit Disorder (ADD), Attention Deficit/Hyperactivity Disorder (AD/HD), behavior disorders, chronic asthma, severe allergies, diabetes, physical handicaps, communicable diseases, and temporary handicapping conditions. These conditions are considered handicaps under the law if a student: 1.) has a physical or mental impairment which substantially limits one or more major activity, 2.) has a record of such impairment, or, 3.) is regarded as having such impairment. "Major activity" includes walking, seeing, speaking, breathing, learning, working, caring for oneself, and performing manual tasks. Such handicaps entitle a student to a modified educational program under contract with the schools to provide what the parents/guardians perceive as necessary instructional support for their child. Under Section 504, instructional accommodations are required without the full procedural requirements outlined in the Individuals with Disabilities Education Act (IDEA), namely, an evaluation, evaluation report (ER), and individualized education program (IEP).[18]

Technically, an AD/HD designation does not guarantee that all legislative criteria are met for services as handicapped or disabled. Accommodations are required, but without an IEP. Section 504 disabilities, such as AD/HD may be included under the IDEA as "other health impaired" if the child has a physical or mental disability, and, as a result of the physical or mental disability, the child is in need of special education. (This would include children with AD/HD who have specific learning disabilities.) Only a diagnosis of "other health impaired" would generate the full range of special education due process provisions including an IEP. The Supreme Court recently held in a related case that "it is apparent that if a person is taking measures to correct, or mitigate, a physical or mental impairment, the effects of those measures – both positive and negative – must be taken into account when judging whether that person is 'substantially limited' in a major life activity." This could have implications for students (AD/HD or other) who neglect to take prescribed medication. The language of the law is interpreted to mean that a person is limited "presently – not potentially or hypothetically."[19]

Evaluation

An evaluation must be conducted prior to assigning any student to a special education program. The evaluation should consist of testing, background information, and any information from outside evaluations.

IQ tests, as a rule, do not constitute substantial evidence[20] for eventual placement in a special program; however, such tests bear weight.[21] Evaluations are valid for two years. This includes evaluations done by independent evaluators and outside evaluations from private schools.[22] Standardized testing and the use of minimum cutoff scores have been held to constitute legitimate criteria for determining giftedness since academic scores and IQ are rationally related to identifying gifted students.[23]

Evaluations are the responsibility of the school district. However, if the parents elect to have the student tested privately, they assume the costs unless the assessment was done as the result of an evaluation disagreement.[24]

If exceptionalities are thought to exist, a request should be made. The school district must obtain permission to evaluate from the parents/guardians and advise them of their substantive and procedural rights under the law (procedural safeguards). When consent is granted to evaluate the student, the school district has 45 school days to complete the evaluation.

The comprehensive evaluation involves appropriate testing and recommendations by a multidisciplinary team consisting of the parent/guardian, teachers, and a school district representative. (The new IDEA requirements stress the need to include at least one regular education teacher in addition to the special education teacher.) An evaluation report (ER) must be completed by the school district within ten days after the evaluation; and it must be reported to the parent/guardian within five school days at an evaluation.

Once the special need is identified, an individualized educational program (IEP) must be developed within 30 calendar days. The IEP team must consist of the parent/guardian, regular and special education teachers,[25] and a representative of the school district.

An appropriate educational placement can only occur after the parent/guardian signs a Notice of Recommended Educational Placement (NOREP). This authorizes the school district to provide the necessary accommodations for the student. Once the placement is accepted and the NOREP is signed, the IEP must be implemented no sooner than five but no later than ten school days, unless the parents execute a written waiver indicating otherwise. It comes as no surprise that one court declared that a twenty-one month delay in implementation of an IEP was excessive and a violation of a school district's responsibility.[26] When there are delays in providing appropriate placement and services, school districts must report them promptly to the state.[27]

If a parent/guardian does not approve of the placement, (s)he may request a pre-hearing conference, mediation, or a due process hearing. In extreme cases, the results of the hearing may be appealed.

An appeal to the Secretary of Education is an option to a special education hearing. However, if an evaluation decision on a student is on appeal prior to a hearing, the decision of the hearing is final and not subject to review by the Secretary of Education.[28] In either case, the results of the hearing or opinion by the Secretary of Education may be appealed to the appropriate court of jurisdiction. In all cases, before the full range of procedural safeguards kicks in, there must be a diagnosis of each child's exceptionality and a determination made as to an appropriate placement.[29]

Appropriate Placement

An appropriate education is characterized as placement in the least restrictive environment where instruction and support services are designed to meet the unique needs of the handicapped (or gifted child) and are consistent with the goals of the I.E.P.[30] Placement of gifted children need only be rationally related to a legitimate school purpose to be upheld by the courts.[31] A district does not have to devise a program that makes "best use" of a student's abilities; it needs to develop programs appropriate to the needs of the child.[32] If parents feel that placement in an academic program is inappropriate after the standard procedural guidelines have been followed, the burden of proof is on the parents and not the school district.[33]

What is considered appropriate can be seen in light of the concept of education in the least restrictive environment (LRE). The concept of LRE was born in Pennsylvania with the *PARC* decision so that institutionalized children might maintain contact with and socially interact with normal children, thereby enhancing the mentally retarded child's opportunity to re-enter society. Institutionalization has not been held to be the LRE.[34] Indeed, it remains the final option to special needs placement.

In 1982, the United States Supreme Court decided *Rowley v. Hendrick Hudson School District* where the court declared that schools were not required to provide handicapped children with the "best" or "perfect" education, just a "ground floor" opportunity. The Supreme Court further emphasized that the education must "to the maximum extent appropriate" be with other children who are not handicapped.[35] The educational accommodation(s) must be meaningful, not minimal, even if other accommodations might prove to be superior.[36] Challenges to placements by school districts on these grounds have been numerous. However, as long as procedural guidelines were followed, the placements are generally sustained. Even a child's removal from the public school and subsequent progress in a private school did not suggest that an inappropriate placement occurred while the student was attending the public school.[37] The value of placement in the LRE in a regular school setting with non-handicapped students has been affirmed in subsequent litigation.[38]

School officials should keep in mind that if an alternative placement is appropriate, it must be made regardless of the financial implications to the school district.[39] The consideration of cost is irrelevant as a determinant to alternative placement if there is only one "appropriate" option. Cost only becomes relevant when there are a number of potentially appropriate placements.[40] Given more than one option, schools will generally choose the financially most prudent alternative placement.

The least restrictive environment (LRE) issue has been involved in a number of court cases. The standard was set in a 1989 decision by the Fifth Circuit, *Daniel R. R. v. State Board of Education*.[41] Here, the court outlined factors to consider when determining the least restrictive environment. The first consideration is whether the child can satisfactorily be accommodated in the regular classroom using supplemental aids and services. Can modifications to the regular classroom and/or the curriculum be made? What about the addition of an aide? Another consideration is whether placement in regular education will benefit the child beyond academics...in areas such as language development, behavior, and/or socialization. A third consideration is the potential harm that mainstreaming or inclusion might have on the child. Lastly, the placement of the special needs child must be considered in light of the potentially harmful impact that it might have on regular education students. For example, if a disruptive student consumes so much of a teacher or an aide's time so as to cause the educational process of the rest of the class to suffer, placement in another setting would be appropriate.[42] If the child can be educated in the regular classroom under the conditions set forth in *Daniel R. R.*, the child cannot be removed from the regular classroom placement.[43]

School districts and parents must keep in mind that education is not an all-or-nothing proposition. A pullout may be appropriate to some learning situations, and other learning situations may dictate inclusion. Partial inclusion or mainstreaming should always remain an option.

No student should have to choose between an appropriate education and emotional well-being. In a case where a student's parents refused to permit testing on the advice of the child's psychologist, the court upheld the refusal based upon the potential risk of psychopathology to the child. The child, who received special education services for a learning disability, speech impairment, and an emotional impairment, was on homebound instruction subsequent to hospitalization as a result of severe hazing by his classmates. Fearing a relapse, the parents maintained that the risk of harm to the child in returning to the school for a comprehensive evaluation violated his constitutional right to privacy. The court concurred.[44]

In 1993, *Oberti v. Clementon Board of Education* focused on the issue of LRE in terms of inclusion for all children with disabilities, not just mental retardation. The Third Circuit declared that school districts must consider placing children with physical disabilities in regular classroom settings with appropriate support mechanisms before considering any alternative placement.[45] Relying on *Daniel R. R.*, the court declared: 1.) the school's efforts to make a reasonable, honest effort to accommodate the child in the regular classroom is essential, 2.) the comprehensive educational benefit to the child in the regular classroom placement exceeds the benefit provided in a special education class, and 3.) the regular placement, with support mechanisms in place, cannot be destructive of the educational process of the regular education students. All efforts to sustain a child in the mainstream must be made before a child can be removed from the regular classroom setting (the least restrictive environment).

Thus, a free and appropriate education requires individual attention to the needs of each child,[46] the "best interests of the child,"[47] or the "recognized needs of the child."[48] The regulations do not require approval of a more appropriate program when an appropriate one exists nearby.[49]

Automatic placement based on a singular evaluative criterion will violate the law.[50] Likewise, parental preference alone is insufficient to warrant a particular placement.[51]

The essence of the educational program for special needs students is the Individualized Education Program (IEP). The IEP shall include statements concerning the present level of achievement, annual goals, short-term instructional goals, and specific educational services including related services. It must contain a description of the extent of participation in regular education as well as dates for initiation and duration of the program. The IEP must also contain objective criteria for evaluation. The IEP is critical. An IEP written in generalized terms without sufficiently recognizing the needs of the particular student is not legitimate. It must focus on the best interests of the student.[52] And as long as the IEP is "reasonably calculated to enable the child to receive educational benefits" at the time of its creation, it will be upheld.[53] Finally, although the IEP governs the delivery of educational services in any given year, a service identified in one year's IEP cannot be presumed to be automatic in subsequent years.[54]

Just how far a school must go to accommodate an exceptional student in an IEP has been a continuing subject of litigation. In a due process hearing of a severely mentally retarded child, parents contested a school district's determination that the student was ineligible for an extended school year (ESY) program. The school district was required to show substantial evidence that the proposed change was necessary.[55] However, it is clear that refusal to implement all or a portion of an IEP will result in a judgment against the district. An extended school year is not limited to children with "severe" disabilities. It must be considered for all children. Furthermore, factors other than regression and recoupment can qualify a child for ESY.

In Pennsylvania where gifted students are considered to be exceptional, two cases involving the IEP's are worth noting. In one case, the school district argued that conducting a state approved enrichment program is sufficient for gifted students. This, the school maintained, precluded the need for an individualized program. The parents countered that the program did not offer accelerated instruction in academic areas such as reading and math, subjects where the child was at least two years ahead. The enrichment program was a total of 150 minutes per week and the parents contended that their child wasn't gifted for 150 minutes. The child was gifted all week. The court upheld the parents' claim by holding that the existence of an approved enrichment program does not invalidate the school district's duty to provide an appropriate education for exceptional students.[56] In a more narrow view, another court upheld a school district's contention that a gifted student was not entitled to special math during the school year since he would have the equivalent math exposure in science and computer courses according to the IEP.[57] The court did not answer whether a district must provide courses in excess of the regular curriculum.

Disciplinary changes in placement for special needs students are addressed in Chapter 4, "Due Process."

Related Services

The term related services is defined in federal regulations as transportation and other "such developmental, corrective and other supportive services required to assist a handicapped child to benefit from special education." Existing facilities must be readily accessible and usable by those persons having a disability. School districts are required to make physical accommodations unless the accommodation(s) result in a fundamental alteration in the nature of the program or create undue financial or administrative burdens on the school. Structural modifications must be readily achievable and are made on an individual basis. If changes are required, the district must establish a transition plan that would include outlining the steps to achieve the accommodation and a schedule indicating completion.

Auxiliary aids and services must also be provided under the same criteria as structural accommodations. They must be readily achievable and not impose an undue financial or administrative burden or fundamentally alter the nature of the program. These services extend to providing a handicapped child with catheterization where the absence of such a service would prevent the child from participating in a regular public school program. [58] Catheterization, [59] sign language interpretation, [60] and tracheostomy services [61] are related services consistent with the requirements for an appropriate education within the school's educational capability and health service capability. In a 1997 case, parents successfully challenged a school district's contention that tracheostomy services are excluded from the definition of medical services under the IDEA. An Illinois court granted a preliminary order for the school district to provide a "competent adult" to perform the service as needed on a school bus as the student was being transported to and from school. [62] The United States Supreme Court settled the issue recently in *Cedar Rapids v. Garrett F*[63] where related services are defined as services that can be performed by someone other than a physician. For issues involving methodology, where there is a legitimate professional disagreement among experts, the school district is generally given the benefit of the doubt. [64]

Related services do not include teacher training in specific areas of competency. Parents are not permitted to insist on a teacher-training component for their special needs student even though one had been included in a previous IEP and subsequently dropped.[65]

Records

Maintenance and security requirements for the records of an exceptional child are essentially the same as those of a regular student. However, because of the sensitivity associated with special placement, there are some differences. Access to directory information (Category "A" data) is the same as for regular students requiring only representational consent. Likewise, the complete educational record (consisting of Category "A" and Category "B" data) requires specific consent. When the consent is legitimate for any given situation, access records must be maintained. They include: a record of each party and a date of access and purpose. No record of access is required for authorized employees of the school or agency, parents, or anyone having "proper consent" to review the educational records.

Proper consent is required for the exchange of oral information concerning special education students.

The question sometimes arises in the matter of grades. A report card may indicate that a student has been graded differently (i.e. "modified curriculum," or "modified content") when the curriculum or learning outcomes have been altered. This does not violate the student's right to privacy since the purpose of grade reports is to communicate with the family. A school, however, may not release information to an employer or post-secondary school (*vis a vis* a transcript) that indicates special education status without proper consent. See Chapter 14, "Confidentiality," for more details on who may access information and what constitutes proper consent.

Implications

<u>Teachers and Administrators:</u>

- Schools are required to make reasonable modifications in school programs for accommodating special needs students.

- The exceptionality of each special needs student must be diagnosed and a determination as to appropriate placement must be made on an individual basis.

- The entire IEP process should take no longer than 60 days: 45 days to complete the evaluation and 15 days to develop an ER and report it to the parents/guardians before collaborating to develop the program. Once a NOREP is signed, implementation should occur no sooner that five, or more than ten, school days.

- Due process is essential to any consideration of special needs services: the right to education, evaluation, appropriate placement, related services, and record keeping.

- A diagnosis of attention deficit disorder (ADD) or attention deficit/hyperactivity disorder (AD/HD) does not automatically qualify a child as handicapped. Accommodations must be made, but not to the extent of a full range of special education services or an IEP.

<u>Parents and Students:</u>

- A free and appropriate education requires individual attention to the needs of each particular child.

- Automatic placement by a school district based on a single evaluative criterion will violate the law. Evaluations must include comprehensive testing and pertinent background information.

- A parent's preference to a particular educational placement is, of itself, insufficient grounds for placement.

- Schools may consider cost when there is more than one option to alternative placement. If there is only one alternative placement option, cost cannot be a factor in the decision to place the child.

- Related services must be provided for special needs students as long as they are readily achievable and not impose an undue financial burden on the school district.

- Parents of special needs students may not insist that an IEP include specific training for teachers. Schools, however, may offer to provide such training.

Chapter 20 Endnotes

[1] Pennsylvania Association for Retarded Citizens v. Commonwealth, 343 F. Supp. 279 (Pa. 1972).

[2] Mills v. Board of Education of the District of Columbia, 348 F. Supp. 866 (D.D.C. 1972).

[3] Smith v. Robinson, , 79 L. Ed. 2d 304 (1984).

[4] Cyrex v. Ascension Parish School Board, 31 IDELR 54 (5th Cir. 1999).

[5] 20 U.S.C. 1412 (5) (B).

[6] Southeastern Community College v. Davis, 442 U.S. 397, 99 S. Ct. 2361, 60 L. Ed. 2d 980 (1979); Cavallaro v. Ambach, 575 F. Supp. 771 (W.D. N.Y. 1983).

[7] Timms v. Metropolitan School District, 722 F.2d 1310 (7th Cir. 1983).

[8] Davis, *supra*.

[9] West Chester Area School District v. Commonwealth, Secretary of Education, 401 A.2d 610, 43 Pa. Cmwlth. 14 (1979).

[10] Smith v. Webb, 420 F. Supp. 600 (D.C. Pa. 1976).

[11] Central York School District v. Commonwealth, Department of Education, 399 A.2d 167, 41 Pa. Cmwlth. 383 (1979).

[12] Student Roe by Roe v. Commonwealth of Pennsylvania, 638 F. Supp. 929 (E.D. Pa. 1986).

[13] This has been clearly demonstrated by the enactment of Pennsylvania's Chapter 16.

[14] 34 CFR 300.454.

[15] Hooks v. Clark County School District, No. 00-1261 (2001).

[16] 34 CFR 300.122(a)(3)

[17] 34 CFR 300.503.

[18] Lyons by Alexander v. Smith, 829 F. Supp. 414 (D.D.C. 1993).

[19] Sutton v. United Airlines, Inc., 119 S. Ct. 2139 (1999).

[20] Levy v. Commonwealth, Department of Education, 399 A.2d 159, 41 Pa. Cmwlth. 356 (1979).

[21] Silvio v. Commonwealth, Department of Education, 439 A.2d 893, 64 Pa. Cmwlth. 192 (1982).

[22] Student Doe v. Commonwealth of Pennsylvania, 593 F. Supp. 54 (D.C. Pa. 1984).

[23] Student Roe, *supra*.

[24] Kozak v. Hampton Township School District, 855 A.2d 641 (Pa. Cmwlth. 1995).

[25] Brimmer v. Traverse City Area Public Schools, 872 F. Supp. 447 (W.D. Mich. 1994).

[26] Pires by Pires v. Commonwealth, Department of Education, 467 A.2d 79, 78 Pa. Cmwlth. 127 (1983).

[27] Cordero v. Commonwealth of Pennsylvania, 795 F. Supp. 1352 (M.D. Pa. 1992).

[28] Muth v. Smith, 646 F. Supp. 280 (E.D. Pa. 1986).

[29] Frederick L. v. Thomas, 578 F.2d 513 (D.C. Pa. 1976).

[30] Clevenger v. Oak Ridge School Board, 573 F. Supp. 349 (E.D. Tenn. 1983).

[31] Student Roe, *supra*.

[32] Shanberg v. Commonwealth, Secretary of Education, 426 A.2d 232, 57 Pa. Cmwlth. 384 (1981).

[33] Fitz v. Intermediate Unit No. 29, 403 A.2d 138, 43 Pa. Cmwlth. 370 (1979).

[34] Halderman v. Pennhurst State School and Hospital, 673 F.2d 647 (3rd Cir. 1982).

[35] Rowley v Hendrick Hudson School District, 458 U.S. 176, 102 S. Ct. 3034, 73 L. Ed. 2d 690 (1982).

[36] Polk v. Central Susquehanna Intermediate Unit #16, 853 F.2d 171 (3rd Cir. 1988).

[37] Fuhrman v. East Hannover Board of Education, 993 F.2d 1031 (3rd Cir. 1993).

[38] Roncker v. Walter, 700 F.2d 1058 (6th Cir. 1983); Springdale School District #50 of Washington County v. Grace, 693 F.2d 41 (8th Cir. 1982).

[39] Ojai Unified School District v. Jackson, 4 F.3d 1467 (9th Cir. 1993).

[40] Creameans v. Fairland Local School District, 633 N.E. 2d 570 (4th Dist. 1993).

[41] Daniel R.R. v. State Board of Education, 874 F.2d 1036 (5th Cir. 1989).

[42] Clyde K. and Sheila K. v. Puyallup School District, 35 F.3d 1396 (9th Cir. 1994).

[43] Mavis v. Sobol, 839 F. Supp. 968 (N.D.N.Y. 1993).

[44] Andress v. Cleveland Independent School District, 832 F. Supp. 1086 (E.D. Tex. 1993).

[45] Oberti v. Clementon Board of Education, 995 F.2d 1204 (3rd Cir. 1993).

[46] Battle v. Commonwealth of Pennsylvania, 629 F.2d 269, on remand 513 F. Supp. 425, *certiorari* denied Scanlon v. Battle, 101 S. Ct. 3123, 452 U.S. 968, 69 L. Ed. 2d 981 (1980).

[47] Grkman v. Scanlon, 563 F. Supp. 793 (D.C. Pa. 1983).

[48] Centennial School District v. Commonwealth, Department of Education, 503 A.2d 1090 (Pa. Cmwlth. 1986).

[49] Krawitz v. Commonwealth, Dept. of Ed., 408 A.2d 1202, 48 Pa. Cmwlth. 155 (1979).

[50] Rowley, *supra*; Roncker, *supra*.

[51] Brougham by Brougham v. Town of Yarmouth, 823 F. Supp. 9 (D. Me. 1993).

[52] Grkman, *supra*.

[53] Fuhrman, *supra*.

[54] Board of Education of Downer's Grove Grade School District No. 58 v. Steven L. and Christine L., 23 IDELR 36 (N.D. Ill. 1995); Sioux Falls School District v. Koupal, 526 N.W. 2d 248, 22 IDELR 26 (S.D. 1994).

[55] Conway v. Wilburn, 488 A.2d 92, 87 Pa. Cmwlth. 611 (1985).

[56] Centennial, *supra*.

[57] Scott S. v. Department of Education, 512 A.2d 790 (Pa. Cmwlth. 1986).

[58] Tokarcik v. Forest Hills School District, 665 F.2d 443, *certiorari* denied Scanlon v. Tokarcik, 458 U.S. 1121, 102 S. Ct. 3508, 73 L. Ed. 2d 1383 (1981).

[59] Irving Independent School District v. Tatro, S. Ct. 3371, 82 L.Ed. 2d 664 (1984).

[60] West Virginia *ex rel.* Lambert v. West Virginia State Board of Education, 447 S.E.2d 901 (W.Va. 1994); Zobrest v. Catalina Foothills School District, 113 S. Ct. 2462 (1993).

[61] Neely v. Rutherford County Schools, 851 F. Supp. 888 (M.D. Tenn. 1994).

[62] Skelly v. Brookfield LaGrange Park School District 95, 968 F. Supp. 385 (Ill. 1997).

[63] Cedar Rapids Community School District v. Garrett F., (96-1793), 106 F3d 822, affirmed.

[64] Moubry v. Independent School District No. 696, 9 F. Supp.2d 1086 (D. Minn. 1998).

[65] Sioux Falls School District v. Koupal, 526 N.W. 2d 248, 526 N.W. 2d 248; (S.D. 1994).

NOTES

Chapter 21: Course Content and Instructional Materials

Sources:

> First Amendment
> Fourth Amendment
> Individuals with Disabilities Education Act, 20 U.S.C. 1400-1485
> Section 504 of the Rehabilitation Act of 1973, 29 U.S.C. 794
> The Civil Rights Act, 42 U.S.C. 1983
> The Hatch Act, 20 U.S.C. 1232h

Each state enacts laws that determine what must be taught in the public schools.[1] While mandated curriculum cannot be eliminated,[2] the courts generally reserve the right to determine methodology or techniques to the local board of school directors.[3] Courts have been liberal in interpreting the implied powers of local school boards in matters of curriculum. Historically, they view non-mandated curriculum as an administrative function of the local school board. Accordingly, no constitutional right is violated if a school does not offer a course that is not required by state law,[4] even if it is offered in another school district.[5] Decisions about what is taught are solely reserved for the board of school directors who have the implied power to revise curriculum to meet changing educational conditions.[6]

School District Authority

Broad discretion is given to local school districts over course content as long as the district does not interfere with fundamental individual freedoms. This holds true even where the course content creates controversy, i.e., sex education,[7] drug and alcohol education,[8] and AIDS education.[9]

As a general rule, school programs that comply with the state's mandate may not be challenged.[10] For the most part, parental control over the curriculum is limited to making reasonable course selections for their child.

School boards may determine course content based upon district needs[11] and must assure that parents have access to information about the curriculum as well as a process for the review of instructional materials.[12] This right is guaranteed by the Hatch Act, a federal law that confers rights to parents or guardians to review materials used with students in the schools. The right of review applies to materials only and not the teaching method or technique. When challenges arise, the State Department of Education usually decides on a case-by-case basis taking into consideration the "primary purpose" of the activity in question.

Under the Pennsylvania School Code, school boards are granted the right to adopt textbooks *with* the recommendation of the superintendent and a majority vote of the board.[13] An adoption *without* the recommendation of the superintendent requires a two-thirds vote of the board. School districts are advised to follow procedures that have been approved by the board of school directors as a matter of policy.

The process for handling textbook adoptions and challenges usually includes selection and review committees. Even so, parents and teachers may question recommendations by such committees.[14] However, the board still retains the authority to act apart from their recommendations. If provisions exist in a negotiated agreement specifying certain actions by the school board to remove books, it must follow the collective bargaining agreement.[15]

Even though large sums of money may be expended for textbooks, textbook selections are exempt from the advertising and bidding regulations that apply to the purchase of other school equipment and supplies in Pennsylvania.[16] As long as school district procedures are followed and the board takes appropriate action, an adoption will satisfy statutory guidelines.

Course Content

Over the years, conservative forces have taken an adversarial position to what is being taught in public schools. Curricular challenges began in the 1920's with anti-evolution statutes that required teaching the biblical account of creation. These early legislative efforts developed into "equal time" legislation in the 1970's and 1980's when several states passed laws requiring that the theory of evolution be balanced with the teaching of creation science. Today, the courts are confronting claims by Christian fundamentalists that "secular humanism" infringes on the free exercise of religion. These attempts to shape what is taught in the public schools stem from the Fundamentalist belief in the literal interpretation of the Bible.

Anti-Evolution Statutes

In the 1920's, Arkansas, Tennessee, and Mississippi were states whose fundamentalist fervor prompted legislation that criminalized the teaching of any theory that denied the biblical account of creation. Initially, these laws were upheld as was the case in the famous *Scopes* Monkey Trial that resulted in a guilty verdict by the Tennessee Supreme Court against a teacher who sought the right to teach the theory of evolution in the classroom.[17] Later, the United States Supreme Court declared these laws unconstitutional.

Addressing an Arkansas anti-evolution statute, the Supreme Court stated in *Epperson v. Arkansas*: "the vigilant protection of constitutional freedoms is nowhere more vital than in the community of American schools."[18] Acknowledging that it was "clear that fundamentalist, sectarian conviction was and is the law's reason for existence," the Court declared that the effect of this anti-evolution statute was to prefer a particular religious viewpoint. Ever since the Supreme Court determined that the Arkansas statute violated the Establishment Cause of the First Amendment, anti-evolution statutes have been removed from the books.

Equal Time

Equal time statutes support the notion that a school's science curriculum should give equal emphasis to different theories on the origin and creation of humans including, but not limited to, the biblical account found in Genesis. This notion has been unsupported by the courts over the years. In 1972, *Wright v. Houston*[19] rejected the contention that equal time was necessary for students to be able to practice their faith. Two years later, a Tennessee law was held to be unconstitutional in both the Federal District Court level and on the State Supreme Court level because of the law's preferential stance on the biblical version as opposed to the scientific version.[20]

The equal time issue was revisited six years in *McLean v. Arkansas,*[21] which declared that the 1981 Arkansas Balanced Treatment Act (mandating equal treatment for "creation science" and "evolution science" in the classroom) was unconstitutional on all three prongs of the

Lemon test.[22] In arriving at its decision, the court first cited evidence that the law's language followed the biblical language of Genesis. Furthermore, even though the legislature stated its secular intent, the presence of certain biblical references to creation science was sufficient to invalidate the law as not having a legitimate secular purpose. Second, the court felt that "creation science" was a religious viewpoint and not actually a science. Therefore, the only real effect of the law was to advance religion. Third, the court declared that the law would create excessive entanglement by forcing the state to monitor "classroom discussion in order to uphold the Act's prohibition against religious instruction."

The United States Supreme Court finally put the balanced treatment issue to rest in *Edwards v. Aguillard*.[23] *Edwards* invalidated Louisiana's Balanced Treatment for Creation Science and Evolution-Science in Public School Instruction Act in much the same manner that the Federal District Court handled *McLean*. The Louisiana creationism act also failed the *Lemon* test. The Court "identified no clear secular purpose," recognized that the law advanced "the religious viewpoint that a supernatural being created humankind," and declared that the law sought "to employ the symbolic and financial support of the government to achieve a religious purpose."

Free Exercise

The failure to provide equal time for creation science in *Wright*, *McLean*, and *Edwards* set the stage for challenges based on the Free Exercise Clause of the First Amendment. Constitutional claims have now become the preferred alternative to legislative attempts to align curriculum with fundamentalist Christian beliefs.

Secular humanism has become the basis for most free exercise challenges. Since secular humanism has no specific definition, it is an umbrella term used by fundamentalists to describe opposition to their beliefs. To fundamentalists, secular humanism is an intentional and systemic threat that manifests itself in humanistic ideas such as free choice, rationalism, free inquiry, separation of church and state, feminism, and the primacy of scientific inquiry, to name a few.

The secular humanism argument took on significance in *Wright v. Houston* where the court rejected the plaintiff's claim that the school district sanctioned the "religion of secular humanism." The court was "convinced that the connection was too tenuous a thread upon which to base a First Amendment complaint."[24] In *Wright,* the plaintiff contended that the failure of the school district to permit the teaching of creation science impaired one's constitutional right to practice his/her religion as a violation of Section 1983 of the Civil Rights Act. The court would not accept this reasoning saying that teaching the theory of evolution does not as a matter of law prevent students from practicing their religion. The court stated: "All that can be said is that certain textbooks…present what the plaintiffs deem a biased view in support of the theory [of evolution]."

More recently, *Mozert v. Hawkins* tested the secular humanism argument against the use of a particular reading series. The court held that exposure to different ideas and values is not the same as teaching or indoctrinating.[25] Indeed, although critical reading, judgments, and choices were present in the reading series, students were not compelled to make decisions in areas of their faith where the bible was used as the source of decision-making.

Attacks on public school curriculum have recently focused on attempts to establish secular humanism as a religion. While the courts have intentionally avoided the sticky issue of what constitutes a religion, the accepted judicial interpretation is that evolution is not a religion and creationism is not a science.[26] Nevertheless, a California high school Biology teacher recently invoked the secular humanist argument to justify the teaching of creation science in his classroom.[27] Where earlier challenges involved alleged infringement on students' religious beliefs, this challenge sought clarification on a teacher's free exercise of religion. The case, *Peloza v. Capistrano Unified School District*, relied on *Edwards* and held that the belief in a divine creator is clearly a religious belief, not a scientific theory. Furthermore, the court concluded that neither "evolutionism" nor "secular humanism" is considered a religion and there was no merit to the argument that teaching evolution as a valid scientific theory violated the Free Exercise or Establishment Clause of the First Amendment.

Another dimension to the secular humanism controversy was settled when *Grove v. Mead* interpreted the constitution as eliminating pro-religious as well as anti-religious bias from the classroom. The court reasoned that even if secular humanism were a religion, there would be no infringement upon the free exercise of the plaintiff's own religion. Simply exposing one to literature that depicts a poor black adolescent whose life situation prompts her to question the process of prayer or benevolence of God "does not constitute establishment of religion or anti-religion."[28]

Textbooks

Textbook adoptions have been challenged on a number of grounds. Free speech is one of them. In *Keyeshian v. Board of Regents*, the United States Supreme Court affirmed that the classroom is a "marketplace of ideas."[29] However, the Court offered no guidelines. The balance of academic freedom with the school's right to preserve the integrity of the educational environment has been left to the lower courts. In this context, when books have demonstrable literary value, are developmentally appropriate, and do not disrupt the educational environment they will be free from restriction.[30]

In addition to free speech challenges, textbook selections have faced a host of attacks on religious grounds. School districts have broad power to determine the appropriateness of texts in relationship to the school's curriculum. For example, summary judgment for the school district was granted in one West Virginia case when a series of textbooks were challenged as merely offensive to the plaintiff's beliefs. Acknowledging that some material may be offensive, the court allowed the district to use the texts in question because it made supplementary materials available as an academic option.[31] Religious objections to textbooks will not succeed absent a clear violation of the Establishment Clause or Free Exercise Clause.

A school district's authority to select textbooks was similarly affirmed in *Mozert v. Hawkins*.[32] Here, the Sixth Circuit focused on two key issues: the impact of the textbooks on personal religious beliefs and the fact that the school did not provide options to the objectionable material. The court declared that while it is true that the Holt, Rinehart, and Winston basic reading series exposed students to different values and religious beliefs, "neither the textbooks nor the teachers teach, indoctrinate, oppose or promote any particular value or religion." Even though the students were required to read the assigned material without options, the series "did not create an unconstitutional burden under the Free Exercise Clause" since the students were "not required to affirm or deny a belief or engage or refrain from engaging in a practice prohibited or required by their religion." *Mozert's* challenge emphasizes the broad authority granted to schools over curriculum.

In a similar case, *Smith v. Board of Commissioners* dealt with an attempt to enjoin the Alabama public schools from using forty-four textbooks approved by the State Board. These titles were to be included on the State Adopted Textbook List. In what amounted to a continuation of *Wallace v. Jaffee* (an earlier Alabama school prayer case), the plaintiff tried to establish that "secular humanism, evolution, materialism, atheism, and others" were religions in and of themselves.[33] The plaintiff's argument in *Smith* was simple. If the courts can compel schools to purge "God is great, God is good, we thank Him for our daily food" from the classroom (re: *Wallace*), it follows, that the courts should also purge from the classroom things that teach that salvation is obtained through oneself rather than a deity. Put another way: "If the state cannot teach Christianity, how can it teach or advance the Antichrist?" Faced with the possibility of having to define the nature of religion, the court assumed *arguendo* that secular humanism was a religion. This avoided the "delicate question of what constitutes a religious belief under the First Amendment." Having thus framed the issue, the court applied the second *Lemon* criterion, whether the use of the textbooks in question advanced or inhibited religion and held that there was no constitutional violation of the Establishment Clause.

The plaintiffs challenged two groups of textbooks in particular. First, the Home Economics textbooks were attacked on grounds that they contained tenets of humanistic psychology, notably, the steps in the decision-making process. The plaintiffs felt that by dwelling on the individual and suggesting the use of subjective criteria to make decisions, the texts implied that "moral choices are just a matter of preferences" with no theistic certitude. The court countered that under *Lemon* "it is not sufficient that the government action merely accommodates religion...nor is it sufficient that government conduct confers an indirect, remote, or incidental benefit to religion...or that its effect merely happens to coincide or harmonize with the tenets of religion." In order for an impermissible advancement of religion to occur, there must be endorsement. For example, murder is illegal. The fact that it coincides with the morality contained in Judeo-Christian religions does not invalidate the law. The same could be said for adultery, polygamy, theft, and fraud since they all are considered offenses under the Ten Commandments. Since accommodation is not endorsement, the school's adoption of the Home Economics text was entirely appropriate "even though the plaintiffs found some of the material offensive."

Second, the history and social studies textbooks were challenged because they "failed to include a sufficient discussion of the role of religion in history and culture." The court countered this line of reasoning, stating that "mere omission of certain historical facts regarding religion or the absence of a more thorough discussion of its place in…society" does not convey a message of approval of the "religion of secular humanism." The court concluded that the Establishment Clause is not identification *with* religion (which is what would occur if the public schools consciously attempted to fill the curriculum with historical facts of a religious nature) but a separation *from* religion (which is what the United States Constitution dictates). To do otherwise would force the public schools into an affirmative action to speak about religion. By definition, this is contrary to the accepted interpretation of the Establishment Clause.

Elsewhere, another textbook series, *Impressions*, was challenged in two different courts. This series contained 59 books for use with grades one thorough six while extensively incorporating folk tales, myths, and make-believe. In both jurisdictions, the secular humanism arguments against the series were discarded in favor of the school district. Since the use of *Impressions* was a far cry from fostering pagan cults[34] and the selections were a very small part of a clearly non-religious program,[35] the courts found it difficult to see how using the series constituted government endorsed religion.

Library Books

Until recently, removing books from the school library has generated mixed results from the courts. The Second Circuit declared that the removing a book from the school library is an academic decision, not a constitutional one, as long as there is no curtailment of free speech or thought.[36] The Sixth Circuit concurred but added that, although the board may elect to remove a book or books from the shelves, the board's authority is not unlimited. Here, the board was instructed to return *Catch 22* and *Cat's Cradle* to the library shelves cautioning that removal of any books may not be based solely upon the "tastes" of school board members.[37] Similarly, two federal district courts extended to students the right to read and be exposed to controversial ideas. They concluded that the right is a constitutional one and to infringe on that right by restricting books or magazines requires a "compelling government interest."[38] In the Tenth Circuit, *Cary v. Board of Education* upheld a school board's removal of ten books from the school library as a legitimate decision in view of the board's duty to reflect the community's value system.[39] The Seventh Circuit agreed a year later in *Zykan* when it held that a school board's removal of books from the library did not "rise to the level of a constitutional claim" because the board's action was not an attempt at rigid indoctrination. In a rigorous test that granted substantial latitude to school boards over individual students, *Zykan* declared that a constitutional question would not arise unless: 1.) Rigid indoctrination replaced legitimate pedagogical reasoning, 2.) Religious or scientific orthodoxy is imposed as a means of eliminating a particular kind of inquiry, and 3.) Ideological preference excludes a particular type of thought.[40]

These jurisdictional contradictions were clarified by the United States Supreme Court in *Board of Education v. Pico*.[41] Here, the Court reversed a summary judgment by the Second Circuit in favor of removing certain books from the school library. Nine books had been removed from the high school library: *Slaughterhouse Five*, *The Naked Ape*, *Down These Mean Streets*, *Best Short Stories by Negro Writers*, *Go Ask Alice*, *Laughing Boy*, *Black Boy*, *A Hero Ain't Nothin' But a Sandwich*, and *Soul on Ice*. Although no specific test guidelines were offered by the court, *Pico* held that local boards of education "may not remove books from school libraries simply because they dislike the ideas contained in those books."

While *Pico* emphasized that removal cannot be based on what is "orthodox in politics, nationalism, religion, or other matters of opinion," the Court did not deny that boards have a "substantial legitimate role to play in the determination of school library content."[42] Indeed, boards may select books apart from the recommendations of faculty committees[43] since the rights involved belong to the students and parents, not the teachers.[44]

Considering the latitude granted to a school district in determining the nature of its own curriculum, a great deal of care should be used when selecting books for the school library. The courts view removing books already in school libraries less favorably than prohibiting the addition of new books.[45]

This view is evident in more recent court decisions. In *Case v. Unified School District*,[46] a Kansas City gay and lesbian group decided to promote alternative lifestyles by donating two books, *Annie on My Mind* and *All American Boys*, to the school library. The books depict gay and lesbian gender as well as sexual orientations. The group's publicity prior to the donation created a concern in the community that prompted school officials to investigate the books and reassess the media policy in general.

Discovering that two high schools and two junior high schools already had *Annie* on the shelves, the books were put through the school district's media review procedures. Based on the committee's evaluation, *Annie* was judged suitable, while *All American Boys* was not. The district subsequently refused the donation of both books and, in a surprise action, voted to take *Annie* off the shelves, ignoring the committee's recommendation. The case went to trial where the court focused on the board's intent on removing the existing copies of *Annie* from the library. On this matter, the court ruled that the action of the board was motivated by orthodoxy and was, thus, unconstitutional. To arrive at this conclusion, the court conducted a comprehensive review of the records and discovered that the board members acted with singular purpose based on their personal "disagreement with the ideas expressed in the book." One board member felt that only factual books should be placed in the library. Since works of fiction like *Annie* were not factual, they should be removed. (The record revealed that a certain board member felt that factual books, such as the Bible, would be more appropriate.) Secondly, while the court viewed the board's procedural violation as an issue, it felt that it did not rise to the level of a Constitutional violation of due process. Instead, it held that the board's procedural violation was evidence of "viewpoint discrimination." While the board claimed that its intent was based on the "educational suitability" of the material, the court disagreed, declaring that discrimination occurred because the district refused to consider less restrictive remedies such as placing the book on reserve.

The Fifth Circuit reached the same conclusion under a similar set of facts. After examining the record, the court discovered questionable motivation on the part of the school board. The record in this instance revealed that school officials had ignored the recommendation of the district's review committee. Furthermore, many members of the board had not even read the book while others had read only selected portions of the book provided them by the Christian Coalition.[47]

Obscenity Guidelines

Textbook adoptions may be challenged on the basis of obscenity and vulgarity. An example of the extent to which this might impact the schools was felt when the superintendent of a Florida school district recommended the removal of a text based on the objections of the parent of a female student who was a minister. The school board agreed with the superintendent and the parents' contention that selections from Aristophanes' *Lysistrata* and Chaucer's *Miller's Tale* contained sexually explicit and vulgar references. The text was removed even though the

Textbook Committee supported the selections as having undisputed literary value. In a lawsuit filed to reinstate the text, the District Court upheld the school's broad discretion to remove the text based on the district's responsibility to inculcate community values. The school's decision to eliminate the text was held to be "reasonably related to pedagogical concerns" and well within its right to protect its students from vulgar and obscene material based on community standards.[48]

Books may also be removed from the school library because they are judged to be obscene or vulgar for minors.[49] It is well established in law that students are to be protected from expressions of vulgarity and obscenity, whether it comes from a person or a book, oral or written. The standard for determining the developmental appropriateness of such expression is the community at large, not individual board members.

Implications

<u>Teachers and Administrators</u>:

- Censorship of materials and textbooks are likely to fail if it can be established that the material is developmentally appropriate, relevant to the curriculum, and that no disruption will occur in the school system by their use.

- If textbooks are selected as a matter of school policy using sound procedures, the courts will uphold their selection as long as the adoption does not violate a fundamental constitutional right. Failing to follow adoption or removal procedures is not a constitutional issue; however, it may be seen as evidence of questionable intent.

- Textbooks may expose students to different values and beliefs as long as they do not teach, indoctrinate, oppose or promote any particular value or religion.

- Books may not be removed from the school library simply because school officials dislike the ideas contained in them.

- The courts view removing books from the library less favorably than failing to add items. School districts should make informed decisions about books prior to adoption and/or placement on library shelves.

- School districts may not ignore state-mandated curricula.

- A school has broad authority to determine the content of curriculum as long as what it teaches and how it teaches does not interfere with individual freedoms.

- Parents and guardians retain a great deal of control over the education of their special needs students.

- To date, attempts to align public school curriculum with fundamentalist Christian beliefs have failed in the courts.

<u>Parents and Students</u>:

- Even though school districts have established review committees to address the use of instructional materials, the rights involved in their use belong to students and parents, not to teachers.

- Students are protected from obscenity and vulgarity whether it comes from a person or text.

- Parents have a right to review "new or unproved" material intended for use in the classroom.

- In order to avoid offensive or intrusive questions, students may opt out of tests or questionnaires as a fundamental right to privacy under the Fourth Amendment.

- Parents and guardians are generally limited to making reasonable course selections for their child unless the student is identified with a special need.

- If a state-mandated program or curriculum that passes constitutional muster is implemented, it may not be challenged.

Chapter 21 Endnotes

[1] 22 Pa. Code 4.

[2] Jones v. Board of Trustees of Culver City School District, 47 P.2d 804 (Cal. App. 1935).

[3] State *ex rel.* Williams v. Avoyelles Parish School Board, 147 So.2d 729 (La. 1962).

[4] Zykan v. Warsaw Community School Corporation, 631 F.2d 1300 (7th Cir. 1980).

[5] Board of Education of Okay Independent School District v. Carroll, 513 P.2d 872 (Okl. 1973).

[6] Jones v. Holes, 6 A.2d 102 (Pa. 1939).

[7] Cornwell v. State Board of Education, 314 F. Supp. 340 (D. Md. 1961), affirmed, 428F.2d 471 (4th Cir.), *certiorari* denied, 400 U.S. 942 (1970); Valent v. N.J. State Board of Education, 274 A.2d 832 (N.J. Sup. Ct. Ch. Div. 1971).

[8] 22 Pa Code 4.21.

[9] Ware v. Valley Stream High School, 545 N.Y.S.2d. 316 (N.Y. App. Div.), appeal denied, 545 N.Y.S. 2d. 539 (N.Y. 1989).

[10] Aubrey v. School District of Philadelphia, 473 A.2d 1306, 63 Pa. Cmwlth. 330 (1981).

[11] 22 Pa. Code 4.4(b).

[12] 22 Pa. Code 4.4(d).

[13] 24 P.S. 803.

[14] Loewen v. Turnipseed, 488 F. Supp. 1138 (N.D. Miss. 1980).

[15] Cary v. Board of Education of the Adams-Arapahoe School District, 427 F. Supp. 945 (D. Colo. 1977), affirmed 598 F.2d 53 (10th Cir. 1979).

[16] 24 P.S. 511, 817.1.

[17] Scopes v. State, 289 S.W. 363 (Tenn. 1927).

[18] Epperson v. Arkansas, 393 U.S. 97 (1968).

[19] Wright v. Houston Independent School District, 366 F. Supp. 1208 (S.D. Tex. 1972).

[20] Daniel v. Walters, 515 F.2d 485 (6th Cir. 1975); Steele v. Waters, 527 S.W.2d 72 (Tenn. 1975).

[21] McLean v. Arkansas, 529 F. Supp. 1255 (D. Ark. 1981).

[22] Lemon v. Kurtzman, 403 U.S. 602 (1972). Briefly, the three-pronged test requires that:
1. The law has no secular legislative purpose
2. The law neither inhibits or advances religion
3. The law does not create excessive government entanglement

[23] Edwards v. Aguillard, 482 U.S. 578 (1989).

[24] Wright at 1209.

[25] Mozert v. Hawkins County Public Schools, 827 F.2d 1058 (6th Cir. 1987), *certiorari* denied, 484 U.S. 1066 (1988).

[26] McLean, *supra*.

[27] Peloza v. Capistrano Unified School District, 37 F.3d 517 (9th Cir. 1994).

[28] Grove v. Mead, 733 F.2d 1528 (9th Cir. 1985).

[29] Keyishian v. Board of Regents, 385 U.S. 589 (1967).

[30] Parducci v. Rutland, 316 F. Supp. 352 (M.D. Ala. 1970).

[31] Williams v. Board of Education of Kanawha County, 388 F. Supp. 93 (S.D. W. Va. 1975) affirmed 530 F.2d 972 (4th Cir. 1975).

[32] Mozert, *supra*.

[33] Smith v. Board of School Commissioners of Mobile County, 827 F.2d 684 (11th Cir. 1987).

[34] Fleischfresser v. Directors of School District No. 200, 15 F.3d 680 (7th Cir. 1994).

[35] Brown v. Woodland Joint Unified School District, 27 F.3d 1373 (9th Cir. 1994).

[36] President's Council v. Community School Board District No. 25, 457 F.2d 289 (2d. Cir.), *certiorari* denied 409 U.S. 998 (1972).

[37] Minarcini v. Strongsville City School District, 541 F.2d 577 (6th Cir. 1976).

[38] The Right to Read Defense Committee of Chelsea v. School Committee of the City of Chelsea, 454 F. Supp. 703 (D. Mass. 1978); Salvail v. Nashua Board of Education, 469 F. Supp. 1269 (D. N.H. 1979).

[39] Cary, *supra*.

[40] Zykan, *supra*.

[41] Board of Education of the Island Trees Union Free School District v. Pico, 457 U.S. 853 (1982).

[42] Pico at 893.

[43] Minarcini, *supra*.

[44] Johnson v. Stuart, 702 F.2d 193 (9th Cir. 1983).

[45] Pratt v. Independent School District No. 831, 670 F.2d 771 (8th Cir. 1982); Pico, *supra*.

[45] Campbell v. St. Tammany Parish School Board, 64 F.3d 183 (5th Cir. 1995).

[46] Case v. Unified School District, 908 F. Supp. 864 (D. Kan. 1995).

[47] Campbell, *supra*.

[48] Virgil v. School Board, 677 F. Supp. 1547 (M.D. Fla. 1988).

[49] Wexner v. Anderson Union High School District Board of Trustees, 228 Cal.Rptr. 28 (Ct. App. 1989).

Standard Citations and Abbreviations

Federal Court Reporters

F.Supp., **Federal Supplement**	U.S. District Court
F.2d, **Federal Reporter** (2d signifies 2nd edition)	U.S. Court of Appeals
L.Ed., **Lawyers Edition**	U.S. Supreme Court
S. Ct., **Supreme Court Reporter**	U.S. Supreme Court
U.S., **United States Reporter**	U.S. Supreme Court

State Court Reporters

<u>National Reporting System</u>: *In addition to the national reporting system, each state has its own official reporter.*

A.2d, **Atlantic Reporter**:	Conn., Del., D.C., Maine, Md., N. Hampshire, N. Jersey, Pa., R. Island, V.
Cal. Rptr.2d, **California Reporter**:	California
N.E.2d, **North Eastern Reporter**:	Ill., Ind., Mass., N. Y., Ohio
N.W.2d, **North Western Reporter**:	Iowa, Mich., Minn., Neb., N. D., S. D. Wis.
N.Y.S.2d, **New York Supplement**:	New York
P.2d, **Pacific Reporter**:	Ak., Az., Cal., Col., Haw., Idaho, Kan., Mont., N. Mex., Nev., Ore., Ok., Utah, Wash., Wyo.
S.E.2d, **South Eastern Reporter**:	Ga., N. C., S. C., Va., W. Va.
So.2d, **Southern Reporter**:	Ala., Fla., La., Miss.
S.W.2d, **South Western Reporter**:	Ark., Ky., Mo., Tenn., Texas

<u>Pennsylvania</u>: *Each County also has its own reporter, i.e., Mont. (Montgomery).*

Pa.	**Pennsylvania Supreme Court**
Pa. Cmwlth.	**Pennsylvania Commonwealth Court**
Pa. Super.	**Pennsylvania Superior Court**
D. & C.	**Pennsylvania Court of Common Pleas**

Other Sources

SLIE	**School Law Information Exchange**
IDELR	**Individuals with Disabilities in Education Law Review**

Statutes

U.S.C.	**United States Code**
C.F.R.	**Code of Federal Regulations**
P.S.	**Pennsylvania Statutes**
Pa. C.S.	**Pennsylvania Consolidated Statutes**
Pa C.S.A	**Pennsylvania Consolidated Statutes Annotated**
Pa. Code	**Pennsylvania Code**

Glossary of Legal Terms Commonly Used in School Law

Action - An ordinary proceeding in a court where one party prosecutes another. In common language, a "lawsuit."

Appellant - The party who takes an appeal from one court to another.

Arbitrary - Not supported by fair cause and without reason given.

Assault - An attempt to inflict violence upon another, without touching; an offer to attempt to commit a battery. See Battery.

Battery - An unlawful or other wrongful physical violence inflicted upon another without consent.

Bona fide - In good faith.

Breach of contract - Failure, without legal excuse, to perform part or the whole of a contract.

Civil action - An action brought to recover some civil right or to obtain redress for some wrong.

Certiorari - a writ of review or inquiry, usually in an appellate proceeding to re-examine the action of an inferior tribunal

Class action - A case in which one or more in a numerous class, having a common interest in the issue, sue in behalf of themselves and all others of the class.

Code - A compilation of statutes, formally arranged into chapters, subheadings and sections.

Common law - As used here, legal principles derived from usage and custom or from court decisions affirming such usage and custom.

Compensatory damages - compensation for actual loss caused by a wrongdoing; synonymous with actual damages.

Contract - A deliberate engagement between competent parties, upon a consideration, to perform or abstain from performing some act.

Criminal action - Proceeding by which a party charged with a crime is brought to trial and punishment.

Damages - Monetary compensation recovered in court by the person who has suffered loss or injury through the unlawful act, omission, or negligence of another.

Defendant - The party against whom relief or recovery is sought in a court action.

Defense - That which is offered and alleged by the defendant as a reason in law or act why the plaintiff should not recover.

De novo - retrial.

Dictum - (In plural form, *dicta*) statements or comments in a court opinion that are not essential to the determination of the case.

Dissent - The disagreement of a judge or judges from the majority of the court.

Due process - The exercise of the power of government in such a way as to protect individual rights. Due process may be substantive or procedural.

Duress - Unlawful constraint.

Emancipation of child - Surrender of the right to care, custody, and earnings of a child by his or her parents who at the time renounce parental duties.

En banc - A meeting of all the judges of a court as opposed to a single judge presiding over a cause of action

Enjoin - To require a person, by writ of injunction from a court of equity, to perform, to abstain or desist from, some act.

Estop - To prevent.

Et seq. - Abbreviation of *et sequentes(ia)* meaning "and the following."

Ex rel. - Abbreviation for ex relations, meaning on relation or information; a type of court decision.

Exception - In civil procedure, a formal objection to the action of the court when it refuses a request or overrules an objection, implying that the party excepting does not acquiesce in the court's ruling and may base an appeal thereon.

Exemplary damages - See Punitive Damages.

Hearsay evidence - Testimony given by a witness who relates what others have said or what was heard or said by others rather than what is known personally.

In loco parentis - In place of the parent; charged with some of the parent's rights, duties, and responsibilities.

In re - Concerning. When used in a title of a court case, it designates a type of case.

Injunction - A prohibitive writ issued by the court forbidding the defendant to act.

Laches - failure to assert a right for an unreasonable and unexplained length of time.

Liability - The state of being bound or obliged in law to do, pay or make something good; legal responsibility.

Majority opinion - The statement of reasons for the views or the majority of the members of the bench in a decision in which some of them disagree.

Malfeasance - Performance of an act prohibited by law.

Misfeasance - The performance of an act that might lawfully be done, in an improper manner, by which another person receives an injury.

Negligence - An unintentional act (or omission) that causes injury to one's person , property, or reputation.

Nolo contendere - A pleading by a defendant literally signifying that "I will not contest it."

Nonfeasance - The non-performance of some act that ought to be performed.

Plaintiff - Person who brings an action; he who sues by filing a complaint.

Precedent - A decision considered as furnishing an example or authority for an identical or similar case afterward arising on a similar question of law.

Prima facie - An argument where the evidence is so strong that the adverse party can overthrow it only with sufficient rebutting evidence.

Punitive damages - (Exemplary Damages) Damages over and above actual damages intended to solace the injured party while making an example of the aggravated behavior of the wrongdoer.

Quid pro quo - Something for something.

Remand - To send a case back to the court from which it came for further proceedings after an appellate decision.

Right - A power or privilege in one person against another.

Sine qua non - An indispensable requisite.

Statutory - Created or defined by a statute; required by statute.

Summary judgment - Decision on the matter at hand without the formality of a full proceeding.

Tenure - In its general sense, a mode of holding a position, especially with respect to time.

Tort - The intentional commission or omission of an act by one without right, whereby another is injured, directly or indirectly, in person, property, or reputation.

Writ - A court order requiring the performance of an act or granting the authority to perform an act.

Cases

A berant v. Wilkes-Barre Area School District, 492 A.2d 1186 (Pa. Cmwlth. 1985).

Abrahams v. Wallenpaupak Area School District, 422 A.2d 1201, 54 Pa. Cmwlth. 637 (1980).

Abremski v. Southeastern School District Board of Directors, 421 A.2d 485, 54 Pa. Cmwlth. 292 (1980).

Acker v. Spangler, 500 A.2d 206, 92 Pa. Cmwlth. 616 (1985).

Ademek v. Pennsylvania Interscholastic Athletic Association, Inc., 426 A.2d 1206, 57 Pa. Cmwlth. 261 (1981).

Adler v. Duval County School Board, 851 F. Supp. 446 (M.D. Fla. 1994).

Alabama and Coushatta Tribes of Texas v. Trustees of Big Sandy Independent School District, 817 F.2d 1319 (E.D. Tex. 1993).

Alabama H.S.S.A.A. v. Scaffidi, 564 So.2d 910 (Ala. 1990).

Alex v. Allen, 409 F. Supp. 379 (D.C. Pa. 1976).

Alexander v. Holmes County Board of Education, 396 U.S. 19 (1969).

Aliquippa Education Association v. School District of Borough of Aliquippa, 437 A.2d 1039, 63 Pa. Cmwlth. 91 (1981).

Allegheny Intermediate Unit v. Jarvis, 410 A.2d 389, 48 Pa. Cmwlth. 636 (1980).

Allegheny Valley School District v. Allegheny Valley Education Association, 360 A.2d 762 (Pa. Cmwlth. 1977).

Alman v. Fox Chapel School District, 4 D. & C.3d 288 (Pa. 1977).

American Civil Liberties Union of New Jersey v. Black Horse Pike Regional Board of Education, Civil No. 93-02651.

Andress v. Cleveland Independent School District, 832 F. Supp. 1086 (E.D. Tex. 1993).

Anthony v. Conemaugh Township Area School District, 29 Som. 309 (Pa. 1974).

Appalachia Intermediate Unit #8 Education Association v. Appalachia Intermediate Unit #8, PLRB Case No. PERA-C-88-406W (1988).

Appeal of Chester Upland School District, 423 A.2d 437, 55 Pa. Cmwlth. 102 (1980).

Appeal of Jones, 375 A.2d 1341 (Pa. Cmwlth. 1977).

Appeal of McClellan, 475 A.2d 867, 82 Pa. Cmwlth. 75 (1984).

Appeal of Rose Tree Media School District, 442 A.2d 23 (Pa. Cmwlth. 1982).

Arkansas Activities Association v. Meyer, 805 S.W.2d 394 (Ark. 1991).

Armijo v. Wayon Mound Public Schools, 159 F.3d 1253 (10th Cir. 1998).

Armstrong v. Kline, 476 F. Supp. 583 (D.C. Pa. 1979).

Armstrong v. School District of Philadelphia, 597 F. Supp. 1309 (Pa. Cmwlth. 1984).

Arthur v. Nyquist, 712 F.2d 816 (2nd Cir. 1983).

Association for Retarded Children v. Commonwealth, 343 F.Supp 279 (Pa. 1972).

Atlanta International Insurance Company v. School District of Philadelphia, 786 F.2d 136 (3rd.Cir. 1986).

Aubrey v. School District of Philadelphia, 473 A.2d 1306, 63 Pa. Cmwlth. 330 (1981).

Auerback v. Council Rock School District, 459 A.2d 1376 (Pa. Cmwlth. 1983).

Aurelia D. v. Monroe County Board of Education, 862 F. Supp. 363 (M.D. Ga. 1994).

Axtell v. LaPenna, 323 F. Supp. 1077 (D.C. Pa. 1971).

Ayala v. Philadelphia Board of Education, 305 A.2d 877, 453 Pa. 584 (1959).

Babcock School District v. Potocki, 466 A.2d 616, 502 Pa. 349 (1983).

Baker v. Downey City Board of Education, 307 F. Supp. 517 (C.D. Cal. 1969).

Baker v. School District of City of Allentown, 371 A.2d 1028, 29 Pa. Cmwlth. 458 (1977).

Bales v. Clarke, 523 F. Supp. 1366 (E.D. Va. 1981).

Balog v. McKeesport Area School District, 484 A.2d 198, 86 Pa. Cmwlth. 132 (1984).

Balsbaugh v. Rowland, 290 A.2d 85, 447 Pa. 423 (1972).

Bannister v. Paradis, 306 F. Supp. 189 (D.N.H. 1970).

Barker v. Hardaway, 394 U.S. 905 (1966).

Barndt v. Board of School Directors of Wissahickon School District, 368 A.2d 1355, 28 Pa. Cmwlth. 482 (1977).

Bassion v. Northeast Bradford School District, 31 SLIE 88 (1994).

Battle v. Commonwealth of Pennsylvania, 629 F.2d 269, on remand 513 F. Supp. 425, *certiorari* denied Scanlon v. Battle, 101 S. Ct. 3123, 452 U.S. 968, 69 L.Ed.2d 981 (1980).

Baughman v. Frienmuth, 478 F.2d 1345 (4th Cir. 1973).

Baxter v. Vigo County School Corporation, 26 F.3d 728 (7th Cir. 1994).

Beegle v. Greencastle-Antrim School District, 401 A.2d 374, 41 Pa. Cmwlth. 605 (1979).

Belasco v. Board of Education of School District of Pittsburgh, 486 A.2d 538, 87 Pa. Cmwlth. 5 (1985).

Belle Vernon Area School District v. Gilmer, 415 A.2d 121, 51 Pa. Cmwlth. 603 (1980).

Bellefonte Area School District v. Lipner, 473 A.2d 741 (Pa. Cmwlth. 1984).

Belnier v. Lund, 438 F. Supp. 47 (N.D. N.Y. 1977).

Bender v. Williamsport Area School District, 741 F.2d 538 (3rd.Cir. 1984), vacated on other grounds 475 U.S. 534 (1986).

Bennett v. Kline, 486 F. Supp. 36, affirmed 633 F.2d 209 (D.C. Pa. 1980).

Bensalem Township School District v. Bensalem Township Education Association, 512 A.2d 802 (Pa. Cmwlth. 1986).

Berman by Berman v. Philadelphia Board of Education, 456 A.2d 545 (Pa. Super. 1983).

Bersani by Bersani v. School District of Philadelphia, 456 A.2d 151 (Pa. Super. 1982).

Bethel Park School District v. Krall, 455 A.2d 1377 (Pa. Cmwlth. 1982).

Bethel School District No. 403 v. Fraser, 478 U.S. 675, 686 (1986).

Beussink v. Woodland R-IV School District, 30 F.Supp 2d 1175 (E.D. MO 1998).

Big Beaver Falls Area School District v. Big Beaver Falls Area Education Association, 492 A.2d 87 (Pa. Cmwlth. 1985).

Big Spring School District Board of Directors v. Hoffman by Hershey, 489 A.2d 998, 88 Pa. Cmwlth. 462 (1985).

Billman v. Big Spring School District, 27 D. & C.3d 488 (Pa. 1983).

Bishop v. Colaw, 450 F.2d 1069 (8th Cir. 1971).

Black v. Indiana Area School District, 985 F.2d 707 (3rd Cir. 1993).

Blackwell v. Issaquena County Board of Education, 363 F.2d 749 (5th Cir. 1966).

Blascovich v. Board of School Directors of Shamokin Area School District, 410 A.2d 407, 49 Pa. Cmwlth. 131 (1980).

Blue v. New Haven, 552 EHLR 401 (1981).

Board of Education of Central School District No. 1 v. Allen, 392 U.S. 236 (1968).

Board of Education of Downer's Grove Grade School District No. 58 v. Steven L. and Christine L., 23 IDELR 36 (N.D. Ill. 1995).

Board of Education of Hendrick Hudson Central School District v. Rowley, 458 U.S. 176, 102 S. Ct. 3034, 73 L.Ed.2d 690 (1982).

Board of Education of Okay Independent School District v. Carroll, 513 P.2d 872 (Okl. 1973).

Board of Education of Oklahoma City Public Schools v. Dowell, 111 S. Ct. 630 (1991).

Board of Education of the Island Trees Union Free School District v. Pico, 457 U.S. 853 (1982).

Board of Education of Westside Community Schools v. Mergens, 493 U.S. 182 (1990).

Board of Education v. Ambach 45 N.Y.S. 2d 77 (1983).

Board of Education v. Associated Teachers of Huntington, 30 N.Y.S.2d 122 (N.Y. 1972).

Board of Education v. Frey, 392 A.2d 392 (Conn. 1978).

Board of Education v. Middle Island Teacher's Association, 407 N.E.2d 411 (N.Y. 1980).

Board of Education v. Regala, 589 A.2d 993 (Md. App. 1991).

Board of Public Education of School District of Pittsburgh v. Pyle, 390 A.2d 904, 37 Pa. Cmwlth. 386 (1978).

Board of School Directors of Centennial School District v. Secretary of Education, 376 A.2d 302, 31 Pa. Cmwlth. 307 (1977).

Board of School Directors of Eastern York School District v. Fasnacht, 441 A.2d 481, 64 Pa. Cmwlth. 571 (1982).

Board of School Directors of Fox Chapel Area School District v. Rossetti, 411 A.2d 486, 488 Pa. 125 (1978).

Board of School Directors of Riverside Beaver County School District, Beaver County v. Howe, 389 A.2d 1214, 37 Pa. Cmwlth. 241 (1978).

Boehm v. Board of Education of School District of Pittsburgh, 373 A.2d 1372, 30 Pa. Cmwlth. 468 (1977).

Bohenek v. Valley View School District, 25 SLIE 45 (1988).

Bolling v. Sharpe, 347 U.S. 497 (1954).

Bond v. Philadelphia School District, 27 SLIE 87 (1990).

Bottorf v. Waltz, 369 A.2d 332, 245 Pa. Super. 139 (1976).

Bovino v. Board of School Directors of Indiana School District, 377 A.2d 1284, 32 Pa. Cmwlth. 105 (1977).

Boynton v. Casey, 543 F. Supp. 995 (D. Me. 1982).

Boucher v. School Board of the School District of Greenfield, 7th Circuit Court of Appeals No. 97-3433 (1998).

Bravo v. Bd. of School Directors of the Wellsboro Area School Dist., 504 A.2d 418 (Pa. Cmwlth. 1986)

Breen v. Kahl, 419 F.2d 1034 (7th Cir. 1969).

Bridgeman v. New Trier High School, 128 F.3d 1146 (7th Cir. 1997).

Brimmer v. Traverse City Area Public Schools, 872 F. Supp. 447 (W.D. Mich. 1994).

Bronx Household of Faith v. New York City Board of Education, 127 F.3d 207 (1997).

Brougham by Brougham v. Town of Yarmouth, 823 F. Supp. 9 (D. Me. 1993).

Brown v. Board of Education of Topeka, Shawnee County, Kansas, 347 U.S. 294, 74 S. Ct. 686 (1954).

Brown v. Board of Education of Topeka, Shawnee County, Kansas, 349 U.S. 294, 75 S. Ct. 753 (1955).

Brown v. Quaker Valley School District, 486 A.2d 526, 86 Pa. Cmwlth. 496 (1984).

Brown v. Woodland Joint Unified School District, 27 F.3d 1373 (9th Cir. 1994).

Bruckner v. Lancaster County Area Vocational-Technical Joint School Operating Committee, 453 A.2d 384 (Pa. Cmwlth. 1982).

Bull v. Dardanelle Public School District No. 15, 745 F. Supp. 1455 (E.D. Ark. 1990).

Bunger v. Iowa High School Athletic Association, 197 N.W.2d 535 (Iowa 1972).

Burch v. Barker, 861 F.2d 1149 (9th Cir. 1988).

Burns by and Through Burns v. Hitchcock, 683 A.2d 1322 (Pa. 1996).

Burnside v. Byers, 363 F.2d 744 (5th Cir. 1966).

Burrow by and Through Burrow v. Postville Community School District, 929 F. Supp. 1193 (Iowa 1996).

Bystrom v. Fudley High School, 822 F.2d 747 (8th Cir. 1987).

Cadonic v. Northern Area Special Progress Schools, 426 A.2d 208 (Pa. Cmwlth. 1981).

Caffas v. Board of School Directors of Upper Dauphin Area, 353 A.2d 898, 23 Pa. Cmwlth. 578 (1976).

Calandra by Calandra v. State College Area School District, 512 A.2d 809 (Pa. Cmwlth. 1986).

California v. Chapman & McGee, 679 P.2d 62 (1984).

Campbell v. St. Tammany Parish School Board, 64 F.3d 183 (5th Cir. 1995).

Campbell v. U. S. Civil Service Commission, 539 F.2d 58, (10th Cir. 1976).

Canutillo Independent School District v. Leija, 101 F.3d 393 (5th Cir.1996).

Cardinal Mooney High School v. Michigan H.S.A.A., 467 N.W.2d 21 (Mich. 1991).

Carey v. Piphus, 435 U.S. 247, 98 S. Ct. 1042 (1978).

Carmichaels Area School District v. Harr, 429 A.2d 126, 59 Pa. Cmwlth. 191 (1981).

Cary v. Board of Education of the Adams-Arapahoe School District, 427 F. Supp. 945 (D. Colo. 1977), affirmed 598 F.2d 53 (10th Cir. 1979).

Case v. Unified School District, 908 F. Supp. 864 (D. Kan. 1995).

Casilli v. Board of Public Education of the School District of Pittsburgh, 23 SLIE 7 (1985).

Cavallaro v. Ambach, 575 F. Supp. 171 (W.D. N.Y. 1983).

Cedar Rapids Community School District v. Garrett F., (96-1793), 106 F.3d 822, affirmed.

Centennial School District v. Commonwealth, Department of Education, 503 A.2d 1090 (Pa. Cmwlth. 1986).

Centennial School District v. Commonwealth, Department of Education, 503 A.2d 1090 (Pa. Cmwlth. 1986).

Central Susquehanna Intermediate Unit Education Association v. Central Susquehanna Intermediate Unit No. 16, 459 A.2d 889 (Pa. Cmwlth. 1983).

Central York School District v. Commonwealth, Department of Education, 399 A.2d 167, 41 Pa. Cmwlth. 383 (1979).

Central York School District v. Commonwealth, Department of Education, 399 A.2d 167, 41 Pa. Cmwlth. 383 (1979).

Central York School District v. Ehrhart, 387 A.2d 1006, 36 Pa. Cmwlth. 278 (1978).

Cestari v. School District of Cheltenham Township, 520 A.2d 110 (Pa. Cmwlth. 1987).

Chandler v. McMinnville School District, 978 F.2d 529 (9th Cir. 1992).

Chodkowski v. Beck, 106 P.L.J. 115 (Pa. 1958).

City of Peoria v. Illinois, 531 F. Supp. 148 (C.D. Ill. 1982).

Clairton School District v. Strinich, 413 A.2d 26, 50 Pa. Cmwlth. 389, aff'd 431 A.2d 267, 494 Pa. 297, *certiorari* denied 102 S. Ct. 2254 (1981).

Clark v. Colonial School District, 387 A.2d 1027, 36 Pa. Cmwlth. 419 (1978).

Clark County School District v. Breeden, No. 00-866 (S. Ct. 2001).

Clevenger v. Oak Ridge School Board, 573 F. Supp. 349 (E.D. Tenn. 1983).

Close v. Voorhees, 446 A.2d 728 (Pa. Cmwlth. 1982).

Clyde K. and Sheila K. v. Puyallup School District, 35 F.3d 1396 (9th Cir. 1994).

Cochran v. Louisiana State Board of Education, 281 U.S. 370 (1930).

Coffman v. State, 782 S.W. 2d 249 (Tex. App. 1989).

Cohen v. California, 403 U.S. 15 (1971).

Coladonato v. Southern Columbia Area School Board, 5 D. & C.3d 101 (Pa. 1977).

Colburn v. Upper Darby, 946 F.2d 1017 (3rd Cir. 1991).

Colorado Independent School District v. Barber, 846 S.W.2d 806 (Tex. App.- Eastland 1993).

Columbus Board of Education v. Penick, 443 U.S. 449 (1979).

Commonwealth *ex rel.* School District of Pittsburgh v. Ross, 330 A.2d 290, 17 Pa. Cmwlth 105 (1975).

Commonwealth v. Allen, 1 D. & C.3d 742 (Pa. 1976).

Commonwealth v. Carey, 554 N.E. 2d 1199 (Mass. 1990).

Commonwealth v. Cass, 709 A.2d 350 (1998).

Commonwealth v. Feeser, 364 A.2d 1324, 469 Pa. 173 (1976).

Commonwealth v. Grace, 48 D. & C.2d 331 (Pa. 1969).

Commonwealth v. Hall, 455 A.2d 674 (Pa. Super. 1983).

Commonwealth v. Mangini, 386 A.2d 482, 478 Pa. 147 (1978).

Commonwealth v. Oxford Area School District, 356 A.2d 857, 24 Pa. Cmwlth. 421 (1976).

Commonwealth v. Pasceri, 98 Montg. 276 (Pa. 1974).

Commonwealth v. Phillips, 366 A.2d 306, 244 Pa. Super. 42 (1976).

Commonwealth v. Smoker, 110 A 2d 740, 177 Pa. Super. 435 (1955).

Commonwealth, Labor Relations Board v. Uniontown Area School District, 367 A.2d 738, 28 Pa. Cmwlth. 61 (1977).

Commonwealth v. Snyder 597 N.E. 2d 1363 (Mass. 1992).

Confluence Borough School District v. Ursina Borough School District, 88 Pa. Super. 299 (1926).

Connally v. General Construction Co., 269 U.S. 385 (1926).

Connecticut v. Teal 651 F.2d 222 (4th Cir. 1981).

Conway v. Wilburn, 488 A.2d 92, 87 Pa. Cmwlth. 611 (1985).

Cooper v. Aaron, 358 U.S. 1 (1958).

Cordero v. Commonwealth of Pennsylvania, 795 F. Supp. 1352 (M.D. Pa. 1992).

Cornelius v. NAACP Legal Defense and Education Fund, 473 U.S. 788 (1985).

Cornfield by Lewis v. Consolidated High School District No. 230, 991 F. 2d 1316 (7th Cir. 1993).

Cornwell v. State Board of Education, 314 F. Supp. 340 (D. Md. 1961), affirmed, 428F.2d 471 (4th Cir.), *certiorari* denied, 400 U.S. 942 (1970).

Coronado v. State, 835 S.W. 2d 636 (Tex. Crim. App. 1992).

Covert v. Bensalem Township School District, 104 Pa. Cmwlth. 441 (1987).

Craig v. Boren, 429 U.S. 190 (1976).

Crane v. I.H.S.A.A., 975 F.2d 1315 (7th Cir. 1992).

Crawford-El v. Britton, 000 U.S. 96-827 (1998).

Crawshaw v. Meadeville Area School District, 11 Crawford 39 (Pa. 1970).

Creameans v. Fairland Local School District, 633 N.E. 2d 570 (4th Dist. 1993).

Crestwood School District v. Redgate, 508 A.2d 391 (Pa. Cmwlth. 1986).

Crossland v. Bensalem Township School District, 464 A.2d 632 (Pa. Cmwlth. 1983).

Cyrex v. Ascension Parish School Board, 31 IDELR 54 (5th Cir. 1999).

D.R. v. Middle Bucks Area Vocational Technical School, 972 F.2d 1364 (3rd Cir. 1992).

Dallas v. Cumberland Valley School District, 391 F. Supp. 358 (M.D. Pa. 1975).

Dallas School District v. Richard C., 24 IDELR 241 (Pa.) May 23, 1996).

Dangler v. Yorktown Central Schools, 777 F. Supp. 1175 (S. D. N.Y. 1991).

Daniel R.R. v. State Board of Education, 874 F.2d 1036 (5th Cir. 1989).

Daniel v. Walters, 515 F.2d 485 (6th Cir. 1975).

Daniels v. Williams, 106 S. Ct. 662, 88 L.Ed.2d 662 (1986).

Danson v. Casey, 399 A.2d 360, 484 Pa. 415 (1979).

Danville Education Association v. Danville Area School District, 467 A.2d 644, 78 Pa. Cmwlth. 238 (1983).

Davenport by Davenport v. Randolph County Board of Education, 730 F.2d 1395 (11th Cir. 1984).

Davidson v. Cannon, 106 S. Ct. 668, 88 L.Ed.2d 677 (1986).

Davies v. Barnes, 503 A.2d 93 (Pa. Cmwlth. 1986).

Davis v. Central Dauphin School District School Board, 466 F. Supp. 1259 (D.C. Pa. 1979).

Davis v. Meek, 344 F. Supp. 298, (N.D. Ohio 1972).

Davis v. Monroe County Board of Education, 74 F.3d 1186 (11th Cir. 1996).

Davis v. School District of Philadelphia, 496 A.2d 903 (Pa. Cmwlth. 1985).

Dayton Board of Education v. Brinkman, 443 U.S. 526 (1979).

Deal v. Cincinnati, 369 F.2d 55 (6th Cir. 1966).

DeLeon v. Susquehanna Community School District, 747 F.2d 149 (3rd Cir. 1984).

Denno v. School Board of Volusia County, 218 F3d 1267 (11th Cir. 2000).

Derry Township School District v. Finnegan, 498 A.2d 474 (Pa. Cmwlth. 1985).

DeShaney v. Winnebago County Department of Social Services, 489 U.S. 189 (1989).

Desilets v. Clearview Regional Board of Education, 627 A.2d 667 (N.J. Super A.D. 1993).

Diaz v. San Jose Unified School District, 733 F.2d 660 (9th Cir. 1984), *certiorari* denied, 471 U.S. 1065 (1985).

Doe v. Aldine Independent School District, 563 F. Supp. 883 (S.D. Tex. 1982).

Doe v. Board of Education of Montgomery County, 453 A.2d 814, 295 Md. 67 (1982).

Doe v. Duncanville Independent School District, 994 F.2d 160 (8th Cir. 1988).

Doe v. Koger, 480 F. Supp. 225 (N.D. Ind. 1979).

Doe v. Petaluma City School District, 830 F. Supp. 1560 (N.D. Cal. 1993).

Doe v. Renfrow, 451 U.S. 1022 (1981).

Doe v. Shenandoah County School Board, 737 F.Supp 913 (W. D. Va. 1990).

Doe v. Syracuse School District, 508 F. Supp. 333 (N.D. N.Y. 1981).

Doe v. Taylor Independent School District, 15 F.3d 443, (5th Cir. 1994).

Dohanic v. Department of Education, 111 Pa. Cmwlth. 193 (1987).

Donellan v. Mt. Lebanon School District, 377 A.2d 1054 (Pa. Cmwlth. 1977).

Donohue v. Copiague Union Free School District, 47 N.Y.2d 440, 418 N.Y.S.2d 375, 391 N.E.2d 1352 (1979).

Duncan v. Rochester Area School District, 529 A.2d 48 (Pa. Cmwlth. 1987).

Earls v. Board of Education of Tecumseh Public School District, No. 00-6128 (6th Cir. 2001).

East Pennsboro Area School District v. Commonwealth, Pennsylvania Labor Relations Board, 467 A.2d 1356, 78 Pa. Cmwlth. 301 (1983).

Edwards v. Aguillard, 482 U.S. 578 (1989).

Eisner v. Stamford Board of Education, 440 F.2d 803 (2nd Cir. 1971).

Ellwood City Area School District v. Secretary of Education, 9 Pa. Cmwlth. 477 (1973).

Emmett v. Kent School District No. 415, 92 F. Supp.2d 1088 (WD Wash. 2000).

Engle v. Vitale, 370 U.S. 421 (1962).

Epperson v. Arkansas, 393 U.S. 97, 89 S. Ct. 266 (1968).

Everett v. Marcase, 426 F. Supp. 398 (D.C. Pa. 1977).

Everson v. Board of Education of Ewing Township, 330 U.S. 1, 67 S. Ct. 504 (1947).

F. P. v. State, 528 So.2d 1253 (Fla. App. 1st Dist. 1988).

Fairview School District v. Fairview Education Association, 368 A.2d 842, 28 Pa. Cmwlth. 366 (1977).

Falvo v. Owasso Independent School District, 2000 U.S. App. Lexis (10th Cir. 2000).

Fenton v. Stear, 423 F. Supp. 767 (W.D. Pa. 1976).

Ferndale Area School District v. Shawley, 313 A.2d 366, 11 Pa. Cmwlth. 185 (1973).

Ferrel v. Dallas Independent School District, 392 F.2d 697 (5th Cir. 1968).

Figuero v. Thompson, 1 D.& C.3d 266 (Pa. 1975).

Fink v. Board of Education of Warren County Sch. Dist., 442 A.2d 837 (Pa. Cmwlth. 1982).

Fitz v. Intermediate Unit No. 29, 403 A.2d 138, 43 Pa. Cmwlth. 370 (1979).

Fleischfresser v. Directors of School District No. 200, 15 F.3d 680 (7th Cir. 1994).

Foderaro v. School District of Philadelphia, 531 A.2d 570 (Pa. Cmwlth. 1987) appeal denied 518 Pa. 644.

Fontes v. Irvine Unified School District, 30 Cal. Rptr. 521 (Cal. App. 4th Dist. 1994).

Fowler v. Williamson, 251 S.E. 2d 889 (N.C. Ct. App. 1979).

Franklin v. Gwinnett County Public Schools, 112 S. Ct. 1028 (1992).

Frederick L. v. Thomas, 578 F.2d 513 (D.C. Pa. 1976).

Frederick v. Thomas, 557 F.2d 373 (3rd Cir. 1977).

Frick v. Lynch, 491 F. Supp. 381 (D.R.I. 1980).

Fuhrman v. East Hannover Board of Education, 993 F.2d 1031 (3rd Cir. 1993).

Fujishima v. Board of Education, 460 F.2d 1355 (7th Cir. 1972).

Galford v. Mark Anthony B., 433 S.E.2d 41 (W.Va. 1993).

Gano v. School District No. 411, 674 F. Supp. 796 (D. Idaho 1987).

Garcia v. Miera, 817 F.2d 650 (1987).

Garnett v. Renton School District No. 403, 987 F.2d 641 (9th Cir. 1993).

Gay and Lesbian Students Association v. Cohn, 850 F.2d 361 (8th Cir. 1988).

Gearon v. Loudoun County School Board, 844 F. Supp. 1097 (E.D. Va. 1993).

Genco v. Bristol Borough School District, 423 A.2d 36, 55 Pa. Cmwlth. 78 (1980).

George v. Department of Education, 325 A.2d 819 (Pa. Cmwlth. 1984).

George v. Union Area School District, 350 A.2d 918, 22 Pa. Cmwlth. 547 (1976).

Gilbert v. School District of Philadelphia, 511 A.2d 258 (Pa. Cmwlth. 1986).

Giles v. Marple Newton School District, 367 A.2d 399, 27 Pa. Cmwlth. 588 (1976).

Girard School District v. Pittenger, 392 A.2d 261, 481 Pa. 91 (1978).

Gobla v. Board of School Directors of Crestwood School District, 414 A.2d 772, 51 Pa. Cmwlth. 539 (1980).

Goluba v. School District of Ripon, 847 F. Supp. 242 (E.D. Wisc. 1994).

Gong Lum v. Rice, 275 U.S. 78, 48 S. Ct. 91 (1927).

Good News Club v. Milford Central School, 121 S. Ct. 2093 (2001).

Good News/Good Sports Club v. School District of the City of Ladue, Missouri, 28 F.3d 1501 (8th Cir. 1994).

Gorski v. Dickson City Borough School District, 113 A.2d 334 (1955).

Grace Bible Fellowship v. Maine School Administrative District No. 5, 941 F.2d 45 (1st Cir. 1991).

Graham v. Houston Independent School District, 335 F. Supp. 1162 (S.D. Tex. 1970).

Graham v. Mars Area School District, 415 A.2d 924, 52 Pa. Cmwlth. 116 (1980).

Grandinetti v. Commonwealth, Unemployment Compensation Board of Review, 486 A.2d 1040, 87 Pa. Cmwlth. 133 (1985).

Grant v. Board of School Directors of Centennial School District, 471 A.2d 1292, 80 Pa. Cmwlth. 481 (1984).

Greater Johnstown Area Vocational-Technical School v. Greater Johnstown Area Vocational-Technical Education Association, 450 A.2d 787 (Pa. Cmwlth. 1982).

Greater Johnstown Area Vocational-Technical School v. Greater Johnstown Area Vocational-Technical Education Association, 489 A.2d 945, 88 Pa. Cmwlth. 141 (1985).

Green v. County School Board of New Kent County, Virginia, 391 U.S. 430 (1968).

Greenwald v. McKeesport Area School District, 19 D. & C.3d 79 (Pa. 1980).

Gregoire v. Centennial School District, 907 F.2d 1366 (3rd Cir. 1990).

Griffin v. County School Board of Prince Edward County, 377 U.S. 218 (1964).

Grkman by Grkman v. Scanlon, 563 F. Supp. 793 (D.C. Pa. 1983).

Grkman v. Scanlon, 528 F. Supp. 1032 (1981).

Grove City College v. Bell, 465 U.S. 555 (1984).

Grove v. Mead, 733 F.2d 1528 (9th Cir. 1985).

Gurmakin v. Costanza, 411 F. Supp.. 982 (E.D. Pa. 1976), affirmed 556 F.2d 184 (3rd. Cir. 1977), affirmed in part, vacated and remanded in part 626 F.2d 1115 (3rd Cir. 1980), *certiorari* denied 450 U.S. 923 (1981).

Guyer v. School Board of Alachua County, 634 So.2d 806 (Fla. App. 1st Dist. 1994).

Guzik v. Drebus, 431 F.2d 594 (6th Cir.).

Halderman v. Pennhurst State School and Hospital, 673 F.2d 647 (3rd Cir. 1982).

Hamburg v. Commonwealth, Department of Education, 458 A.2d 288 (Pa. Cmwlth. 1983).

Hamburg v. North Penn School District, 484 A.2d 867, 86 Pa. Cmwlth. 371 (1984).

Hammond v. Board of Education of Carrol County, 639 A.2d 223, 100 Md. App. 60 (Md. 1994).

Harborcreek School District v. Harborcreek Education Association, 441 A.2d 807 (Pa. Cmwlth. 1982).

Hark v. School District of Philadelphia, 505 F. Supp. 727 (D.C. Pa. 1980).

Harlow v. Fitzgerald, 457 U.S. 800, 102 S. Ct. 272 (1982).

Harmon v. Mifflin County School District, 32 SLIE 1 (1995).

Harper v. Edgewood Board of Education of School District No. 228, 655 F. Supp. 1353 (S.D. Ohio 1987).

Harris v. Commonwealth, Secretary of Education, 372 A.2d 953, 29 Pa. Cmwlth. 625 (1977).

Harris v. Forklift Systems, 114 S. Ct. 367 (1993).

Harris v. Joint School District No. 241. 41 F.3d 447 (9th Cir. 1994).

Harrison v. Capital Area Intermediate Unit, 479 A.2d 62, 84 Pa. Cmwlth. 344 (1984).

Hatch v. Goerke, 502 F.2d 1189 (10th Cir. 1974).

Hazelton Area Education Association v. Commonwealth, Pennsylvania Labor Relations Board, 503 A.2d 71, 93 Pa. Cmwlth, 646 (1985).

Hazelwood v. Kuhlmeier, 484 U.S. 260 (1988).

Healy v. James 408 U.S. 169 (1972).

Helms v. Cody. 856 F. Supp. 1102 (E.D. La. 1994).

Hemry by Hemry v. School Board of Colorado School District No. 11, 760 F. Supp. 856 (D. Colo. 1991).

Hernandez v. School District #1, 315 F. Supp. 289 (D. Colo. 1970).

Hixson v. Greater Latrobe School District, 421 A.2d 474, 52 Pa. Cmwlth. 92 (1980).

Hoffman v. Board of Education, 49 N.Y.2d 121, 400 N.E.2d 317, 424 N.Y.S.2d 376 (1979).

Hoffman v. West Chester Area District School Board, 397 A.2d 482, 40 Pa. Cmwlth. 374 (1979).

Hohman v. Blue Ridge School District, 405 A.2d 572 (Pa. Cmwlth. 1979).

Hoot by Hoot v. Milan Area Schools, 853 F. Supp. 243 (E.D. Mich. 1994).

Hoots v. Commonwealth of Pennsylvania, 672 F.2d 1107 (1982), *ceriorari* denied 457 U.S. 824, 103 S. Ct. 55 (1982).

Hooks v. Clark County School District, No. 00-1261 (S. Ct. 2001).

Hoppock v. Twin Falls School District, 772 F. Supp. 1160 (D. Idaho 1991).

Horton v. Goose Creek Independent School District, 690 F.2d 470 (5th Cir. 1982).

Horton v. Jefferson County DuBois Area Vocational Technical School, 157 Pa. Cmwlth. 424 (1993).

Hosler v. Bellefonte Area School District, 395 A.2d 289, 38 Pa. Cmwlth. 429 (1978).

Howard H. v. Wentzel, 372 A.2d 30, 29 Pa. Cmwlth. 362 (1977).

Human Relations Commission v. Chester School District, 233 A.2d 290, 427 Pa. 157 (1967).

Husted v. Canton Area School District, 458 A.2d 1037 (Pa. Cmwlth. 1983).

Illinois v. Gates, 462 U.S. 213 (1983).

In Interest of Doe, 887 P. 2d 645 (Hawaii 1994).

In Interest of S.F., 607 A.2d 793 (PA. Super. 1992).

In re Appeal of Cowden, 486 A.2d 1014 (Pa. Cmwlth. 1985).

In re Feldman, 395 A.2d 602, 38 Pa. Cmwlth. 634 (1978).

In re Gault, 387 U.S. l, 87 S. Ct. 1428, 18 L.Ed.2d 527 (1967).

In re Giles, 367 A.2d 399, 27 Pa. Cmwlth. 588 (1976).

In re Indebtedness of Avoca Borough School District, 85 D.& C. 102 (Pa. 1953).

In re S.K., 647 A.2d 952 (Pa. Super. 1994).

In re the Matter of Gregory M., 82 N.Y. 2d 588 (1993).

In the Interest of Guy Dumas, 515 A.2d 984 (Pa. Super. 1986).

In the Interest of Jessica Mae Curry, 79 Westmoreland 207 (1997).

Independent School District No. 8 v. Swanson, 553 P.2d 496 (Okla. 1976).

Ingraham v. Wright, 97 S. Ct. 1401, 51 L.Ed.2d 711 (1977).

Interest of L.L. v. Circuit Court, 28 N.W.2d 343 (WI S. Ct. App. 1979).

Irving Independent School District v. Tatro, 104 S. Ct. 3371, 82 L.Ed.2d 664 (1984).

J. M., Jr. v. Montana H.S.A.A., 875 P.2d 1026 (Mont. 1994).

J.N. by and through Hager v. Bellingham School District No.501, 871 P.2d 1106 (Wash. App. Div. 1 1994).

Jackson v. Centennial School District, 501 A.2d 218 (Pa. 1985).

Jackson v. Dorrier, 424 F.2d 213 (6th Cir.), *certiorari* denied, 400 U.S. 850 (1970).

Jackson v. Franklin County School Board, 765 F.2d 535 (1985).

Jacobs v. Board of School Commissioners, 490 F.2d 601 (7th Cir. 1973).

Jacobs v. State College Area School District, 26 SLIE 91 (1989).

Jager v. Douglas County School District, 862 F.2d 824 (11th Cir. 1989).

Jefferson v. Ysleta Independent School District, 817 F.2d 303 (1987).

Jeffery v. Marple-Newton School District, 23 SLIE 88 (1986).

Jeffrey v. O'Donnell, 702 F. Supp. 513 (M.D. Pa. 1987).

Jeglin v. San Jacinto Unified School District, 827 F. Supp. 1459 (C.D. Cal. 1993).

Jobson v. Pennsylvania Interscholastic Athletic Association, 18 D. & C.3d 347 (1981).

John Doe v. Board of Education of Oak Park and River Forest High School District, (No. 663014 7th Cir. 1997).

Johnson v. Clark, 418 N.W.2d 466 (Mich. App. 1987).

Johnson v. Stuart, 702 F.2d 193 (9th Cir. 1983).

Johnson v. United School District Joint School Board, 201 Pa. Super. 375 (1963).

Johnson-Loehner v. O'Brien, 859 F. Supp. 575 (M.D. Fla. 1994).

Jones v. Board of Trustees of Culver City School District, 47 P.2d 804 (Cal. App. 1935).

Jones v. Clear Creek Independent School District, 977 F.2d 963 (5th Cir. 1992).

Jones v. Holes, 6 A.2d 102 (Pa. 1939).

Jones v. Latexo Independent School District, 497 F. Supp. 223, (E.D. Tex. 1980).

Jordan by and through Jones v. I.H.S.A.A., 813 F. Supp. 1372 (N.D. Ind. 1993).

Jordan v. School District of City of Erie, Pa., 583 F.2d 91 (D.C. Pa. 1978).

Joy v. Penn-Harris-Madison School Corporation, 212 F.3d 1052 (7th Cir. 2000).

Judiciary Committee v. Freedom of Information Commission, 473 A.2d 1248, 39 Conn. Sup. 176, (1983).

Kaelin v. Grubbs, 682 F.2d 595 (6th Cir. 1982).

Kaplan v. Philadelphia School District, 388 Pa. 213 (1957).

Karabian v. Columbia University, 14 F.3d 773 (2nd Cir. 1994).

Karcher v. May, 484 U.S. 72 (1987).

Karp v. Becker, 477 F.2d 171 (9th Cir. 1973).

Kasper v. Girard School District, 361 A.2d 471, 25 Pa. Cmwlth. 552 (1976).

Katz v. McAulay, 438 F.2d 1058)2nd Cir. 1971).

Katzman by Katzman v. Cumberland Valley School District, 479 A.2d 671, 84 Pa. Cmwlth. 474 (1984).

Keating v. Board of School Directors of Riverside School District, 513 A.2d 547, 99 Pa. Cmwlth. 337 (1986), appeal denied 514 Pa. 626 (1987).

Kelley v. Johnson, 425 U.S. 238 (1976).

Keyes v. School District No. 1, Denver Colorado, 413 U.S. 189 (1973).

Keyishian v. Board of Regents, 385 U.S. 589 (1967).

Killian v. Franklin Regional School District, 136 F. Supp. 2d 446 (WD Pa. 2001).

King v. Hempfield Area School District, 8 D.& C.4th 48 (Pa. 1983).

Kite v. Marshall, 661 F.2d 1027 (1981), *certiorari* denied, 50 U.S.L.W. 3982 (1982).

Kleczek v. Rhode Island Interscholastic League, Inc., 612 A.2d 734 (D.R.I. 1992).

Klein v. Smith, 635 F. Supp. 1440 (D. Me. 1986).

Knudsen v. Delaware County Regional Water Quality Control Authority, 478 A.2d 533, 84 Pa. Cmwlth. 36 (1984).

Koppel v. Levine, 347 F. Supp. 456 (E.D. N.Y. 1972).

Kozak v. Hampton Township School District, 855 A.2d 641 (Pa. Cmwlth. 1995).

Krawitz v. Commonwealth, Department of Education, 408 A.2d 1202, 48 Pa. Cmwlth. 155 (1979).

Kriss v. Brown, 390 N.E.2d 193 (Ind. App. 1979).

Kromnick v. School District of Philadelphia, 739 F.2d 894 (3rd Cir. 1984), *certiorari* denied, 105 S. Ct. 782 (1985).

Kudasik v. Board of Directors, Port Allegany School District, 455 A.2d 261 (Pa. Cmwlth. 1983).

L amb's Chapel v. Center Moriches School District, 770 F. Supp. 91 (A.D. N.Y. 1991).

Landeman v. Churchill Area School District, 200 A.2d 20, 414 Pa. 530 (1964).

Lander v. Seaver, 32 Vt. 114 (Vt. 1859).

Landi v. West Chester Area School District, 353 A.2d 895, 23 Pa. Cmwlth. 586 (1976).

Langley v. Uniontown Area School District, 367 A.2d 736, 28 Pa. Cmwlth. 69 (1976).

Lanner v. Wimmer, 662 F.2d 1349 (10th Cir. 1981).

Lee v. School District of Philadelphia, 51 D.& C.2d 504 (Pa. 1971).

Lee v. Weisman, 112 U.S. 2649 (1992).

Leechburg Area School District v. Dale, 424 A.2d 1309, 492 Pa. 515 (1981).

Leechburg Area School District v. Leechburg Education Association, 380 A.2d 1203, 475 Pa. 413 (1977).

Lemmon Education Association v. Lemmon School District #52-2, 478 N.W.2d 821 (S.D. 1991).

Lemon v. Kurtzman, 403 U.S. 602 (1972).

Lenker v. East Pennsboro School District, 632 A.2d 969 (Pa. Cmwlth. 1993).

Leslie v. Oxford Area School District, 420 A.2d 764, 54 Pa. Cmwlth. 120 (1980).

Levy v. Commonwealth, Department of Education, 399 A.2d 159, 41 Pa. Cmwlth. 356 (1979).

Lewis by Keller v. Hatboro-Horsham School District, 465 A.2d 1090 (Pa. Cmwlth. 1983).

Lewis v. Board of Education, 537 N.E.2d 435 (Ill. App. 1989).

Lindsay v. Thomas, 465 A.2d 122, 77 Pa. Cmwlth. 171 (1983).

Lisa H. v. State Board of Education, 467 A.2d 1127, 502 Pa. 613 (1983).

Loewen v. Turnipseed, 488 F. Supp. 1138 (N.D. Miss. 1980).

Lowman By and Through Lowman v. Indiana Area School District, 507 A.2d 1270 (Pa. Cmwlth. 1986).

Lubbock Civil Liberties Union v. Lubbock Independent School District, 669 F.2d 1038 (5th Cir. 1982).

Lucciola v. Commonwealth, Secretary of Education, 360 A.2d 310, 25 Pa. Cmwlth. 419 (1976).

Lushen v. Peters Township School District, 65 D. & C. 2d 712 (Pa. 1974).

Lyons by Alexander v. Smith, 829 F. Supp. 414 (D.D.C. 1993).

M.M. v. Anker, 607 F.2d 588 (2nd Cir. 1979).

MacKnight v. Beaver Area School District, (C.P. Beaver County Pa. 1982).

Magill v. Appalachia Intermediate Unit No. 8, 646 F. Supp. 339 (W.D. Pa. 1986).

Marinaro v. Cheltenham Township School District Board, Teacher Tenure Appeal, No. 7-88.

Mark v. Borough of Hatboro, 51 F.3d 1137 (3rd Cir. 1995).

Mathias v. Richland School District, 592 A.2d 811 (Pa. 1991).

Matter of Lewisburg Area Education Association, 371 A.2d 568 (Pa. Cmwlth. 1977).

Mavis v. Sobol, 839 F. Supp. 968 (N.D.N.Y. 1993).

Maxwell v. The School District of Philadelphia, 1999 WL 313764 (E.D. Pa. 1999).

McCloskey by McCloskey v. Abington School District, 515 A.2d 642 (Pa. Cmwlth. 1986).

McCorkle v. Bellefonte Area Board of School Directors, 401 A.2d 371, 41 Pa. Cmwlth. 581 (1979).

McCracken v. Central Susquehanna Intermediate Unit, 382 A.2d 1293 (Pa. Cmwlth 1978).

McDonnell Douglas v. Green, 411 U.S. 792 (1983).

McKee v. Southeast Delco School District, 512 A.2d 28, 354 Pa. Super. 433 (1986).

McKeesport Area School District Board of Directors v. Collins, 423 A.2d 1112, 55 Pa. Cmwlth. 548 (1980).

McKnight v. City of Philadelphia, 445 A.2d 778, 299 Pa. Super. 327 (1982).

McLaurin v. Oklahoma State Regents, 339 U.S. 637 '1950).

McLean v. Arkansas, 529 F. Supp. 1255 (D. Ark. 1981).

Meek v. Pittenger, 421 U.S. 349 (1975).

Melson v. Board of School Directors of State College Area School District, 415 A.2d 1024, 52 Pa. Cmwlth. 531 (1980).

Merritt v. Board of Education of School District of Philadelphia, 513 A.2d 504 (Pa. Cmwlth. 1986).

Messina v. Blairsville-Saltsburg School District, 503 A.2d 89 (Pa. Cmwlth. 1986).

Mifflin County School District v. Monsell, 504 A.2d 1357 (Pa. Cmwlth. 1986).

Mifflin County School District v. Stewart by Stewart, 503 A.2d 1012 (Pa. Cmwlth. 1986).

Miller v. California, 413 U.S. 15 (1973).

Miller v. Emelson, 520 A.2d 913 (Pa. Cmwlth. 1987).

Milliken v. Bradley, 418 U.S. 717 (1974).

Milliken v. Bradley, 433 U.S. 267 (1977).

Mills v. Board of Education of the District of Columbia, 348 F. Supp. 866 (D.D.C. 1972).

Milonis v. Williams, 691 F.2d 931 (1982), certiorari denied, 460 U.S. 1069 (1983).

Minarcini v. Strongsville City School District, 541 F.2d 577 (6th Cir. 1976).

Minersville Area School District v. Commonwealth, Pennsylvania Labor Relations Board, 475 A.2d 962, 82 Pa. Cmwlth. 506 (1984).

Missouri *ex rel.* Gaines v. Canada, 305 U.S. 337 (1938).

Missouri State High School Activities Assn. v. Schoenlaub, 507 S.W. 2d 394 (Mo. 1974).

Missouri v. Jenkins, 495 U.S. 33 (1996).

Mitchell v. Helms, 120 S. Ct. 2530 (2000).

Moiles v. Marple-Newton School District, 37 SLIE No. 33 (Pa, Secretary of Education 2000).

Molitor v. Kaneland Community Unit School District No. 302, 163 N.E.2d 89, 18 Ill.2d 11 (1959).

Monaca School District Appeal, 52 D.& C.2d 447 (Pa. 1971).

Monell v. New York City Department of Services, 436 U.S. 658 (1978).

Moody v. Cronin, 484 F. Supp. 270 (C.D. Ill. 1979).

Moody v. P.I.A.A., 11 Crawford 45 (Pa. 1970).

Mooney by Mooney v. North Penn School District, 493 A.2d 795 (Pa. Cmwlth. 1985).

Mope v. Hazleton Area School District, 506 A.2d 1345 (Pa. Cmwlth. 1986).

Moreland v. Western Pennsylvania Interscholastic Athletic League, 572 F.2d 121 (C.A. Pa. 1978).

Moriarta v. State College Area School District, 601 A.2d 872 (Pa. Cmwlth. 1981).

Moubry v. Independent School District No. 696, 9 F. Supp.2d 1086 (D. Minn. 1998).

Mozert v. Hawkins County Public Schools, 827 F.2d 1058 (6th Cir. 1987), *certiorari* denied, 484 U.S. 1066 (1988).

Murphy v. Commonwealth, Department of Education, 460 A.2d 398 (Pa. Cmwlth. 1983).

Murray v. Pittsburgh Board of Education, 759 F. Supp. 1178 (W.D. Pa. 1991).

Murray v. West Baton Rouge Parish School Board, 472 F.2d 438 (5th Cir. 1973).

Muth v. Smith, 646 F. Supp. 280 (E.D. Pa. 1986).

Nabozny v. Podlesny, et al., 92 F.3d 446 (7th Cir. 1996).

Nagy v. Belle Vernon Area School District, 412 A.2d 172, 49 Pa. Cmwlth. 452 (1980).

Nancy M. v. Scanlon, 666 F. Supp. 723, (E.D. Pa. 1987).

Nartowicz v. Clayton County School District, 736 F.2d 646 (11th Cir. 1984).

Near v. Minnesota, 283 U.S. 697 (1931).

Neely v. Rutherford County Schools, 851 F. Supp. 888 (M.D. Tenn. 1994).

Nelson v. Moline School District No. 40, 725 F. Supp. 965 (C.D. Ill. 1989).

Nelson v. Tuscarora Intermediate Unit No. 11, 426 A.2d 1234, 57 Pa. Cmwlth. 514 (1983).

Neshaminy Federation of Teachers v. Neshaminy School District, 428 A.2d 1023, 59 Pa. Cmwlth. 63 (1981).

Neshaminy Federation of Teachers v. Neshaminy School District, 462 A.2d 629 (Pa. 1983).

Neuhaus v. Federico, 505 P.2d 939 (Ore. 1973).

New Castle Area School District v. Bair, 368 A.2d 345, 28 Pa. Cmwlth. 240 (1977).

New Jersey v. T.L.O., 469 U.S. 325, 105 S. Ct. 733, 83 L.Ed.2d 720 (1985).

Newkirk v. School District of Philadelphia, 261 A.2d 305, 437 Pa. 114 (1968).

Nicole M. v. Martinez United School District, _____F. Supp._____ (Cal. 1997).

Nitzberg v. Parks, 525 F.2d 378 (4th Cir. 1975).

Norristown Area School District v. A.V. By and Through V.V., 495 A.2d 990 (Pa. Cmwlth. 1985).

North Haven Board of Education v. Bell, 456 U.S. 512 (1982).

Northwest Tri-County Intermediate Unit No. 5 Education Association v. Northwest Tri-County Intermediate Unit No. 5, 465 A.2d 89 (Pa. Cmwlth. 1983).

Norwin School District v. Belan, 507 A.2d 373, 510 Pa. 255 (1986).

Norwin School District v. Commonwealth, Unemployment Compensation Bd. of Review, 471 A.2d 904, 80 Pa. Cmwlth. 67 (1984).

Oberti v. Clementon Board of Education, 995 F.2d 1204 (3rd Cir. 1993).

Occhipinti v. Board of School Directors of Old Forge School District, 408 A.2d 1189, 48 Pa. Cmwlth. 56 (1983).

O'Grady v. Centennial School District, 401 A.2d 1388, 43 Pa. Cmwlth. 187 (1979).

Ojai Unified School District v. Jackson, 4 F.3d 1467 (9th Cir. 1993).

O'Leary v. Wisecup, 364 A.2d 770, 26 Pa. Cmwlth. 538 (1976).

Oleson v. Board of Education of School District No. 228, 676 F. Supp. 820 (N.D. Ill. 1987).

Olson v. Board of School Directors Methacton School District, 478 A.2d 954, 84 Pa. Cmwlth. 189 (1984).

Olson v. Warren County School District, 11 D. & C.3d 243 (1978).

Oncale V. Sundowner Offshore Services, Inc., 523 U.S. 75 (1998).

O'Rourke v. Walker, 120 Conn. 130 (1925).

Paladino v. Adelphi University, 89 A.D.2d 85, 454 N.Y.S.2d 868 (1982).

Parducci v. Rutland, 316 F. Supp. 352 (M.D. Ala. 1970).

Parents Against Abuse v. Williamsport, 594 A.2d 796 (Pa. Cmwlth. 1991).

Parratt v. Taylor, 451 U.S. 527, 101 S. Ct. 1908, 68 L.Ed.2d 420 (1981).

Patrick Shaw et al. v. John McCracken, Superintendent, and the Corry Area School District (W.D. Pa. 1995).

Pease v. Millcreek Township School District, 195 A.2d 104, 412 Pa. 378 (1963).

Pedersen v. South Williamsport Area School District, 667 F.2d 312 (3rd Cir. 1982).

Peloza v. Capistrano Unified School District, 37 F.3d 517 (9th Cir. 1994).

Penn-Delco School District v. Urso, 382 A.2d 162, 33 Pa. Cmwlth. 501 (1978).

Pennsylvania Association of Retarded Citizens (PARC) v. Commonwealth of Pennsylvania, 343 F. Supp. 279 (Pa. 1972).

Pennsylvania Human Relations Commission v. Chester School District, 426 Pa. 360 (1967).

Pennsylvania Human Relations Commission v. Uniontown School District, 445 Pa. 52 (1973).

Pennsylvania Interscholastic Athletic Association, Inc. Greater Johnstown School District, 463 A.2d 1198 (Pa. Cmwlth. 1983).

Pennsylvania State Education Association v. Appalachia Intermediate Unit No. 8, 460 A.2d 1234 (Pa. Cmwlth. 1983).

Pennsylvania State Education Association v. Baldwin Whitehall School District, 372 A.2d 960, 30 Pa. Cmwlth. 149 (1977).

Pennsylvania State Education Association v. Commonwealth, Department of Public Welfare, 449 A.2d 89 (Pa. Cmwlth. 1982).

Penzenstadler v. Avonworth School District, 403 A.2d 621, 43 Pa. Cmwlth. 571 (1979).

People in the Interest of P.E.A., 754 P.2d 382 (Colo. 1988).

People of the State of Illinois *ex rel.* McCollum v. Board of Education of School District No. 71, Champaign County, 333 U.S. 203 (1948).

People v. Dillworth, 640 N.E. 1009 (Ill. App. 3d Dist. 1994).

People v. Price, 431 N.E.2d 267 (N.Y. 1981).

Pequa Valley School District v. Pennsylvania Department of Education, 99 S. Ct. 3091, 443 U.S. 901, 61 L.Ed.2d 869 (1979).

Perkiomen Valley Education Association v. Perkiomen Valley School District, 460 A.2d 896 (Pa. Cmwlth. 1983).

Perry Education Association v. Perry Local Educator's Association, 460 U.S. 37 (1983).

Persi v. Aliquippa Borough School District, 15 D. & C.3d 52 (Pa. 1979).

Personnel Administrator of Massachusetts v. Feeney, 442 U.S. 256 (1979).

Peter W. v. San Francisco Unified School District, 60 Cal. App. 3d 814, 131 Cal. Rptr. 854 (1976).

Petition of Wellsboro Area School District, 467 A.2d 1197, 78 Pa. Cmwlth. 467 (1983).

Petition of Woodland Hills School District, 473 A.2d 257 (Pa. Cmwlth. 1984).

Pfieffer v. Marion Center Area School District et. al., 917 F.2d 799 (3rd Cir. 1990).

Philadelphia Federation of Teachers Local No. 3 AFT, AFL-CIO v. Board of Education of School District of Philadelphia, 414, A.2d 424, 51 Pa. Cmwlth. 296 (1980).

Philadelphia Federation of Teachers, Local No. 3 v. Thomas, 436 A.2d 1228, 62 Pa. Cmwlth. 286 (1981).

Philadelphia School District Board of Education v. Kushner, 109 Pa. Cmwlth. 120 (1987).

Philadelphia School District Board of Public Education v. Beilan, 386 Pa. 82 (1956), affirmed 357 U.S. 1414 (1958), rehearing denied 358 U.S. 858 (1958).

Phillips v. Trinity Area School District, 29 SLIE 40 (1992).

Pickens v. Oklahoma Municipal Separate School District, 594 F.2d 433 (5th Cir. 1979).

Pires by Pires v. Commonwealth, Department of Education, 467 A.2d 79, 78 Pa. Cmwlth. 127 (1983).

Pittsburgh Federation of Teachers, Local 400 v. Langer, 546 F. Supp. 434 (W.D. Pa. 1982).

Pittston Area School District v. Pittston Area Federation of Teachers, Local 1590, 456 A.2d 1148 Pa. Cmwlth. 1983).

Planned Parenthood v. Clark County School District, 941 F.2d 817 (9th Cir. 1991), en banc affirming, 887 F.2d 935 (9th Cir. 1985).

Plessy v. Ferguson, 163 U.S. 537, 16 S. Ct. 138 (1896).

Pliscou v. Holtville Unified School DIstrict, 411 F. Supp. 842 (J.D. Cal. 1976).

Plyler v. Dow, 457 U.S. 202 (1982).

Poe v. Hamilton, 565 N.E.2d 887 (Ohio App. 1990).

Poling v. Murphy, 872 F.2d 757 (6th Cir. 1989).

Polk v. Central Susquehanna Intermediate Unit #16, 853 F.2d 171 (3rd Cir. 1988).

Pookman v. Upper St. Clair School District, 483 A.2d 1371 (Pa. 1963).

Popp v. Western Beaver County School District, 9 D. & C.3d 514 (1979).

Port Jefferson Station Teachers' Association v. Brookhaven Comswogue Union Free School District, 383 N.E. 553 (N.Y. 1978).

Porter v. Board of School Directors of Clairton School District, 445 A.2d 1386 (Pa. Cmwlth. 1982).

Pottgen v. Missouri State Activities Association, 857 F. Supp. 654 (E.D. Mo. 1994).

Pottsville Area School District v. Marteslo, 423 A.2d 1336 (Pa. Cmwlth. 1980).

Pratt v. Independent School District No. 831, 670 F.2d 771 (8th Cir. 1982).

President's Council v. Community School Board District No. 25, 457 F.2d 289 (2d. Cir.), *certiorari* denied 409 U.S. 998 (1972).

Proch v. New Castle Area School District, 430 A.2d 1034, 60 Pa. Cmwlth. 111 (1981).

Q uarterman v. Byrd, 453 F.2d 54 (4th Cir. 1971).

Quier v. Quakertown Community School District, 27 Bucks Co. L. Rep. 199 (Pa. 1975).

R .A.V. v. City of St. Paul, 505 U.S. 377 (1992).

R. R. v. Shore Regional High School District, 263 A.2d 184 (N.J. Super. 1970).

Rauer v. State University of New York, 552 N.Y.S.2d 983 (A.D. 3d Dept. 1990).

Rawdin v. Bristol Township School District, 44 D. & C.2d 713 (Pa. 1968).

Reed v. Reed, 404 U.S. 71 (1971).

Reitmeyer v. Unemployment Compensation Board of Review, 602 A.2d 505 (Pa. Cmwlth. 1992).

Reynolds v. United States, 98 U.S. 145 (1979).

Rhoades v. Abington Township School District, 424 Pa. 202, 226 A.2d 53 (1967).

Rhodes v. Laurel Highlands School District, 118 Pa. Cmwlth. 119 (1988).

Rich v. Kentucky Country Day, Inc., 793 S.W.2d 832 (Ky. App. 1990).

Richland Education Association v. Richland School District, 418 A.2d 787, 53 Pa. Cmwlth. 367 (1980).

Richland School District v. Commonwealth, Pennsylvania Labor Relations Board, 454 A.2d 649 (Pa. Cmwlth. 1983).

Ridley School District v. Ridley Education Association, 479 A.2d 641, 84 Pa. Cmwlth. 117 (1984).

Rike v. Commonwealth, Secretary of Education, 494 A.2d 1388 (Pa. 1985).

Ringgold School District v. Abramski, 426 A.2d 707, 57 Pa. Cmwlth. 33 (1981).

Rivera v. East Otero School District, R-1, 721 F. Supp. 1189 (D. Colo. 1989).

Riverview School District v. Riverview Education Association, 639 A.2d 974 (Pa. Cmwlth. 1994).

Roberts v. City of Boston, 59 Mass. 198 (Mass. 1849).

Roberts v. Colorado State University, 814 F. Supp. 1507 (D. Colo. 1993).

Robinson v. Abington Education Association, 423 A.2d 1014, 492 Pa. 218 (1980).

Robison v. Clearfield Area School Directors, 3 D. & C.3d 508 (Pa. 1977).

Robson v. Penn Hills School District, 437 A.2d 1273, 63 Pa. Cmwlth. 250 (1981).

Rogers, Arkansas v. McCluskey, 102 S. Ct. 3469 (1982).

Roman v. Appleby, 558 F. Supp. 449 (D.C. Pa. 1983).

Romano v. Harrington, 725 F. Supp. 687 (E.D. N.Y. 1989).

Roncker v. Walter, 700 F.2d 1058 (6th Cir. 1983).

Rosen v. Montgomery County Intermediate Unit, 495 A.2d 217, 90 Pa. Cmwlth. 335 (1985).

Ross v. Blue Mountain School District Board of School Directors, 21 SLIE 21 (1985).

Rosso v. Board of School Directors of Owen J. Roberts School District, 380 A.2d 1328, 33 Pa. Cmwlth. 175 (1977).

Rowe v. Daviess County, 655 S.W.2d 28 (Ky. Ct. App. 1983).

Rowinsky v. Bryan Independent School District, 80 F.3d 1006 (5th Cir. 1996).

Rowley v. Hendrick Hudson School District, 458 U.S. 176, 102 S. Ct. 3034, L.Ed. 2d 690 (1982).

Rudi v. Big Beaver Falls Area School District, 74 Pa. D. & C.2d 790 (1976).

Rural Housing Alliance v. U. S. Department of Agriculture, 498 F.2d 73 (D.C. Cir. 1974).

Rutter v. Northeastern Beaver County School District, 437 A.2d 1198, 496 Pa. 590 (1981).

S.A.F.E. v. Detroit Board of Education. 815 F. Supp. 1045 (E.D. Mich. 1993).

S.C. v. State, 583 So.2d 188 (Miss. 1991).

S.W.2d 707 (Mo. App. S.D. 1993).

S-1 v. Turlington, 635 F.2d 342 (5th. Cir. 1981).

Sadler v. Board of Education of Cabool School District, 851 S.W.2d 707 (Mo. App. S.D. 1993).

Salvail v. Nashua Board of Education, 469 F. Supp. 1269 (D. N.H. 1979).

Santa Fe Independent District v. Doe, No. 99-62 (S. Ct. 2000).

Save Our School v. Colonial School District, 1993 W. L. 24361.

Savka v. Commonwealth, Department of Education, 403 A.2d 142, 44 Pa. Cmwlth. 62 (1979).

Schaill ex. rel. Kross v. Tippecanoe County School Corporation, 679 F. Supp. 833 (N.D. Ind. 1988).

Schobert v. Marcase, 428 A.2d 739,, 58 Pa. Cmwlth. 595 (1981).

School Board of the County of Prince William v. Malone, 762 F.2d 1210 (4th Cir. 1985).

School District of Abington Township, Pennsylvania v. Schemmp, 374 U.S. 203 (1973).

School District of City of Pittsburgh v. Zebra, 325 A.2d 330, 15 Pa. Cmwlth. 203 (1974).

School District of Erie v. Erie Education Association, 447 A.2d 686 (Pa. Cmwlth. 1982).

School District of Harrisburg v. P.I.A.A., 309 A.2d 353 (Pa. 1973).

School District of Millcreek Township v. Millcreek Education Association, 440 A.2d 673, 64 Pa. Cmwlth. 389 (1982).

School District of Philadelphia v. Brockington, 511 A.2d 944 (Pa. Cmwlth. 1986).

School District of Philadelphia v. Pennsylvania Human Relations Commission, 294 A.2d 410, 6 Pa. Cmwlth. 281 (1972).

School District of Philadelphia v. Rochester, 405 A.2d 1142, 46 Pa. Cmwlth. 123 (1979).

School District of Philadelphia v. Twer, 447 A.2d 222, 498 Pa. 429 (1982).

School District of Pittsburgh v. Commonwealth, Department of Education, 382 A.2d 772, 33 Pa. Cmwlth. 535 (1978).

School District of Pittsburgh v. Pennsylvania Department of Education, 99 S. Ct. 3091, 443 U.S. 901, 61 L.Ed.2d 869 (1979).

Sciotto v. Marple-Newton School District, 1999 WL 740691 (E.D. Pa. 1999).

Scopes v. State, 289 S.W. 363 (Tenn. 1927).

Scotchlas v. Board of School Directors of Haverford Township School District, 496 A.2d 916 (Pa. Cmwlth. 1985).

Scott S. v. Department of Education, 512 A.2d 790 (Pa. Cmwlth. 1986).

Scott v. Philadelphia Parking Authority, 166 A.2d 278 (1960).

Scoville v. Board of Education of Joliet Township, 425 F.2d 10 (7th Cir. 1970).

Scranton Federation of Teachers v. Scranton School District, 445 A.2d 260 (Pa. Cmwlth. 1982).

Scranton School Board v. Scranton Federation of Teachers, Local 1147, A.F.T., 365 A.2d 1339, 27 Pa. Cmwlth. 152 (1982).

Sertik v. School Board of the City of Pittsburgh, 584 A.2d 390, 136 Pa. Cmwlth. 594 (1990).

Seyfried v. Walton, 668 F.2d 214 (3rd Cir. 1981).

Shade Central City School District v. Class of 1974, 1 D.& C.3d 376 (Pa. 1976).

Shaffer v. Board of School Directors of Albert Gallatin Area School District, 570 F. Supp. 698 (Pa. 1983), reversed by 730 F.2d 910 (Pa. 1984).

Shaler Area School District v. Salakas, 406 A.2d 243, 45 Pa. Cmwlth. 556, affirmed 432 A.2d 165, 494 Pa. 630 (1979).

Shamberg v. State, 762 P.2d 488 (Alaska App. 1988).

Shanberg v. Commonwealth, Secretary of Education, 426 A.2d 232, 57 Pa. Cmwlth. 384 (1981).

Shanley v. Northeast Independent School Districtm 462 F.2d 960 (5th Cir. 1972).

Shaw, Patrick v. John McCracken, Superintendent, and the Corry Area School District, (W.D. Pa. 1995).

Sherman v. Community Consolidated District 21, 980 F.2d 437 (7th Cir.1992).

Sherman v. Community Consolidated School District 21, 8 F.3d 1160 (7th Cir. 1993).

Sherry v. New York State Education Department, 479 F. Supp. 1328 (W.D. N.Y. 1979).

Shestack v. General Braddock Area School District, 437 A.2d 1059 (Pa. Cmwlth. 1981).

Shoup v. Forest Area School District, 30 SLIE 84 (1993).

Silanao v. Sag Harbor Unified School District, 42 F.3d 719 (2nd Cir. 1994).

Silvio v. Commonwealth, Department of Education, 439 A.2d 893, 64 Pa. Cmwlth. 192 (1982).

Simonetti by Simonetti v. School District of Philadelphia, 454 A.2d 1038 (Pa. Super, 1982).

Singer by Singer v. School District of Philadelphia, 513 A.2d 1108 (Pa. Cmwlth. 1986).

Sioux Falls School District v. Koupal, 526 N.W. 2d 248; 22 IDELR 26 (S.D. 1994).

Skelly v. Brookfield LaGrange Park School District 95, 968 F. Supp. 385 (Ill. 1997).

Sloan v. Lemon, 413 U.S. 825 (1972).

Slotterback by Slotterback v. Interboro School District, 766 F. Supp. 280 (E.D. Pa. 1991).

Smith v. Board of School Commissioners of Mobile County, 827 F.2d 684 (11th Cir. 1987).

Smith v. Crim, 240 S.E.2d 884 (Ga. 1977).

Smith v. Robinson, 104 S. Ct. 3457, 79 L.Ed.2d 304 (1984).

Smith v. School District of Hobart, 811 F. Supp. 966 (N.D. Ind. 1993).

Smith v. Webb, 420 F. Supp. 600 (D.C. Pa. 1976).

Snow v. State of New York, 61 N.Y.2d 608, 475 N.Y.S.2d 1026, 468 N.E.2d 1004 (1984).

Southeastern Community College v. Davis, 442 U.S. 397, 99 S. Ct. 2361, 60 L.Ed.2d 980 (1979)

Spence v. Washington, 418 U.S. 406 (1974).

Spitler v. Eastern Lebanon County School District, SLIE, Vol. 38, No. 18 (2001).

Springdale School District #50 of Washington County v. Grace, 693 F.2d 41 (8th Cir. 1982).

Springer v. Fairfax County School Board, 27 IDELR 367 ((4th Cir.) January 23, 1998).

Springfield School District, Delaware County v. Department of Education, 397 A.2d 1154, 483 Pa. 539, (1979).

Sporie v. Eastern Westmoreland Area Vocational-Technical School, 408 A.2d 888, 47 Pa. Cmwlth. 390 (1979).

Stanley v. Northeast Independent School District, 462 F.2d. 960 (5th Cir. 1972).

State ex rel. Dresser v. Board of School District No. 1, 116 N.W. 232 (Wis. 1908).

State ex rel. Kelley v. Ferguson, 144 N.W. 1039, 95 Neb. 63 (1914).

State *ex rel.* Sheibley v. School District No. 1, 48 N.W. 393, 31 Neb. 552 (1891).

State *ex rel.* Williams v. Avoyelles Parish School Board, 147 So.2d 729 (La. 1962).

State of Arizona v. Serna, 860 P.2d 1320 (Ariz. App. Div 1 1993).

State v. D.T.W., 425 So.2d 1383 (Fla. Dist. Ct. App. 1983).

State v. Moore, 603 A.2d 513 (N.J. Super. A.D. 1992).

State v. Slattery, 787 P. 2d 932 (Wash. App. 1990).

Staub v. Southwest Butler County School District, 398 A.2d 204, 263 Pa. Super. 413, affirmed 413 A.2d 1082, 489 Pa. 196 (1979).

Steele v. VanBuren Public School District, 845 F.2d 1492 (8th Cir. 1988).

Steele v. Waters, 527 S.W.2d 72 (Tenn. 1975).

Steffen v. Board of Directors of South Middletown Township School District, 377 A.2d 1381, 32 Pa. Cmwlth. 187 (1977).

Stein v. Philadelphia Federation of Teachers Local 3, AFT, AFL-CIO, 464 A.2d 606 (Pa. Cmwlth. 1983).

Stern v. New Haven Community Schools, 529 F. Supp. 31 (E.D. Mich. 1981).

Stobaugh v. Wallace, 757 F. Supp. 653 (W.D. Pa.).

Stoneking v. Bradford Area School District, 882 F.2d 720 (3rd Cir. 1989).

Strauder v. West Virginia, 100 U.S. 303 (1879).

Stroudsburg Area Board of Education v. Pennsylvania Labor Relations Board, 395 A.2d 622 (Pa. Cmwlth. 1978).

Stuart v. School District No.1 of the Village of Kalamazoo, 30 Mich. 69 (1874).

Stuart v. Nappi, 443 F. Supp. 1235 (D. Conn. 1978).

Student Coalition for Peace v. Lower Merion School District Board, 776 F.2d 431 (3rd Cir. 1985).

Student Doe v. Commonwealth of Pennsylvania, 593 F. Supp. 54 (D.C. Pa. 1984).

Student Roe by Roe v. Commonwealth of Pennsylvania, 638 F. Supp. 929 (E.D. Pa. 1986).

Sullivan v. Houston Independent School District, 438 F.2d 1058 (2nd Cir. 1971).

Sutterby v. Zimer, 594 N.Y.S.2d 607 (N.Y. 1993).

328

Sutton v. United Airlines, Inc., 119 S. Ct. 2139 (1999).

Sutton v. Utah State School for the Blind, 173 F.3d 1226 (10th Cir. 1999).

Swann v. Charlotte-Mecklenburg Board of Education, 402 U.S. 1, 91 S. Ct. 1267 (1971).

Swartley v. Tredyffrin Easttown School Dist., 430 A.2d 1001, 287 Pa. Super. 499 (1981).

Sweatt v. Painter, 339 U.S. 629 (1950).

Tarter v. Raybuck, 742 F.2d 977 (6th Cir. 1984).

Tate v. Board of Education of Jonesboro, Arkansas, 453 F.2d 975 (8th Cir. 1972).

Tennessean Newspapers, Inc. v. Levi, 403 F. Supp. 1318 (M.D. Tenn. 1975).

Texas v. Johnson, 491 S. Ct. 397 (1989).

The Right to Read Defense Committee of Chelsea v. School Committee of the City of Chelsea, 454 F. Supp. 703 (D. Mass. 1978).

Thomas v. Board of Education, 607 F.2d 1043 (2nd Cir. 1979) *certiorari* denied, 444 U.S. 1081 (1980).

Thompson v. Waynesboro Area School District, 673 F. Supp. 1379 (M.D. Pa. 1987).

Thrasher v. General Casualty Co. of Wisconsin, 732 F. Supp. 966 (W.D. Wis. 1990).

Timms v. Metropolitan School District, 722 F.2d 1310 (7th Cir. 1983).

Tinker v. Des Moines Independent Community School District, 393 U.S. 503, 89 S. Ct. 733, 21 L.Ed.2d 731 (1969).

Tipper v. New Castle Area School District, (W.D. Pa. 1994).

Todd v. Rush County Schools, 133 F.3d 984 (7th Cir. 1998).

Tokarcik v. Forest Hills School District, 665 F.2d 443, *certiorari* denied Scanlon v. Tokarcik, 458 U.S. 1121, 102 S. Ct. 3508, 73 L.Ed.2d 1383 (1981).

Tomlinson by Tomlinson v. Pleasant Valley School District, 479 A.2d 1169, 84 Pa. Cmwlth. 518 (1984).

Torres v. Little Flower Children's Services, 64 N.Y.2d 119, 485 N.Y.S.2d 15, 474, N.E.2d 223 (1984).

Trachtman v. Anker, 563 U.S. 512 (2nd Cir. 1977) *certiorari* denied, 435 U.S. 925 (1978).

Trainer V. Chichester School District, 455 A.2d 1270, 72 Pa. Cmwlth. 47 (1983).

Travis v. Teter, 370 Pa. 326 (1952).

Trinity Area School District v. Trinity Area Education Association, 412 A.2d 167 (Pa. Cmwlth. 1980).

Twin Valley School Dist. v. Student Activity Fund of the Twin Valley High School Class of 1981, et al. (Pa. C.P. Berks).

Unionville-Chadds Ford School District v. Rotteveel, 487 A.2d 109, 87 Pa. Cmwlth. 334 (1985).

United States v. Montgomery County Board of Education, 395 U.S. 225 (1969).

Upper Bucks County Area Vocational-Technical School Joint Committee v. Upper Bucks County Vocational-Technical School Education Association, 482 A.2d 274, 85 Pa. Cmwlth. 115 (1985).

Upper Merion Area School District v. Upper Merion Education Association, 482 A.2d 274, 85 Pa. Cmwlth. 115 (1984).

Usher v. Upper St. Clair School District, 487 A.2d 1022, 87 Pa. Cmwlth. 461 (1985).

Vail v. Board of Education, 706 F.2d 1435 (7th Cir. 1988), affirmed 104 S. Ct. 2144 (1989).

Vail v. Portsmouth School District, 354 F. Supp. 592 (D.N.H. 1973).

Valent v. N.J. State Board of Education,274 A.2d 832 (N.J. Sup. Ct. Ch. Div. 1971).

Valentine v. Joliet High School District, 802 F.2d 981 (7th Cir. 1986).

Van Hooser v. Warren County Board of Education, 807 S.W.2d 230 (1991).

Vann v. Board of Education of School District of Philadelphia, 464 A.2d 684 (Pa. Cmwlth. 1983).

Verbina United Methodist Church v. Chilton County Board of Education, 765 F. Supp. 704 (M.D. Ala. 1991).

Vernonia School District 47J v. Acton, 115 S. Ct. 2386 (1995).

Victoria L. v. District School Board, 741 F.2d 369 (11th Cir. 1984).

Vince by Vince v. Ringgold School District, 499 A.2d 1148, 92 Pa. Cmwlth. 598 (1985).

Virgil v. School Board, 677 F. Supp. 1547 (M.D. Fla. 1988).

Visco v. Cheltenham Township School District, 27 SLIE 17 (1990).

Wallace v. Ford, 346 F. Supp. 156 (E.D. Ark. 1972).

Wallace v. Jaffree, 472 U.S. 38 (1985).

Walter v. West Virginia Board of Education, 610 F. Supp. 1161 (S.D. W.Va. 1985).

Walton v. Pittsburgh School District, 28 SLIE 86 (1991).

Ward v. Board of Education of School District of Philadelphia, 496 A.2d 1352 (Pa. Cmwlth. 1985).

Ware v. Valley Stream High School, 545 N.Y.S. 2d. 316 (N.Y. App. Div.), appeal denied, 545 N.Y.S. 2d 539 (N.Y. 1989).

Warren County School District of Warren County v. Carlson, 418 A.2d 810, 53 Pa. Cmwlth. 568 (1980).

Washegesic v. Bloomingdale Public Schools, 813 F. Supp. 559 (W.D. Md. 1994), *certiorari* denied 115 S. Ct. 1822.

Washington v. Seattle School District No. 1, 458 U.S. 457 (1982).

Waslo v. North Allegheny School District, 549 A.2d1359 (Pa. Cmwlth. 1988).

Wayne Highlands Education Association v. Wayne Highlands School District, 498 A.2d 1375, 92 Pa. Cmwlth. 114 (1985).

Weeds v. Wright 334 F.2d. 369 (5th Cir. 1964).

Weiss v. Scranton School District, 537 A.2d 910 (1988), affirmed 521 Pa. 528 (1988).

West Chester School Board v. West Chester Area Education Association, 28 SLIE 16 (CP Chester 1991).

West Chester Area School District v. Commonwealth, Secretary of Education, 401 A.2d 610, 43 Pa. Cmwlth. 14 (1979).

West Chester Area School District v. West Chester Area Education Association, 449 A.2d 824 (Pa. Cmwlth. 1982).

West Middlesex Area School District v. Commonwealth, Pennsylvania Labor Relations Board, 423 A.2d 781, 55 Pa. Cmwlth. 404 (1980).

West Shore Education Association v. West Shore School District, 456 A.2d 715 (Pa. Cmwlth. 1983).

West Shore School District v. Bowman, 409 A.2d 474, 48 Pa. Cmwlth. 104 (1979).

West Shore School District v. West Shore Education Association, 519 A.2d 552 (Pa. Cmwlth. 1986).

West Virginia *ex rel* Lambert v. West Virginia State Board of Education, 447 S.E.2d 901 (W.Va. 1994).

West Virginia State Board of Education v. Barnette, 319 U.S. 624 (1943).

Westhafer v. Cumberland Valley School District, SLIE, Vol. 38, No. 19 (2001).

Wexner v. Anderson Union High School District Board of Trustees, 228 Cal.Rptr. 28 (Ct. App. 1989).

White v. School District of Philadephia, 553 Pa. 214 (1998).

White by White v. Salisbury Township School District, 588 F. Supp. 608 (D.C. Pa. 1984).

Widener v Frye, 809 F. Supp. 35 (S.D. Ohio 1993).

Widmer v. Vincent, 454 U.S. 263 (1981).

Wiemerslage v. Maine Township High School District 207, 824 F. Supp. 136 (N.D. Ill. 1993).

Wilcher v. State of Texas, 867 S.W.2d 466 (Tex. App. 1994).

Williams v. Board of Education , 626 S.W.2d 361 (Ark. 1982).

Williams v. Board of Education of Kanawha County, 388 F. Supp. 93 (S.D. W. Va. 1975) affirmed 530 F.2d 972 (4th Cir. 1975).

Williams v. Duquesne School District, 131 P.L.J. 325 (C.P. Allegheny County Pa. 1983).

Williams v. School District of Bethlehem, 998 F.2d 168 (3rd Cir. 1993).

Wilson Area Education Association v. Wilson Area School District, 494 A.2d 506 (Pa. Cmwlth. 1985).

Wimbish v. School District of Penn Hills, 430 A.2d 710, 59 Pa. Cmwlth. 620 (1981).

Wisconsin v. Yoder, 406 U.S. 205, 92 S. Ct. 1526 (1972).

Wissahickon School District v. McKown, 400 A.2d 899, 42 Pa. Cmwlth. 169 (1979).

Wolff v. Board of School Directors of Chichester School District, 429 A.2d 129, 59 Pa. Cmwlth. 196 (1981).

Wolman v. Walter, 433 U.S. 229 (1977).

Wood v. Strickland, 420 U.S. 308 (1975).

Woodland Hills School District v. Commonwealth, Department of Education, 516 A.2d 875 (Pa. Cmwlth. 1986).

Woodring v. School Directors of Bald Eagle Area School District, 56 D.& C.2d 401 (Pa. 1972).

Wooster Republican Printing Company v. City of Wooster, 383 N.E.2d 124, 56 Ohio St. 2d 126, (1978).

Wright v. Houston Independent School District, 366 F. Supp. 1208 (S.D. Tex. 1972).

Wyoming Valley West Education Association v. Wyoming Valley West School District, 500 A.2d 907, 92 Pa. Cmwlth. 365 (1985).

Yaris v. Special School District of St. Louis County, 558 F. Supp. 545 (E.D. Mo. 1983).

Yaris v. Special School District of St. Louis County, 558 F. Supp. 545 (E.D. Mo. 1983).

Young v. Armstrong School District, 344 A.2d 738, 21 Pa. Cmwlth. 203 (1975).

Zamora v. Pomeroy, 639 F.2d 662 (10th Cir. 1981).

Zebra v. School District of the City of Pittsburgh, 296 A.2d 748, 449 Pa. Cmwlth. 432 (1972), appeal after remand, 325 A.2d 330, 15 Pa. Cmwlth. 203.

Zeller v. Donegal School District No. 15, 517 F.2d 600 (3rd Cir. 1975).

Ziccardi v. School District of Philadelphia, 498 A.2d 452 (Pa. Cmwlth. 1985).

Zobrest v. Catalina Foothills School District, 113 S. Ct. 2462 (1993).

Zorach v. Clauson, 343 U.S. 306 (1952).

Zykan v. Warsaw Community School Corporation, 631 F.2d 1300 (7th Cir. 1980).